Schools and Work
Technical and Vocational Education in France since
the Third Republic

Schools and Work traces the development of vocational and technical education in France since the late nineteenth century, detailing its history and situating it in the broader context of educational development and economic modernization. Charles Day analyses the changes in industrial technology as well as the rise and decline of Fordism and Taylorism and their replacement by new techniques of flexible specialization and lean production. He demonstrates that, confronted with the challenges of globalization, increased competition, and deindustrialization, state and industry have been forced to redefine skill requirements, reform schools and programs, and establish new forms of cooperation, notably in creating work-study, continuing education, and apprenticeship programs like those available in Germany and other European countries.

In the half century since World War II, France has developed from a conservative, semi-rural society in which the great majority of the population had only a primary education to a highly developed modern one with a remarkably well-educated and well-trained citizenry and labour force. Technical and vocational training, which before 1960 were confined to an enclave within the French education system, now permeate the entire system. Business and industry, long isolated from education, play a major role in educational decision making. The French educational system today meets the demand for skilled personnel in almost all fields while maintaining "a complement of general culture."

The first book in English to treat the important subject of technical education in France, *Schools and Work* places technical education within the larger field of French public education, including the administrative and political backdrop, European industrial development, the nature of work, and global competitiveness.

CHARLES R. DAY is professor of history at Simon Fraser University.

Schools and Work

*Technical and Vocational Education
in France since the Third Republic*

CHARLES R. DAY

McGill-Queen's University Press
Montreal & Kingston · London · Ithaca

© McGill-Queen's University Press 2001
ISBN 0-7735-2147-X

Legal deposit second quarter 2001
Bibliothèque nationale du Québec

Printed in Canada on acid-free paper

This book has been published with the help of
a grant from the Humanities and Social
Sciences Federation of Canada, using funds
provided by the Social Sciences and
Humanities Research Council of Canada.

McGill-Queen's University Press
acknowledges the financial support of the
Government of Canada through the Book
Publishing Industry Development Program
(BPIDP) for its activities. It also acknowledges
the support of the Canada Council for the
Arts for its publishing program.

Canadian Cataloguing in Publication Data

Day, Charles R.
　　Schools and work: technical and vocational
　　education in France since the Third Republic
　　Includes bibliographical references and index.
　　ISBN 0-7735-2147-X
　　1. Technical education – France – History –
　　20th century. 2. Vocational education – France
　　– History – 20 th century. I. Title.
　　T121.D393 2001　　607.1'044　　C00-901719-4

This book was typeset by Dynagram Inc.
in 10/12 Palatino.

MP

For my sons, Stephen and Andrew

Contents

Acknowledgments

I have been fortunate to be invited several times to the Laboratoire d'analyse secondaire et de méthodes appliquées à la sociologie (LAS-MAS), a branch of the Centre national de la recherche scientifique, in Paris. I wish to thank my colleagues in that group for the kindness they have shown me over the years and especially during my association with the institute, and with the École des Hautes Études en Sciences Sociales, as directeur d'études in 1998. Above all, I would like to thank André Grelon of LASMAS and the CNRS for his help and friendship over the years.

I would also like to thank Sofia Oberti and Joan MacDonald for their help in the preparation of the text.

Abbreviations

AFDET   Association française pour le développement de l'enseignement technique

Bac pro   Baccalauréat professionnel

BEP   Brevet d'enseignement professionnel (brevet de l'éducation professionnelle)

BTS   Brevet de technicien supérieur

CAP   Certificat d'aptitude professionnelle

CAPES   Certificat d'aptitude au professorat de l'enseignement supérieur

CAPET   Certificat d'aptitude au professorat de l'enseignement technique

CEREQ   Centre d'études et de recherches sur les qualifications

CES   Collège d'enseignement secondaire

CET   Collège d'enseignement technique

CFA   Centre de formation d'apprentis

CFPT   Centre de formation des professeurs de l'enseignement technique

CGT   Confédération générale du travail

CNPF   Conseil national du patronat français

CPA   Classe préparatoire à l'apprentissage

CPC   Commission professionnelle consultative

CPPN   Classes préprofessionnelles de niveau

DEUG   Diplôme d'études universitaires générales

DEUST   Diplôme d'études universitaires de sciences et techniques

DNTS   Diplôme national de technologie spécialisée

DUT   Diplôme universitaire de technologie

ENNA   École normale nationale d'apprentissage

ENP École nationale professionnelle

ENSET École normale supérieure de l'enseignement technique

EPCI École pratique de commerce et d'industrie

EPS École primaire supérieure

FEN Fédération de l'éducation nationale

IUFM Institut universitaire de formation des maîtres

IUP Institut universitaire professionnalisé

IUT Institut universitaire de technologie

LEGT Lycée d'enseignement général et technologique

LP Lycée professionnel

LEP Lycée d'enseignement professionnel

MENESR Ministère de l'éducation nationale, de l'enseignement supérieur et de la recherche

OCDE Organisation de coopération et de développement économiques

ONISEP Office national d'information sur les enseignements et les professions

SGEN Syndicat général à l'éducation nationale

SIVP Stages d'initiation à la vie professionnelle

SMIC Salaire minimum interprofessionnel de croissance

SNALC Syndicat national autonome des lycées et collèges

SNES Syndicat national des enseignements du second degré

SNETAA Syndicat national de l'enseignement technique et de l'apprentissage autonome (enseignement professionnel)

STS Section de technicien supérieur

UER Unité d'enseignement et de recherche

UIMM Union des industries métallurgiques et minières

Schools and Work

Thou has most traitorously corrupted the youth of the realm in erecting a grammar-school; and whereas, before, our forefathers had no other books but the score and the tally, thou hast caused printing to be used; and, contrary to the King, his crown, and dignity, thou has built a paper-mill. It will be proved to thy face that thou hast men about thee that usually talk of a noun and a verb, and such abominable words as no Christian ear can endure to hear.

William Shakespeare, King Henry VI, Act 4, Scene 4

Introduction

J'avais toujours un extrême désir d'apprendre à distinguer le vrai d'avec le faux, pour voir clair en mes actions et marcher avec assurance en cette vie.

Descartes

The study of the history of technical education presents many challenges to the historian, who must not only write educational history but also analyse the relationship between two quite different worlds: that of the schools, which are static and self-contained, with stated standards and requirements, and that of the productive sector, which is dynamic and adaptable, with constantly changing demands. The historian of technical education must know the history of techniques and of work and must be informed about socio-professional categories, social relations, science and technology, and general versus technical culture. He or she must also identify a multitude of actors: employers, workers, educators, administrators, students and their associations, and various other political, industrial, and professional groups.

The history of technical education is also a history of employment practices, which involves the deployment of labour, career advancement, and the social construction of identity. Under the Old Regime, status was linked to birth and property, but since the Revolution education has become increasingly important in determining social standing. In the last generation or two, as family, community, church, and other intermediary groups decline in importance in our lives, professions have become more important as indicators of status and identity, and this in turn has raised the importance of the transition from school to work force. This is especially true in France, where the school plays an unusually prominent role in vocational training.[1] Technical and vocational schools are particularly expensive to establish and administer.

Professors are difficult to train because they must teach general, technical, and practical subjects to students who are frequently unable to succeed in general studies. The debate on the content of programs and diplomas thus involves questions of pedagogy, vocational training, and the direction of technological change.

Underlying this debate remains the central question of the economic value of education and technical training. Does educational investment increase productivity, profits, labour output, and the standard of living, as the human capital theory of the 1950s and 1960s suggested?[2] Virtually all of the studies that have been done on this question have refuted this theory as too simplistic and as objectifying human labour, but they have produced no decisive evidence for the economic value of technical education, mainly because education and training are social constructs that interact with other institutional factors and activities, such as the systems of industrial relations, ownership patterns, the availability of investment capital, and the ability to adapt technology and market new products. What we can say is that countries where governing and business elites who control the state have concertedly instituted educational and training policies as part of a broader plan for technological and industrial development (Germany, Japan, and more recently Singapore) and who have co-opted labour in one way or another have had considerable success in achieving growth, despite their diverse approaches to development. Other countries, such as the UK, that have placed less emphasis on central economic planning and education and training have ended up with a labour force possessing fewer skills, which may have impeded the introduction of high technology industries. France falls somewhere in between, though since the 1980s it has been increasingly successful in adapting German and Japanese methods. In this book, I will examine education and training as part of the process of industrialization, emphasizing that they are social constructions and that the link between skills and performance must be seen in a social context, as part of the complex interactions of modern life.

The book traces the evolution of manpower training and the education of skilled workers, technicians, and industrial engineers under the government's division of technical education from the 1890s until the division was abolished in 1960, and the rapid development of technical and vocational training at all levels of the educational system from 1960 to the present day. Ideally, technical and vocational education convey knowledge and competence in certain designated areas and impart attitudes to work that promote effective performance. This includes pride in quality output, self-reliance and the ability to adjust to new situations.[3] Prior to the 1980s technical and vocational schools in France did not always achieve these objectives. Until fairly recently they did not produce enough graduates, and their integration with many sectors of business and industry was not always adequate. As a result, industry lacked skilled personnel in many fields and had to promote workers on the job. This meant that French industrial development was hampered by poor manpower training at all but the highest levels, which probably undermined France's adaptation to changing industrial technology.

Since the late 1970s, governments, business, and labour have increasingly collaborated to improve technical training in France, with generally good results. Despite their relatively low prestige, French technical and vocational schools have long been pedagogically innovative, and effective in educating young people deemed unable to advance in general studies. The introduction over the past two decades of many aspects of the German dual system, which combines in-school and on-the-job training has finally ended an approach to vocational training that was overly academic and school-bound, with good results for the training of skilled workers and technicians.

This book differs from others on French technical education in that it examines the history of vocational and technical training in the broader context of economic development and modernization.[4] It involves an analysis of changes in industrial technology, the rise of Taylorism and Fordism (a system of mass production involving long assembly lines and the "scientific management of labour" by trained engineers and experts), their decline in the decades after the war, and their gradual replacement since the 1970s by new techniques of flexible specialization and lean production aimed at building an economy based on high value-added production. I will discuss the reasons for the long isolation of technical education in the educational system, the hostility between educators and businessmen, and the marked improvement in relations over the past twenty years.

Economic changes have had important social and cultural effects in France, especially since the Second World War. The schools, as constituents of a centralized state system, have both reflected these changes and facilitated them. Technical and vocational schools in particular stand at the intersection of numerous, often contradictory, discourses in a hierarchical educational system that directs young people into higher or lower levels, often according to social origins. These schools train skilled personnel for positions that may or may not prove viable in a world of rapidly changing technology. They provide the possibility of social and professional advancement while confirming the marginal status of their mainly lower-class clientele;

they are often depicted as "bridges to success" that achieve meritocratic objectives of social justice and equality, but in practice often
reinforce class distinctions, racial stereotypes, and gender inequality.

I approach the subject thematically, discussing the development of
vocational, technical, and engineering education in France since the
late nineteenth century with a focus on to the economic, social, and
cultural implications of the activities of technical and vocational
schools. Since the time of Napoleon the lycées have taught a "noble"
general culture based on the humanities, with some time spent on
the theoretical sciences and mathematics, and disdaining all that was
utilitarian and mechanical. But at the same time, France was indus-
trializing and needed specialized technical personnel. This led to the
creation of a separate division of technical education under the Ministry of Industry and Commerce in 1895, designed to meet the needs
of business and industry for skilled workers, technicians, and production engineers, discussed in chapter 1. Gradually this division
created a parallel system of technical schools ranging from junior
secondary to higher education. By the end of the Fourth Republic
this system had reached its apogee, as described in chapter 2. Since
the abolition of the division in 1960, technical and vocational education have been increasingly integrated into the larger educational
system and today admit over half of all secondary students and
award 45 per cent of *baccalauréats*. Chapter 3 discusses the development of working class education from 1920 to 1981, the interwar
period to the end of the conservative phase of the Fifth Republic, and
chapter 4 continues the discussion from the election of François
Mitterrand as president in 1981 to the late 1990s. Confined to continuing education courses during the interwar period, the instruction
of workers was moved to schools during the Vichy regime. These
schools continued under various names under the Fourth and Fifth
Republics, as *centres d'apprentissage, collèges d'enseignement technique,
lycées d'enseignement professionnel* and, finally, as *lycées professionnels*,
which have awarded their own *baccalauréat professionnel* since 1985.
Vocational schools and programs for women have existed since the
late nineteenth century, but have tended to be concentrated in a few
tertiary specialties with limited employment opportunities.

Chapter 5 deals with the training of technicians in France since the
First World War. Technicians were originally trained under the Commerce ministry's division of technical education and after 1960 in the
lycées techniques. Since the 1980s the latter have been assimilated into
the general lycées, and their students almost invariably continue their
studies into higher education, so that training ordinary technicians
remains a problem. In chapter 6, I review the training of senior tech-

nicians, industrial engineers and managers within institutions of advanced education. Until fairly recently, the only uniformly well-educated people in business and industry were high-level executives educated in the *grandes écoles*; many skilled workers and technicians were promoted on the job. Since the 1960s, however, governments have created a technical stream in higher education, starting with two-year programs to train senior technicians: the *sections de techniciens supérieurs* (STS) in the lycées techniques and the *instituts universitaires de technologie* (IUT) in the universities. Several technical schools and universities have also been created, and in the early 1990s a system of four-year *instituts universitaires professionnalisés* (IUP) were opened to train industrial engineers at the university level.

France is unique in the world in the extent to which it has attempted to provide technical and vocational training in schools. This book analyses this experiment over the past century and the mixed results it has produced, drawing freely from the examples of other countries, notably that of Germany. Since 1958 the Fifth Republic has seen the modernization of the economy, an increase in the role of business and industry in the educational process, the opening of secondary and higher education to the average person, the integration of technical and vocational studies into an increasingly consolidated secondary system, and some decentralization of education. I argue that technical and vocational training, so universally disdained, has been the most innovative sector of French education and that in recent years France has been increasingly successful in adapting its centralized, rigid, bookish, anti-utilitarian educational system to the needs of the modern world and to a rapidly evolving economy.

1 The Origins of Technical and Vocational Education in France

Enseignement technique: en demander bruyamment le
développement ... et y envoyer les enfants des autres."
Gustave Flaubert, *Dictionnaire des idées reçues*

THE FRENCH REVOLUTION AND NAPOLEON

Technical education in France originated with the creation of specialized engineering schools during the eighteenth century mainly in response to the requirements of military engineering. These included the
École des ponts et chaussées (1747), the École des mines (1783), and the
École du génie de Mézières (1748). The Revolution saw the creation of
the École polytechnique in 1794, which Napoleon transformed into a
high-level military engineering school. The École centrale des arts et
manufactures, the first institution to train civil engineers for industry,
was established privately in 1829 and became public in 1857. With the
exception of the École du génie de Mézières, these schools exist today.
They recruited from an upper class clientele and trained students for
high-level executive positions in the public services and, in the case of
the École centrale, executive engineers for industry.

The Revolution, having abolished the old *collèges royaux* and exiled
the teaching orders, left the new government uncertain as to the type
of school it wanted and could afford. During the early 1790s Con-
dorcet, Talleyrand, and Lakanal introduced plans for a national system of free, compulsory, and lay instruction, which never materialized
because France was concerned with war and inflation. The central
schools (*écoles centrales*) established in 1795, were a promising experiment in modern (non-classical) secondary education, but they never
really had a chance in the face of financial problems, administrative
disorganization, and the hostility of traditionalists toward modern

studies. In 1802 Napoleon replaced them with the lycées, based on the earlier French model of classical secondary education.

Napoleon created the lycées to train highly skilled but obedient civil servants and military officers, drawn from the bourgeoisie, for his growing empire. In 1808 and 1811 he established the *Université*, a highly centralized public education system run by *universitaires*, public education administrators and academics. The head of the Université, the grand master (later minister of Public Instruction), presided over a high council on public education, several inspectors-general, and academy rectors and inspectors.

The lycées, half barracks and half monasteries, were run on rigid, military lines. They offered their own elementary classes, so that young men were cloistered in these institutions from around age ten to eighteen. Only affluent families could afford the high boarding and tuition fees. The "disinterested" *culture générale* taught in the lycées, was based on the study of classical languages, mainly Latin, and was designed to provide leadership qualities as defined in classical literature and bore little relationship to the changing realities of the nineteenth century. The students studied some mathematics but little science.

Although private secondary schools were tolerated and primary education was left to the Church, the Université maintained a monopoly over secondary programs, examinations, and the granting of diplomas. The municipal colleges (*collèges communaux*) were financed locally but received grants from the state. They were subject to inspection, and their professors were required to be certified by the state. The private, mainly Catholic, schools had to prepare students for state examinations and diplomas. The two key diplomas were the *baccalauréat*, which was both the secondary school leaving credential and the first university diploma, and the *agrégation*, which opened the way to professorships in the senior classes of the lycées and higher education. Only three per cent of the age group twelve to eighteen attended secondary schools and even fewer ever obtained the baccalauréat, which became a potent means of social selection. Armed with the baccalauréat, a student could register in any university faculty. Although few attended the almost moribund faculties of arts and sciences, which survived mainly by organizing and grading the baccalauréat and by offering evening courses, the faculties of law and medicine were active.[1]

In the universities the situation of science was no better. The faculties of science were poorly funded and did little research. Napoleon neglected them in favour of the lycées and the grandes écoles. The latter were high-level scientific and professional institutions designed to produce senior civil servants and professors for the state corporations (*grands corps*). The École polytechnique was recast by Napoleon to train senior military engineers, and the École normale supérieure, established in 1795, prepared future lycée professors for the *agrégation*.[2] The agrégation was based on an examination and emphasized memory and facility in language rather than a research thesis, which meant that France's best minds were directed toward teaching and the senior bureaucracy rather than research. By neglecting research in all branches of higher education, France gradually lost its preeminence in science over the nineteenth century to Germany and its excellent universities.[3]

Napoleon also created the first middle-level technical schools, the écoles d'arts et métiers, to train skilled workers, foremen, and shop supervisors for the mechanical industries. These schools were founded at Châlons-sur-Marne in 1806 (originally at Compiègne in 1803) and at Angers in 1815 (originally at Beaupréau in 1811) to train skilled workers and foremen, "les sous-officiers de l'armée industrielle."[4] The Conservatoire national d'arts et métiers was established in 1794 as a laboratory and museum of industrial techniques that offered evening courses in industrial technology.[5]

THE NINETEENTH CENTURY, 1815–75

Although France created technical schools at the higher and intermediate levels during the eighteenth and early nineteenth centuries, primary instruction for young people aged six to twelve was left to local communities, private groups, and to the Church. During the first half of the nineteenth century the great majority of workers received little instruction and training apart from apprenticeship, which was in decline. The Chapelier Law of 1791 abolished the guilds and all forms of working class association, the bodies most likely to organize apprenticeship.

During the first half of the nineteenth century, the new industrial division of labour further undermined apprenticeship. In the machine construction, railway, and metallurgical companies in the 1840s and 1850s, planning offices (*bureaux d'études et de méthodes*) staffed by engineers, technicians, and draftsmen increasingly issued detailed instructions to shop foremen for the manufacture of specialized parts to be carried out to the letter by workers on the factory floor, a foretaste of Taylorism. This system, in which speed of execution was central, made it difficult to train skilled personnel on the job and further undermined apprenticeship. As mechanical precision replaced manual dexterity, the metal fitter (*ajusteur*) began to disappear and the assemblyman (*monteur*) became more important. Although workers became increasingly dequalified, some, perhaps a quarter, needed new skills to read and interpret blueprints and to do finishing, maintenance, and repair on the new tools and machines. Some smaller companies, especially in the luxury trades and the arts, or in precision industries (instruments, clockmaking) also needed skilled workers. But the majority, coming from the countryside, remained unskilled.

The immediate challenge was to provide improved primary instruction, especially in the cities and in backward areas of the west and centre where illiteracy remained high. The Guizot Law of 1833 required every commune with more than 500 people to open a primary school for boys and to pay the teacher at least a minimum wage. The eighty or so departments were required to establish teacher-training schools (écoles normales primaires), and the larger towns and smaller cities of over 6,000 people were obliged to open higher primary schools (écoles primaires supérieures) to provide two or three years of post-primary instruction for the middle and lower middle classes whose children required more than an elementary education but who did not need to spend years learning the classics. These young people would become middle-level supervisors, clerks, and school teachers. However, the higher primary schools failed to appeal to their intended clientele, perhaps because the word "primaire" was too closely associated with the common people to appeal to the upwardly mobile lower middle class. Some of the schools survived as municipal vocational schools in industrial and commercial cities, notably in Amiens, Le Havre, Lille, Lyon, Mulhouse, Nantes, Paris, and Reims.[6]

By mid-century the debate over a non-classical "modern" alternative for the middle and lower middle-classes shifted to the secondary level, which was more prestigious and less associated with manual work. Victor Duruy, education minister from 1863 to 1869, introduced l'enseignement secondaire spécial in 1865 as a four-year program based on French, mathematics, science, history, and geography. The program was designed to appeal to those from the middle classes destined for middle-management positions who needed several years of modern instruction rather than the long course of classical studies. However, it had only mediocre success with this group because of its inferior prestige.[7]

Under the Third Republic, governments gradually transformed l'enseignement spécial into l'enseignement moderne (decrees in 1881, 1886, and 1891), a seven-year program with its own baccalauréat based on French rather than Latin classics. In 1902 moderne was transformed into one of four baccalauréat options, option D, modern languages and science. It appeared at last that modern secondary studies had found their niche in the public education system, but the program was looked down upon by classicists and attracted the weaker students until the Second World War.

Still, the various levels of the middle class were provided with educational institutions designed to meet their needs. The urban working class was not so fortunate. In the middle of the nineteenth century, 568 inhabitants per thousand worked in agriculture, 218 were employed in small companies with fewer than ten workers, and only fifty-eight worked in big industry, making it difficult to focus attention on the plight of industrial workers, particularly in the face of resistance from employers.[8] Nevertheless, concern over the social consequences of child labour led to a law in 1841 forbidding factory work for those under eight and limiting it to eight hours per day for those up to twelve years of age. An apprenticeship law in 1851 reintroduced apprenticeship contracts and included provisions to protect apprentices from their employers.[9] Both laws had provisions guaranteeing a minimum of schooling for young people under thirteen. This, combined with the Falloux Law of 1850 which raised the pay of teachers and required towns of over 800 inhabitants to maintain schools for girls, might have led to substantial improvements in the condition of children. Unfortunately the laws of 1841 and 1851 lacked provisions for enforcement and had little impact, and the Falloux Law was administered in a very conservative manner during the 1850s.

At this time a group of advocates of vocational education appeared under the leadership of General Arthur Morin, director of the Conservatoire des arts et métiers from 1849 to 1880, and centred around the Ministry of Industry and Commerce in Paris.[10] The ministry organized a major inquiry into technical and vocational education in France, which resulted in the publication of two volumes of testimony and statistics in 1865, along with various reports and notes.[11]

The hearings were marked by sharp disagreement over the kind of vocational training that should be given and at what level. One group favoured the model of the École Turgot of Paris, founded in 1837, which offered a mainly general curriculum – an extension of the primary program – with some manual and vocational training, the idea being that the young worker would learn his skills in the factory and shop.[12] Another group argued that vocational schools should train workers and foremen directly for their jobs.[13] Convinced that the Ministry of Public Instruction and the *universitaires* were incapable of understanding the requirements of modern industrial society, they called for the creation of a separate system of public vocational schools under the Commerce ministry, the *Université de l'industrie*, in competition with the schools under the Ministry of Public Instruction.[14]

The Commerce ministry drew up a bill in 1867 that left the initiative for the creation of vocational and technical schools to private groups, municipalities, and the departments but provided a budget to subsi-

dize such schools. It also created a Conseil supérieur de l'enseignement technique and placed all vocational schools and courses under
its own authority. The law was never implemented, and the government contented itself with allocating 150,000 francs to Commerce to
subsidize vocational schools and courses.

Some technical and vocational instruction was given by private individuals, companies, and associations. The Christian Brothers (Frères
des écoles chrétiennes) ran a number of schools that provided apprenticeship and vocational training.[15] Several industrialists, notably the
metallurgist Eugène Schneider at Creusot and the printer Chaix in
Paris, founded factory schools for their workers. Industrial associations in Mulhouse, Reims, and other cities organized evening courses
for workers, as did the Conservatoire des arts et métiers in Paris, the
Société polytechnique (1830), composed of graduates of the École
polytechnique, the Société philotechnique (1848), composed of graduates of the École centrale, and various other philanthropic and religious organizations.[16] But these schools and courses reached no more
than 5 per cent of about 440,000 young people employed in business
and industry.

During the 1870s investigations conducted by the City of Paris
revealed the perilous state of apprenticeship in the industries of the
region.[17] Octave Gréard, inspector general and director of primary
education for the Department of the Seine, organized an excellent
system of primary and higher primary schools in Paris, which served
as a model for the national reforms of the 1880s.[18] He established the
École Diderot on the boulevard de la Villette in 1873 as a model
apprenticeship school to train young men in the metal and wood
crafts.[19] During the 1880s eleven more such schools would be created
in various specialties. These apprenticeship schools were complemented by eight higher primary schools established on the model of
the École Turgot.[20]

THE THIRD REPUBLIC, 1875–1914

Between 1879 and 1886 the triumphant Republic introduced a series
of laws, usually called the Ferry Laws after Jules Ferry who was alter-
natively prime minister and education minister during these years,
rendering French education compulsory, free, and secular for boys
and girls to the age of thirteen. Teacher training was improved and
normal schools and lycées for young women were established in the
departments. The laws required cities and towns of over 6,000 inhabitants to maintain higher primary schools (écoles primaires supérieures)
for boys and girls of modest, usually lower middle class origin, aged

thirteen to fifteen. They were financed and controlled by the municipalities while the Ministry of Public Instruction provided subsidies and general supervision and inspection.

The higher primary schools offered a three-year general program of modern, non-classical studies (French, history-geography, math, science, civic education, plus some manual training) for young people aged 12 to 14 seeking additional education beyond the elementary schools but unable to pursue the lengthy and expensive classical curriculum of the lycées. After attending higher primary schools, most went to work at about 14 years of age, but some continued into the teacher-training schools (écoles normales primaires) to become elementary school teachers or into trade schools such as the Écoles d'arts et métiers to acquire industrial skills in order to qualify as foremen and shop supervisors. Preparing young people for a variety of intermediate positions in business, industry, and the public services, the higher primary schools soon captured the petty bourgeois clientele of l'enseignement spécial and grew steadily over the years.[21]

The success of the Ferry Laws and the higher primary schools in the generation before the First World War can be explained by a social consensus in favour of compulsory and free primary education, which increased the demand for post-primary education. Rapid economic growth and changes in the labour force from the 1880s to 1914 also played a role. The number employed in industry and transport in France in 1856 was 4,384,000. It was still 4,444,000 in 1880 but by 1906 the figure had reached 6,338,000 (up two million or 50 per cent) during a period in which the population was growing slowly. In the half century after the First World War this figure grew only modestly to 6,862,000.[22]

The period between 1881 and 1914 saw annual economic growth average 4.5 per cent. Although French railway and machine tool production declined vis-à-vis her rivals, particularly Germany and the United States, and advancement in new fields such as chemistry was slow, the French led the world in automobiles and aviation and had a respectable record in electricity. Thanks to intensive exploitation of the Briey basin in Lorraine, iron ore production rose by 87 per cent and steel by 152 per cent in the two decades before the war, equal to the pace of Germany and the United States.

Such growth saw the beginnings of a genuine industrial proletariat in France, drawn mainly from the peasantry but also including women (51 per cent of textile workers by the end of the century) and foreigners.[23] The period also saw substantially increased demand for skilled workers, who made up around a quarter of industrial workers, and for foremen and technicians, who were needed to maintain, regulate, and repair machines, handle new kinds of equipment, and to help introduce assembly line techniques using universal machine tools. Qualifications were not easily earned in the factory because of the range of skills involved and the increasing specialization of workers.[24]

In 1878 the deputy and ex-worker Martin Nadaud visited the École Diderot and drew up a bill establishing a similar school in each department.[25] Anthyme Corbon, another ex-worker presented a similar bill in the Senate. Both bills left the creation of vocational schools to local authorities with the state providing subsidies and encouragement. In 1879 the government appointed Gréard and Corbon to a study commission chaired by Henri Tolain, another senator and former worker, to look into establishing a national system of vocational schools.

This study led to the first law on vocational education in France, adopted on 11 December 1880, creating the *écoles manuelles d'apprentissage* to provide pre-apprenticeship training during the late primary school years. Although these were placed under the joint authority of the Minister of Industry and Commerce and the Ministry of Public Instruction, the municipalities and departments were given the authority to establish and finance them. Parliament voted no funds, expecting the local authorities to do so, as Paris had done in the 1870s.[26] The result was that no schools were created during the 1880s, aside from the eleven established in Paris between 1880 and 1887 on the model of the École Diderot.

In the months before the passage of the law enacting the écoles manuelles d'apprentissage, the Ministry of Public Instruction decreed the creation of three schools at Vierzon, Voiron, and Armentières called *Écoles d'enseignement primaire supérieur et d'enseignement professionnel*, the future *écoles nationales professionnelles*, as models for the écoles manuelles d'apprentissage. These were based on Gréard's idea of "l'éducation intégrale" to produce the "complete worker." This meant the creation of multi-purpose schools combining pre-school, primary, vocational, and normal sections on one campus, and emphasizing a blend of theoretical and practical instruction rather than early specialization. The goal was to provide the young worker some vocational instruction as part of a broader general education, avoiding premature exposure to the bad influences of the factory.[27]

In practice, the ministry had only a vague idea as to how these schools should be organized. Members of parliament such as Corbon and Nadaud saw the complete worker in the traditional artisanal mould, and they were willing to accept the vocational school as the means of training workers only because of the inadequacy of the modern factory as a place for learning a trade. A second group, led

by Jules Ferry and Ferdinand Buisson, director of the primary education division in the Ministry of Public Instruction from 1879 to 1896
favoured the ideas of Gréard. They argued that the higher primary
schools, with their general modern programs designed to serve the
needs of young people preparing for middle-level positions in
the economy and public services, should serve as the model for the
higher-primary vocational schools such as the écoles manuelles d'apprentissage and the écoles professionnelles. Although the vocational
schools were to teach skills, they should not become so specialized as
to prevent the young person from acquiring a good general formation preparing him or her for life in a democratic society. A third
group, associated with the Commerce ministry and the Conservatoire national d'arts et métiers, envisaged the vocational school as
training workers capable of being immediately placed in business
and industry, and they were especially keen to train young workers
in the use of the new machine tools that were beginning to appear
in the mechanical and metallurgical industries. All three groups
agreed that these young men should follow in the footsteps of their
working-class fathers. The higher primary school, vocational or general, led only to the workplace and not to the secondary lycée, which
was reserved for the bourgeoisie.

As the republicans proved unable to resolve their differences, in
1886 the government placed the écoles professionnelles and the écoles
manuelles d'apprentissage under the joint authority of the ministries
of Public Instruction and Commerce, called the *Condominium*. Differences of opinion between the two ministries soon came to a head at an
inter-ministerial conference in 1887. Buisson argued that the general
programs of the higher primary schools suited the French economy
with its thousands of small firms, shops, and farms and its varied
business and industrial sectors. He argued that a young person can
"acquire the skills that form the worker without losing, for lack of
exercise, the intellectual capacities that make the man."[28] Like Gréard,
he saw the vocational school as a kind of refuge protecting a young
man from the bad environment of the factory and providing some
additional education, personal development, and a chance to acquire
basic skills.

In contrast, Gustave Ollendorf, director of the office of technical
education in the Commerce Ministry, saw the écoles professionnelles
and the écoles manuelles d'apprentissage as vocational schools training an elite of highly skilled workers capable of adapting to "the
rapid transformation of industry" and aiding France in the "struggle" with foreign competitors. Ollendorf insisted that the programs of
these schools constituted a new *culture technique* deriving from tech-

nological change. He and the Commerce group argued that the higher primary schools, as useless hybrids leading nowhere, should disappear, that their vocational sections should be transformed into vocational schools serving the economic specialties of their regions, and that their general programs should be assimilated into the lycées and collèges.[29]

The *Condominium* remained in force until 1892 when the écoles manuelles d'apprentissage, renamed *écoles pratiques de commerce et d'industrie*, were placed under the exclusive control of the Ministry of Commerce. All other higher primary schools where teaching was "principally industrial or commercial" were to be transferred to Commerce. This proved to be a turning point in the fortunes of the Commerce ministry – the victory of industrialists over pedagogues. The écoles pratiques became more specialized and shop-oriented than the écoles manuelles had been, and they grew rapidly from twelve schools with 1,717 students (1,342 boys) in 1893 to sixty-nine schools with 12,979 students in 1910.[30]

After six years of delay, the Ministry of Public Instruction opened the three *écoles primaires supérieures et professionnelles* in 1887, at Vierzon, Voiron, and Armentières, as *centres scolaires* providing preschool, primary, and higher primary vocational schools, with each division providing some manual work. The vocational schools failed to attract many students from the annexed primary schools; their parents were usually in a hurry to put them to work.[31] By the early 1890s the ministries of Public Instruction and Commerce decided to reorganize the schools as national vocational boarding schools, *écoles nationales professionnelles*, each recruiting regionally rather than locally. In this capacity they attracted more qualified students and began to prosper, but the continuing existence of adjacent primary schools and other institutions prevented them from emerging as clearly technical schools until after 1900.

The three écoles nationales professionnelles at Vierzon, Voiron, and Armentières remained under the *Condominium* during the 1890s. In 1893, the two ministries agreed to a joint commission to deal with programs, personnel, and inspection of the three schools.[32] The commission appeared to be working sufficiently well that in 1898 the government purchased the École Livet, a private professional school in Nantes, for conversion into a fourth école nationale professionnelle. But squabbling between the two ministries was to be such that five weeks before the school was due to open in October 1898, there was no director, no faculty, and no program.[33] The school managed to open in 1899, inadequately staffed, and the first year of operation was chaotic. While the two ministries were trying to cooperate in order to open the ENP in Nantes, the Ministry of Commerce was offering the city council 2,500 francs for "equipment" to convert its higher primary school into an école pratique de commerce et d'industrie.[34] In the midst of such a "petite guerre" cooperation was impossible.

Under the leadership in the Chamber of Deputies of Modeste Leroy, Gauche démocratique (right-centre) deputy from Evreux (Eure), the Commerce group redoubled its attacks in parliament on the *Condominium*. Leroy had made his reputation by attacking the state scholarship system for granting awards mainly to the sons of state bureaucrats destined for the civil service and liberal professions. He pointed out that in 1895 only one-ninth of scholarship holders (107 of 973) were headed for business and industry, and he came within seven votes of overturning the whole program.[35] On 1 February 1899, he suddenly introduced in the Chamber of Deputies an amendment to the budget of 1900 that transferred the budget of the écoles nationales professionnelles of Armentières, Vierzon, Voiron, and Nantes from the Ministry of Public Instruction to the Ministry of Commerce.[36] The Minister of Commerce (1899–1902), Alexandre Millerand, with the backing of business and industrial associations, actively supported the amendment. The Chamber referred the amendment to the budget commission in November 1899, which pronounced in favour of the transfer. The Chamber discussed it on 31 January 1900, and adopted it by a vote of 288 to 255, the Senate ratifying the bill 2 April 1900. In addition to the écoles nationales professionnelles, parliament also transferred the École Diderot and twelve other Paris vocational schools to Commerce.[37]

The reforms of 1892 and 1900 gave the Commerce ministry a complete system of schools ranging from the écoles pratiques and écoles nationales professionnelles at the junior secondary level, to the écoles d'arts et métiers at the senior secondary level, and the école centrale des arts et manufactures in higher education. Millerand assimilated the écoles d'horlogerie at Besançon and Cluses into the newly acquired écoles nationales professionnelles. Two new écoles d'arts et métiers were opened in Lille in 1900 and Cluny in 1901, and a third was planned for Paris, opening in 1912.[38] In 1907 the five écoles d'arts et métiers became engineering schools, and the écoles nationales professionnelles gradually replaced them as schools training industrial technicians, mainly for the machine and mechanical industries. In 1890 the École des hautes études commerciales of Paris and thirteen provincial écoles de commerce were also placed under the Ministry of Commerce, giving the ministry a network of business as well as industrial schools.[39]

The number of schools under Commerce rose steadily during the following years, from thirty-five in 1900 to ninety-six in 1905, while the number of students grew from 5,000 to 18,000.[40] This accompanied a slow but steady rise in the education budget of the ministry from 1.9 million francs in 1883 to 5 million in 1905, reaching almost 10 million francs in 1914.[41] The ministry opened a training section for professors at the École d'arts et métiers of Châlons in 1891 to prepare teachers for these schools. It was transferred to the École d'arts et métiers of Paris in 1912, and in 1934 it became the École normale supérieure de l'enseignement technique (ENSET).[42] The Commerce system that emerged in 1900 resembled in many ways the "Université de l'Industrie" as envisaged in the 1860s by Arthur Morin and his assistant, Henry Tresca.[43]

The rapid development of the technical education system required expansion of its administration under the Ministry of Commerce. The ministry was organized mainly to encourage industry and trade. Its educational budget and bureaucracy were small, and its Conseil supérieur de l'enseignement technique, created in 1870, was semi-official in status, met irregularly, and seldom published its minutes. In 1883, the Commerce minister named a director of the division of technical education, but his successor failed to name one, and the division spent long periods of time without a director until 1895 when the ministry definitely established the division of technical education (*direction de l'enseignement technique*) under Louis Bouquet, aided by an assistant director, inspectors, and councils at the national, regional and departmental levels.[44] The Conseil supérieur de l'enseignement technique included representatives from business, industry, and engineering and alumni associations, who worked closely with officials of the technical education division and the Ministry of Commerce. Business and industry were also well represented on the department committees. By 1900 an autonomous division of technical education had emerged under the ministry separate from the education system under the Ministry of Public Instruction.

The organization of the technical education division during the 1890s brought the various groups supporting technical education together. That led in 1902 to the formation of the independent *Association française pour la défense de l'enseignement technique*, which aggressively pursued the expansion of the schools under Commerce.[45] AFDET had ample contacts in parliament. Almost one fifth of the deputies in the National Assembly in 1912, a total of 114 including seventy-eight from the right-centre (68 per cent), listed technical education as one of their highest priorities.[46]

Proponents of technical education kept up pressure on Public Instruction to abandon technical education. As president of AFDET from 1907 to 1912, Modeste Leroy, deputy from Evreux attacked the Ministry of Public Instruction and the higher primary schools. He described the latter as "boîtes à bachot pour petits fonctionnaires," diverting able young workers from productive industry into economically parasitical positions as clerks and petty bureaucrats, thereby creating a class of potentially discontented "déclassé intellectuals."[47] He dismissed the vocational courses of the higher primary schools as *bricolage* (puttering around), and attacked the Ministry of Public Instruction repeatedly for producing "a devastating plague of bureaucrats" that was undermining the productive forces of the nation in the deadly economic struggle with Germany and other rivals.[48]

Leroy argued that Commerce should be allowed to annex the vocational sections of the higher primary schools and convert them into écoles pratiques de commerce et d'industrie (the general sections to be given to the lycées and collèges). He pointed to the law of 1892 allowing the conversion of any higher primary school into an école pratique when its programs were "principally industrial or commercial."[49] Indeed, backed by AFDET, the Commerce Ministry successfully persuaded a number of industrial cities to convert their higher primary schools with vocational sections into écoles pratiques, which exacerbated tension between the two ministries.[50]

This placed the Ministry of Public Instruction in a very difficult position. Its budget for vocational instruction was small, and the installation of workshops and labs and the training of personnel was expensive. If it introduced practical and vocational programs into the higher primary schools, it risked losing them to Commerce. If it did not, its programs would be attacked as irrelevant to the needs of the modern world and the arms race with Germany.[51]

René Leblanc, inspector-general of vocational education in the Public Instruction Ministry, became the outspoken defender of the ministry and of the higher primary schools. He responded to Leroy's attacks on these schools by attacking the écoles pratiques as overly specialized and reaching only a small portion of the population engaged in industry – roughly those employed in the machine and metallurgical trades, or about 25 per cent of industrial workers – and therefore a minority of students.[52] This criticism had some validity. The programs of the écoles pratiques were designed to train skilled workers and were heavily weighted toward the practical. Students received little general education, yet did not acquire sufficient skills to enable them to adapt quickly to the workplace. The main problem was that the school workshops were designed as small-scale factories with heavy emphasis on workshop and practical instruction, very long work weeks (table 1.1), but relatively few visits to local factories and firms. The goal for Leroy, Ollendorf, and others was to produce a kind of "superworker," the master of his trade, capable of rising up the industrial hierarchy and achieving a middle-class status in the world of work.[53] Leblanc argued that the opposite was happening. Many graduates never used their skills, quitting heavy industry to set themselves up as bicycle merchants, car and motor repairmen, hardware traders, and small subcontractors and suppliers in mechanical parts.[54]

Leblanc also argued that because of the diversity and decentralization of the French economy, the higher primary programs with six or seven hours a week of vocational instruction were suitable to the needs of the country. He cited official statistics indicating that slightly more than 300,000 workers (of a total of three million in the labour force) worked in 151 companies with more than 1,000 employees, while 807,000 worked in 489,000 firms having one to four employees.[55] The great majority of French workers and artisans did not need specialized training but rather a good modern education enabling them to adapt to a variety of conditions. Leblanc pointed out that many of the thirty-six écoles pratiques that existed in 1901 were former higher primary schools – most of the schools located in industrial and commercial areas had already been converted. The stakes were high, for there were about 203 higher primary schools for boys and 93 for girls in 1901.[56] If Commerce were to get control of all of the 129 higher primary schools that offered vocational programs, the system so popular among the working people of France would be "in ruins."[57]

Leblanc was probably wrong, however, in his contention that graduates of the écoles pratiques did not become industrial workers; statistics on the early careers of graduates in 1906 reveal that most became workers and that graduates were frequently promoted to posts as foremen and shop supervisors.[58] Moreover, the higher primary vocational sections do not appear to have been very effective in teaching vocational skills. An English observer, Charles Copland Perry, found on his tour of inspection in 1899 that the higher primary schools provided too little vocational training and that shop teachers were often poorly trained. He concluded that the programs of the écoles pratiques in which students spent 60 per cent of their time in the workshop and 40 per cent taking general and technical courses were more effective, mainly because they were adapted to local economic needs.[59]

On the other hand, the Commerce lobby appears to have been wrong in their argument that the higher primary schools diverted young people from productive industry into bureaucratic positions in various government administrations. In 1900 30 per cent of graduates went into industry, a quarter into business, and 17 per cent into farming, while 21.5 per cent continued their studies in secondary schools, normal schools, or in the écoles d'arts et métiers and other technical and professional schools.[60] While it is doubtless true that many who entered business and industry did so in small family businesses that

Table 1.1
Weekly schedules in post-elementary schools, 1900

School	Workshop Hours			General Program			Total		
Year	1	2	3	1	2	3	1	2	3
Diderot	39	39	48	9	9	6	48	48	54
EPS	4	6	6	26	24	24	30	30	30
ENP	15	20	25	26	26.5	22	41	46.5	47
EPCI	30	30	33	16.5	19.5	18	46.5	49.5	51

Source: AN F 17 14350, Note sur l'organisation de l'enseignement technique, n.d., [1900–1901].
Charles Copland Perry, L'Enseignement technique français jugé par un Anglais, Rapport adressé au
Département des Sciences et des Arts de la Grande Bretagne (Grenoble, 1899), 26. Yves Legoux, Du
compagnon au technicien, 139. Astier & Cuminal, L'enseignement technique, 250. Charlot and Figeat, 157.

were not necessarily very productive, it is also true that half the students of the écoles d'arts et métiers were recruited from the vocational sections of the higher primary schools (the remainder were drawn from the écoles nationales professionnelles, the écoles pratiques, and other technical schools), which indicates that they had received a solid preparation in science, mathematics, and industrial design.

The higher primary schools also produced many students for the new engineering institutes created by the Ministry of Public Instruction in university science faculties during the last two decades of the nineteenth century. Several, at Grenoble, Nancy, Lille, Lyons, and Toulouse, had become schools in chemical, mechanical, and electrical engineering. Like the écoles d'arts et métiers, the École centrale, and the École supérieure d'électricité (1894), they did not require a baccalauréat for admission, which opened secondary and higher education to scientifically oriented young men from the lower classes.[61]

Two tracks thus developed in applied science after 1900 that bypassed the baccalauréat and classical studies: one under the Commerce Ministry and the other, just mentioned, under the primary education division of the Public Instruction Ministry. Students could follow either track, or some combination thereof, in seeking a technician's or engineer's diploma. This promising development was undermined by the quarrel between Commerce and Public Instruction and the constant attacks on each others' schools, which delayed growth at the intermediate level and erected unnecessary barriers and divisions between general studies and the technical and vocational streams. Such quarrels were obviously wasteful, as individuals on both sides gradually came to realize, because they undermined French energies and prevented the more rapid development of popular vocational education.

For a variety of reasons, patriotic and political, a more conciliatory attitude developed in both the Commerce and Public Instruction ministries during the years before the First World War. For one thing, there were no major political or ideological differences dividing supporters of the two sides (as there had been in the church-state quarrel), because most belonged to the Radical Party or to small parties allied to it (Parti Républicain, Gauche démocratique), which, despite the leftist tenor of their names, were moderate, and accepted the need for compulsory primary education and higher primary vocational studies. They shared a concern about the quality of the French labour force compared to that of Germany, where virtually all young German workers benefited from an excellent system of apprenticeship schools run by industry, labour unions, and the states (*länder*).

Among *universitaires*, Ferdinand Buisson (Radical) came increasingly to support technical schools and compulsory continuing education programs to age eighteen for young people working in business and industry. Leblanc himself suggested juxtaposing the higher primary and practical schools, the general sections to be run by the Ministry of Public Instruction and the technical side by the Ministry of Commerce.[62] On the Commerce side, the election in 1912 of Senator Gustave Dron as president of AFDET, replacing Modeste Leroy, signaled growing moderation in policy. As mayor of Tourcoing, Dron had overseen the establishment of both an école pratique and an école primaire supérieure on the same campus, and he favoured cooperation between the two ministries in the field of post-elementary education. A member of the Parti Républicain, close to the Radical party, he worked with former commerce ministers and Radical politicians who had a history of support for the higher primary schools – Alfred Massé, Charles Couyba, and Fernand David – who also advocated reconciliation between the two ministries.[63]

Between 1906 and 1912 parliament recognized the central importance of the higher primary schools, raising their annual budget for vocational training and manual work from 6,000 to 300,000 francs. This made possible substantial improvements in workshops, equipment, and teacher training and remuneration.[64] These reforms blunted the offensive of Commerce and laid the groundwork for the eventual cooperation of the two ministries after the war.

THE NUMBER OF STUDENTS IN TECHNICAL SCHOOLS BEFORE 1914

After 1900 France was reasonably well served by her technical schools at the middle and higher levels. In addition to the elite grandes écoles – Polytechnique, Ponts-et-Chaussées, Mines, and Centrale – newer schools such as the École supérieure d'électricité (1894), the École supérieure d'aéronautique (1909), the École de physique et de chimie industrielles in Paris (1882), and in the provinces, the Institut industriel du Nord (1873), the Écoles de chimie industrielle of Lyon (1883) and of Nancy (1890), the Institut électrotechnique of Grenoble, and the applied science institutes in the universities produced an adequate number of engineers. The École supérieure de Commerce of Paris (1890) and thirteen écoles de commerce in the provinces provided business education to 1,700 students a year. The écoles d'arts et métiers, training industrial engineers, doubled in number from three to six between 1900 and 1912 and had around 1,800 students.[65] The four écoles nationales professionnelles at Vierzon, Voiron, Armentières, and Nantes, with 1,686 students in 1913, filled the role once played by the arts et métiers in training shop supervisors, draftsmen, and technicians. The écoles pratiques grew from thirteen in 1892 to seventy-three in 1913 (fourteen for girls) with 14,700 students.[66] The thirteen Paris municipal schools along with the vocational sections of the higher primary schools and various private écoles de métiers also trained skilled workers who were frequently promoted to positions as foremen and shop supervisors on the job. In all, the system reached around 37,000 young people in 1914.[67] In addition, 45,000 attended the higher primary schools, 97,000 secondary lycées and collèges, and 40,000 higher education. When one considers that there were 5.5 million children attending elementary school, clearly the majority of French children finished school at age thirteen with little or no practical training or post-elementary education and went to work in factory or shop or in the family farm or firm where they usually learned on the job.[68]

The schools under Commerce produced only an elite of skilled workers, technicians, and engineers. There was little or no provision for the education of the average worker beyond private schools operated by companies and associations and evening courses offered by private associations. By 1910 an estimated 88 per cent of young workers had no formal technical training.[69] Since the time of the Second Empire the Ministry of Commerce had recognized and subsidized employers' associations, chambers of commerce, industrial societies, workingmen's unions, and religious and philanthropic groups that organized daytime and evening courses for young workers aged thirteen through seventeen in factories or in schools associated with business and industry. In 1904, 586 such associations offered 4,223 courses for 95,000 auditors in 1905, of whom about 50,000 appear to have attended regularly.[70] Thus almost 87,000 young people under the age of eighteen received some kind of vocational training in schools or

Table 1.2
Students in secondary vocational and technical schools 1913–14

Écoles pratiques de commerce et d'industrie	14,700
Écoles nationales professionnelles	1,686
Écoles nationales d'horlogerie	1,200
Écoles nationales d'Arts et Métiers	1,800
Écoles professionnelles de Paris	4,000
Other ministries, private schools	7,400
EPS, Sections professionnelles	6,000
Sub Total	36,786
Cours professionnels	50,000
Total	86,786

courses, out of 874,941 young people employed in the labour force or 10 per cent, a figure that was rather low, but somewhat higher than Jean-Pierre Guinot's estimate of 70,000 or 8 per cent, on which most subsequent figures have been based.[71]

CONCLUSION

The first generation of the Third Republic saw great progress in education in response to economic growth and rising social demand, in particular the introduction of compulsory, free primary education, the creation of a national system of higher primary schools and normal schools under the Ministry of Public Instruction, and the establishment of a system of public technical schools under the technical education division of the Ministry of Industry and Commerce.

The growth of technical and vocational education began to accelerate after 1900 but was limited by the quarrel between the ministries of Public Instruction and Industry and Commerce over the future of higher primary education. The Ministry of Commerce wanted early specialization of the workforce, and it sought to annex the écoles primaires supérieures with vocational sections to its own system of écoles pratiques. Educators in the Ministry of Public Instruction believed that technical education placed utilitarian considerations above the requirements of civilization and that industrialists were too anxious to encourage young workers to specialize before they had received an adequate general education. Industrialists, on the other hand, were convinced that the *universitaires* did not understand the requirements of industry and that, given the chance, they would divert capable young workers from technical to general studies, producing a class of discontented déclassé intellectuals. While their suspicion seems extreme, it must be remembered that even supporters of vocational education like Gréard, Ferry, and Buisson thought that the best thing they could do for young working class people was to delay their entry into factory and shop for as long as possible, hardly a position likely to endear them to industrialists. The quarrel between the public education and commerce ministries peaked in the 1890s and early 1900s, declining in the years before the First World War. However the suspicion between educators and industrialists continued for over a century from the 1860s into the 1970s, and some of the fears of industrialists about the future of technical education were realized after the abolition of the technical education division in 1960.

Once the technical education division, created officially in 1895, had acquired the écoles pratiques de commerce et d'industrie and the écoles nationales professionnelles in 1892 and 1900, it possessed a full range of schools training skilled workers, draftsmen, foremen, technicians, and production engineers. It came to resemble a mini-education system ranging from higher primary to higher education and staffed by its own bureaucracy, its conseil supérieur de l'enseignement technique, and local and regional committees composed of businessmen, industrialists, school officials, and representatives of the division.

In response to rapid economic growth, the French greatly improved their system of technical schools but failed to do much for the education of the average worker beyond introducing compulsory primary education in 1882. The reigning social idea for the mass of working people, urban and rural, who composed about 90 per cent of the population, was that of Jules Ferry: sons should follow in the footsteps of their fathers and therefore needed no more than a good primary education in French, the three Rs and civics. Moreover, the Third Republic took more credit than it deserved for the introduction of universal primary education, which had been largely attained by the 1870s in most departments.[72] It did reintroduce a good system of higher primary schools, improved female education, and created a small but efficient system of technical and vocational schools under the Ministry of Commerce, mainly at the junior secondary level. It was possible for able young people of lower middle or upper working class origin to obtain schooling beyond the primary level, and even in a few cases to reach advanced education in the form of the new engineering institutes in the university science faculties or the écoles d'arts et métiers without possessing the baccalauréat. These were not inconsiderable achievements within a single generation.

2 The Division of Technical Education from 1920 to 1960

Nous avons un enseignement qui n'est ni primaire ni secondaire
ni supérieur, bien qu'il soit à la fois primaire, secondaire et
supérieur – c'est l'enseignement technique.
Paul Lapie, *Un réquisitoire contre la séparation des ordres*

This chapter discusses the administration of the division of technical
education from the time of its transfer from the Ministry of Commerce to the Ministry of National Education in 1920 to its abolition in
1960. In 1920 technical education became one of four divisions in the
Ministry of Education. The greatest threat to the technical education
division, and indeed to the four divisions of the ministry of education, was the movement favouring the *école unique*, a junior high
school open to all social classes which proposed to absorb the first
cycle of the lycée (secondary division), the higher primary schools
(primary division), and the écoles pratiques and écoles professionnelles (technical education division). Even though some of the best
minds of the day favoured opening junior secondary education to the
common people, the combined hostility of the four divisions (the
three above plus higher education) meant that the école unique only
began to have a serious chance of realization after the abolition of the
divisions in the early 1960s. This meant that the technical education
division survived another forty years as an enclave within the education system, closely connected to the metallurgical, mechanical, and
electrical industries, with around 800,000 students by the late 1950s in
various schools and programs in junior secondary, secondary, and
higher education. Though the system was flourishing at the end of
the Fourth Republic, it had survived only because of interest-group
politics and parliamentary inertia. The arrival of Charles de Gaulle
and the Fifth Republic in 1958, bent on reform and modernization,
meant that its days were numbered.

FROM THE MINISTRY OF COMMERCE
TO THE MINISTRY OF PUBLIC
INSTRUCTION, 1919-20

The Astier Law of 1919 established a national system of continuing education courses for young workers who had left school at the legal age of thirteen. They were obliged to take part-time courses over three years from the age of fourteen to eighteen, to prepare for the Certificat d'aptitude professionnelle (CAP) introduced in 1911 (see chapter 3). Article I of the Astier Law confirmed the placement of the technical education division under the Ministry of Industry and Commerce. Despite better relations with the Commerce Ministry during the pre-war years, the Ministry of Public Instruction, with over 500 vulnerable higher primary schools, feared the growing power of Commerce, which had 80 écoles pratiques under its wing and now controlled a growing national network of vocational courses (500 by 1927).[1]

The new prime minister, Alexandre Millerand, was a long-time supporter of the Commerce position. As minister of commerce from 1899 to 1902, he had vigorously opposed a proposal to transfer the technical education division to Public Instruction, but by 1920 he had changed his mind.[2] The idea of national unity was strong during the post-war period, and it made sense to get technical education out of the Commerce ministry and into the public education system where it would have access to better facilities. In a decree issued on 20 January 1920, his first day as prime minister, Millerand abruptly transferred technical education to the Ministry of Public Instruction. He undid at a stroke three laws passed by parliament. In justifying his actions Millerand cited the importance of national unity and better facilities and financing for technical education, and the need for better coordination between the primary, secondary and technical education divisions. Faced with strong opposition in the Chamber of Deputies and the Senate, he offered to maintain the technical education division as a full-scale *direction* in the ministry under its own secretary of state. He emphasized the importance of bringing together the "bookish and the real," the "cult of the humanities" and the "living realities" represented by technical education.[3]

The technical education lobby, centered in the Association française pour le développement de l'enseignement technique (AFDET) and the business community strongly opposed Millerand's decree. Senator Gustave Dron, AFDET president since 1912, an industrialist and mayor of Tourcoing, wrote to Millerand to approve of the undersecretary but expressed a general "alarm" in industrial circles "caused by the transfer to the Ministry of Public Instruction, which in the past has shown much more interest in general culture than in the technical education favored by the Ministry of Industry and Commerce."[4] Dron and his group and the staff of the technical education division itself were particularly concerned that the division would lose its close contacts with business and professional communities. Modeste Leroy, never one to mince his words, spoke of an "inexplicable abuse of power ... a simple decree, signed by a man who is obviously poorly informed, has just destroyed the effect of three laws."[5]

Dron and Leroy were supported by businessmen who had never forgiven Millerand for a 1900 law limiting factory work to ten hours, and they also resented the 1919 law introducing the eight-hour day. Accordingly, 115 of 125 chambers of commerce petitioned against the transfer from the Ministry of Commerce to Public Instruction (soon renamed Ministry of National Education).[6]

In the Chamber of Deputies, a well organized parliamentary group with close connections to AFDET and to business and industry defended technical education, notably Paul Aubriot, Ferdinand Buisson, Etienne Clémentel, Isidore Cuminal, Fernand David, Paul Doumer, Jules Méline, and Constant Verlot.[7] This group introduced an amendment in the Senate to create the undersecretary of state but keeping it under the Ministry of Commerce.[8]

Millerand got his way by threatening to resign and offering a compromise: to transfer the secretary of state and the technical education division to the Ministry of Public Instruction and to establish an interministerial commission to study administrative coordination and to oversee details of the transfer. The Minister of Commerce was to sit on the Conseil supérieur de l'enseignement technique. The law guaranteed the technical education division its own central administration and budget, its own directors, inspectors, and councils, and its own hierarchy of schools with control over programs and diplomas, teacher training, and placement.[9] This made the division strong enough to hold its own in the Ministry of Public Instruction with the three other *directions* (primary, secondary, and higher education). In the process, Millerand created the Office national des recherches scientifiques.[10]

In practice the transfer worked reasonably well. The assimilation of personnel into the public education system meant easier recruitment, better pay and more prestige for professors and teachers.[11] Most importantly, the long-standing battle between the primary and technical education divisions over the higher primary schools diminished considerably (though did not disappear). The two divisions, now under the same ministry, agreed on a formula whereby technical education had control over the vocational sections of the higher primary schools while the primary division directed the schools and their general programs. This seemingly awkward solution worked well in practice because the two divisions increasingly "twinned" higher primary schools and écoles pratiques (*écoles jumelées*) in urban areas by placing them on the same campus. In smaller towns where separate schools were usually too small to be viable they closed them and created a single school with vocational sections.[12] The 1930s saw the growth of educational centres (*centres scolaires*) bringing together lycées, higher primary schools, écoles pratiques and centres d'apprentissage. In rural areas the technical education division cooperated with the primary division in establishing vocational sections in the more important *cours complémentaires*, which were higher primary sections attached to larger elementary schools.[13] The accord between the primary, secondary, and technical divisions to establish *centres scolaires* made it much easier to introduce vocational orientation, required by law in 1922, and pre-apprenticeship programs to provide transition for children aged thirteen from school to the labour force.[14]

THE ÉCOLE UNIQUE

After the First World War a group of academic war veterans calling themselves the *Compagnons de l'université nouvelle* proposed to extend compulsory education to age fourteen and to introduce a common middle school, an *école unique* open to all social classes and acting as a bridge into senior secondary and higher education.[15] Children would attend primary school until the age of eleven, junior secondary school until fourteen, and (for those continuing their education) senior high school (the lycée) until the age of eighteen. After a period of study together called the *tronc commun* guidance counsellors would move the students into classical or vocational (agricultural and industrial) sections within the école unique.[16]

Supporters of the technical education division opposed the consolidation of junior secondary education as the first step toward abolishing the division and its schools. The Compagnons, educators steeped in Platonic thought, believed that social justice meant streaming young people in line with their natural aptitudes rather than social origins. This raised the fear that they were really trying to recruit the best and brightest from the working classes for the classics, depriving industry of its best recruits.

In response, Ludovic Zoretti, a science professor at the University of Caen, developed a plan for a common middle school based on mixed ability classes and a program of modern studies absorbing the first cycle of secondary education, the higher primary schools, and the intermediate technical schools. His plan became the basis for Socialist party and labour union reform proposals and influenced Jean Zay, the education minister from 1936 to 1939.[17] Paul Lapie, the director of the primary division in the 1920s, also favoured the creation of a genuine middle school, but instead of abolishing the higher primary schools, he favoured making them the basis for a new system of junior secondary schools, absorbing the écoles pratiques and other intermediate schools. Pointing to the advance of democracy and industry, he emphasized the success of the higher primary schools in pioneering a relevant modern and technical pedagogy, and their popularity with their lower middle- and upper working-class clientele.[18]

All plans for an école unique involved the extension of compulsory education from age twelve to fourteen and the reduction of the seven-year Latin program by one or two years. At the age of fifteen the young person would have three options: the classical secondary lycée or collège, the technical school (école nationale professionnelle, second cycle) or the workforce, in which case those employed in industry would take continuing education vocational courses until the age of eighteen. Such reforms threatened to eliminate the first cycle of studies of the lycées, collèges, and the écoles nationales professionnelles, and to eliminate the écoles primaires supérieures and the écoles pratiques de commerce et d'industrie altogether. For this reason the divisions of secondary and technical education formed a tacit alliance against all projects for an école unique, and in particular those of Zoretti and Lapie. Branding the higher primary schools and their modern programs a hybrid, neither classical nor technical, they hoped eventually to absorb these schools, the lycées, their general programs, and the technical schools, their vocational sections. Drawing upon Henri Bergson's idea that "disinterested" classical studies should exist separately from science and especially from applied science, the two divisions foresaw a dual system of secondary schools, classical and technical, under different administrations.[19]

Under the leadership of Edouard Herriot after the war, the Radical Party espoused the idea of the école unique. With the election of the Radical-led cartel des gauches in 1924, Education Minister François Albert created a commission to study the possibility of introducing the école unique. In the deliberations that followed, Paul Lapie and the physicist Paul Langevin favoured the idea, while Francisque Vial, director of secondary education, and Edmond Labbé, director of technical education, teamed up to oppose the idea with the support of

Radical deputy Hippolyte Ducos.[20] Nothing came of the commission's inquiry. All efforts to introduce some form of intermediate comprehensive school were to fail until the 1960s and 1970s.

THE LAW ON SECONDARY EDUCATION OF 1923

The alliance between the secondary and technical divisions was based on their opposition to the advance of modern studies, whether in the higher primary schools or in the lycées. Conservatives especially disliked the law on secondary education of 1902, which had created a modern "bac" alongside three classical ones (Latin-Greek, Latin-modern languages, Latin-sciences) and disrupted the unity of secondary studies. They favoured consolidating the first cycle of secondary education (sixth through the third grades or forms, students aged eleven to fifteen) by requiring every student in the first cycle to take Latin. In 1922, Léon Béard, education minister in the conservative Poincaré government, a *normalien* and a former classics professor, proposed to do away with modern studies during the first cycle of secondary education, making four years of Latin and two years of Greek compulsory for all students. During the second cycle (the last three years of high school: *seconde, première et terminale*), the student would choose between programs leading to a classical or modern baccalauréat, but at that point clearly only inferior students would choose moderne.[21]

The *baccalauréat moderne*, descended from Victor Duruy's *l'enseignement secondaire spécial*, had proved useful in providing educational opportunities for young people of lower middle- and upper working-class origin coming up from the primary, higher primary and normal schools who had not studied Latin but wished to complete their secondary education and have access to the universities. Sometimes they attended a lycée, but more often than not they transferred to a *collège communal*, a local municipal college that relied heavily on *moderne* for survival. Moderne was also essential to women because the female lycées introduced in the 1880s did not offer Latin and Greek. Although Béard proposed a science curriculum common to both the classical and modern programs, the classics were dominant and, as Louis Loucheur pointed out, no one could enter higher education without having taken Latin for a minimum of four years and Greek for a minimum of two.[22]

After intense parliamentary debate, the Béard bill was adopted by a narrow margin in July 1923.[23] Surprisingly, industrial associations such as the UIMM (*Union des Industries Métallurgiques et Minières, de la*

Construction Mécanique, Électrique et Métallique), which had long played a key role in the defense and development of technical education in France, supported the emphasis on classical education. A particularly detailed picture of the reaction to the bill of business and industrial associations survives because the *Association des professeurs des langues vivantes*, bitterly opposed to the bill for obvious reasons, sent a letter on 29 September 1921 to chambers of commerce and industrial associations soliciting support for its campaign against the bill. It warned of the "grave threat" to the country and to the economy posed by the destruction of the modern option.[24]

Of the five industrial associations, twelve chambers of commerce, three educational societies, and one professional association that replied, only two (the chambers of commerce of Carcassonne and Chambéry) defended *moderne*. The others supported classical languages as the best instruction for businessmen and industrialists.[25] While several cited the standard arguments of Latin as the mother tongue of French and Greece and Rome as the cradle of civilization, most defended it on practical and patriotic grounds as capable of training an elite of men of action who would provide renewed, vigorous leadership for France and French industry in the modern age. In other words, businessmen espoused pre-industrial ideas of honour, character, and culture rather than business virtues and utilitarian training.

The directors of the UIMM stated: "By the intellectual discipline that it demands, by the examples it provides, by the sense of tradition it awakens, the study of Latin develops judgment and thought much more fully than do the exact sciences, modern languages, geography, and even history."[26] The directors of the *Comité central des houillères de France* wrote: "The immense effort that the Great War imposed upon our major industries has shown very clearly the superiority of our collaborators whose broad culture and varied instruction had provided them an intellectual flexibility and a capacity for analysis of the most unexpected problems."[27] They argued that the academic preparation for middle-level technical managers or *cadres* could be relatively short because they could learn their specialization on the job: "The true vocational school is the factory, the mine, and the business office." The *cadres supérieurs*, on the other hand, had to be administrators, producers, inventors, businessmen, and leaders of men. Their education must be "une gymnastique savante" based on the classics, which would teach the students to think, to express themselves clearly, and to develop good work habits – the qualities necessary for the modern executive.[28]

Industrialists wanted vocational education for their skilled workers, foremen, technicians, and production engineers but not for themselves. Some, and their senior executives, came from the grandes écoles that recruited not from moderne or technique but from classical studies and that prepared not for business and industry but for the upper civil service (*les grands corps*). Although in theory the École polytechnique and its affiliates the Écoles des mines and ponts-et-chaussées were engineering institutes, in fact their programs were rather general. They were designed to produce executives for government services not technical specialists whom they could hire as needed from lesser schools such as the écoles d'arts et métiers. The key to success was proficiency in passing examinations and fluency in language rather than practical applications or research. French industrialists were thus heavily influenced in their attitudes by the social-cultural training of the elite grandes écoles. Even those not educated there, notably the owners of family businesses, frequently sent their sons to them, thus combining, in Bourdieu's terms, economic and cultural capital (chapter 6). Diplomas signifying the acquisition of a general culture were more sought after than certificates of technical proficiency; and the more specialized a degree, the less prestige it had.[29]

The surprise of the events of 1923 was that education officials rallied in defense of moderne while industrialists favoured classique. Even the Conseil supérieur de l'enseignement, which had originally favoured compulsory Latin, changed its mind.[30] With the election of the Cartel des gauches in 1924, the Herriot government largely nullified the Béard law, restoring moderne in the first cycle and doing away with compulsory Latin and Greek. Henceforth, the baccalauréat program offered three options (instead of four as in the 1902 regime): A (Latin, Greek); A' (Latin, one modern language); and B (two modern languages).[31] The basic disciplines, French, history, geography, science, and mathematics formed a common program for students of all sections. Only in the final years of the secondary program did students choose between philosophy and mathematics, most opting for philosophy while the moderne students took mathematics.[32] This formed a compromise between the Béard legislation and the 1902 law: the baccalauréats A and A' were carried over from the 1923 legislation and moderne B was simply added to them.

The rescue of moderne was not particularly welcome to the technical education lobby because the Béard law had guaranteed the continued existence of a separate technical-vocational system alongside the lycée. The abolition of tuition in the secondary schools several years later was similarly unwelcome because it greatly increased the number of students entering secondary education, which favoured the emergence of the modern junior high school and the eventual consolidation of secondary education. Jean Zay, the education minister from

1936 to 1939, introduced a bill in 1937 creating a comprehensive school, but he ran into such strong opposition from the proponents of secondary and technical studies that he had to withdraw the legislation. He did manage to transfer the higher primary schools from the primary to the secondary division and extended the school-leaving age to fourteen. The technical education division survived attempts by Zay and others at consolidation, thanks in part to its alliance with the secondary division and the support of the UIMM, which could be counted on to defend the classics for the upper classes and vocational training for the lower middle and upper working classes.

THE ADMINISTRATION OF THE TECHNICAL EDUCATION DIVISION

The division had a director and two assistants, plus inspectors (*inspecteurs principaux* and voluntary *inspecteurs de l'enseignement technique*), and departmental committees composed of industrialists, businessmen, local officials, and officials of the division, which mainly administered examinations. The vocational advisory boards (*commissions professionnelles consultatives*), established in 1948, one for each group of professional activities, set curriculum. AFDET, UIMM, and the increasingly powerful alumni associations of the écoles d'arts et métiers and écoles nationales professionnelles worked closely with the division, forming a lobby in defence of their interests and providing volunteers for the departmental commissions.

Edmond Labbé, 1920–33

Between 1895 and 1960 there were seven directors of the technical education division.[33] The period from 1920 to 1944 saw just two: Edmond Labbé from 1920 to 1933 and Hippolyte Luc, who had been Labbé's assistant, from 1933 to 1944. Born in 1868 of working-class origin, Labbé obtained his teaching certificate from the École normale primaire of Douai and began his career as an elementary schoolmaster. He went on to attend the École normale primaire supérieure of Saint-Cloud, a school for professors at the teacher-training schools, and became a professor and then director at the École nationale professionnelle of Armentières. By 1908 he was an inspecteur général in the division of technical education. He remained in Lille throughout the German occupation and assisted Herbert Hoover in rebuilding the region after the war.[34]

Because of his background in primary education, Labbé did not share the prejudices of many in the Commerce group against the education ministry, the *universitaires*, and the higher primary schools. In

1920 he succeeded Henri Tenot as director of the technical education division just as it was being transferred from the Ministry of Commerce to the Ministry of Public Instruction. While Leroy and others in the Commerce lobby strongly opposed the transfer, Labbé grasped the opportunities for technical education in the diverse facilities of the public education system that were not available in the much smaller Ministry of Commerce. He, Gustave Dron, and Gaston Vidal, the first under-secretary of state after the transfer to the Ministry of National Education in 1920 saw the opportunity to make peace with the division of primary education and end the old struggle between the higher primary schools and the écoles pratiques.[35] They supported a policy of twinning higher primary and practical schools and later in creating educational centres offering a variety of post-elementary choices.

Labbé's term of office also saw the introduction of a national system of vocational certificates and vocational guidance counselling, the creation of apprenticeship and vocational courses for young workers in factories and schools, the establishment of many adult evening schools for workers, the reform of the écoles nationales professionnelles and the opening of sixteen new ones, and the assimilation of the écoles municipales professionnelles of Paris into the technical education division. The École des arts et industries textiles de Roubaix, the École nationale supérieure de céramique de Sèvres, and an engineering school in newly recovered Strasbourg were transferred to the technical education division, all three at the level of the écoles d'arts et métiers.[36]

As the demand for skilled workers and technicians grew, Labbé spoke increasingly about the need to teach "les humanités techniques," which he hoped would bridge the gap between classical culture and technical studies. But as programs were already heavily loaded, teachers were encouraged to find ways to integrate cultural teaching into vocational programs. Labbé's pedagogy thus placed the profession at the centre of teaching: "Tout pour la profession, et par la profession," he liked to say, and he recommended drawing examples from practical exercises and the use of tools as a way of teaching language, the precise use of words and their applications, as well as the general principles of science.[37] For this rather rough and ready approach to teaching he was sometimes ridiculed by academics.[38] Labbé, in his turn, had no love of the "culture mongers." He wrote in a moment of exasperation: "Parlons-nous de profession? On nous répond 'culture.' Montrons-nous les besoins de l'industrie française, la concurrence étrangère, la mécanique de précision, l'optique, la coutellerie qu'il faut défendre, créer presque? On n'a qu'un mot: 'Culture! culture! culture! culture! Cela suffit à tout.' "[39]

In the tradition of Octave Gréard, Labbé rejected early specialization, arguing that the worker must become part of the national community and must therefore gain general culture as well as vocational training. At the same time he had to work closely with industrialists and businessmen who demanded early specialization and were largely indifferent to the culture and "personal development" of their workers. Although he worked hard to expand vocational courses for young workers and to reform apprenticeship, resources were few and the cooperation of industrialists was limited, so he concentrated on training foremen, shop supervisors, and technicians for which there was steeply rising demand in the interwar years. He used his limited resources to expand the number of écoles pratiques and écoles nationales professionnelles.

Hippolyte Luc, 1933–44

Labbé's successor, Hippolyte Luc, had a very different upbringing. Of humble origin, he began his studies at the collège d'Avallon then transferred to the prestigious Lycée Louis le Grand in Paris, receiving his agrégation in philosophy in 1913. He became a lycée professor, academy inspector, then Labbé's assistant in the technical education department from 1925 to 1933. Anatole de Monzie, Minister of Education, named him to replace Labbé who retired in 1933. Louis Planté's portrait of him is worth citing:

À première vue, il apparaît fruste, têtu, rude dans ses propos, directe dans ses rapports; il a l'air d'un contre-maître supérieur prêt à se colleter avec ses ouvriers dont il sait le métier mieux qu'eux. Et on le découvre fin, cultivé, curieux de tout; ses lectures sont immenses; seul peut-être il sait dominer sa tâche, concevoir le dessin d'ensemble d'une sorte d'Université parallèle allant de l'humble école artisanale aux chaires savantes du CNAM [Conservatoire national d'Arts et Métiers] que Monzie s'obstine à nommer le Conservatoire du Peuple![40]

Luc pointed out that the city of Bremen in Germany had a larger budget for apprenticeship training than the technical education division had for all of France.[41] One encounters a growing tone of bitterness in his remarks: "In France we pass laws with no means to apply them. We are prolific in texts and sterile in applications."[42] Complaining of "the eternal conflicts that use up French life," he said: "Everyone in France criticizes and nobody wants to do anything. What this country suffers from above all else is the love of criticism. If the love of action was as widespread as the pleasure people take in shooting arrows in all directions, I believe that our situation would be much better than it is."[43] He admonished the Conseil supérieur de l'enseignement technique: "If one could, just once, in the interest of the children, not transform these discussions into continual conflicts, I believe that everyone would be the better for it."[44]

Luc versus Zay

As education minister from 1936 to 1939, Jean Zay sought to consolidate and democratize the education system. He extended the school leaving age to fourteen and organized education into successive "degrees" emphasizing the movement of young people from one level to the next. In a bill presented to parliament in March 1937, he proposed to abolish the *petites classes* (primary classes) in the lycées and to set up a one-year program called the *classe d'orientation* in the first cycle of secondary education for young people aged thirteen. After a year studying a common program, students would be streamed by trained guidance counsellors into one of three sections in the new middle school – literary, scientific or technical – on the basis of aptitude and ability. The senior secondary cycle, for young people aged fifteen to seventeen, consisted of three streams: classical, modern and technical, the first two leading to baccalauréat examinations at age seventeen or eighteen and the latter to various technical and vocational certificates (CAP, BEP, etc.).[45]

The secondary and technical education divisions were opposed to Zay's bill. The former feared reducing Latin from seven to six years and shortening the "long impregnation" necessary to gain the full benefit of classical studies, while the latter feared losing its écoles pratiques and the first cycle of the école nationale professionnelle, which threatened the very existence of the technical education division. Luc wrote an article in the AFDET magazine *L'Enseignement technique* in 1938 titled "Les problèmes actuels de l'enseignement technique" in which he defended the division as "an economic enclave in the public education system" and argued for *verticalisme*, or the partition of public education into four separate divisions, each with its own hierarchy of schools. This, he said, was the only way of protecting technical education from control by the *universitaires*, who since the time of Napoleon had shown little comprehension of the technical and scientific realities of the modern world.[46] Wedded to an outdated classical conception of learning, their roots firmly anchored in the past, public education officials could not be trusted to administer technical education.

Luc asserted the intellectual and cultural value of a technical education, of a *culture technique* and "a community of spirit" uniting all levels of the technical education division. This made possible the development of an "active pedagogy" based on an understanding of the real world in contrast to the sterile theoretical approaches of an exam-ridden education system. The technical schools also assured able young people of modest origin a chance of advancement and gave industry access to well-trained personnel.

Zay's bill of 1937 split his own Radical party, bringing forth such former professors as Edouard Herriot,[47] Albert Bayet, and Hippolyte Ducos in defense of the technical education division.[48] They, in alliance with Alfred Jules-Julien, the secretary of state for the division (1935–37), undermined Zay's bill. Such political activities provoked considerable annoyance in Zay's cabinet, whose members complained of "La guerre Formation professionnelle … Est-il admissible que l'Enseignement technique fasse combattre par son organe et sous la plume de Jean Luc, Chef-adjoint du Cabinet de M. Julien [sic], une réforme qui est l'oeuvre du Ministre et qui a l'approbation du Gouvernement … Est-ce que le Sous-Secrétaire d'État est décidé à défendre le projet du gouvernement? La petite guerre va-t-elle continuer?"[49] Thus undermined within the government and by fellow members of his own party, Zay had to give up on his legislation – his bill never got out of committee. He did introduce 200 experimental classes d'orientation in the sixth and fifth classes (involving around 5,000 students aged eleven to twelve) in which teachers from the primary, secondary, and technical divisions cooperated in defining new approaches to education.[50] This program was continued after the war by Zay's colleague Gustave Monod, inspector-general and then director of secondary education from 1945 to 1951, as the classes nouvelles (18,000 students).[51]

Despite the failure of his bill and the fall of two Popular Front governments, Zay continued as education minister until 1939. When war broke out in 1939, he resigned to report to his reserve regiment. Partly Jewish, he was arrested by the Nazi-backed Vichy government and murdered by its militia in 1944 while being transferred from prison.[52] Hippolyte Luc continued as director of the technical education division under Vichy until 1944. In 1941 Education Minister Jérôme Carcopino transformed the écoles pratiques de commerce et d'industrie into collèges techniques, still under the technical education division, and converted the higher primary schools into collèges modernes. The term collèges, replacing the pejorative écoles, signaled a promotion to the secondary system, though these schools remained clearly inferior to the lycées. The new collèges techniques absorbed some of the vocational sections of the former higher primary schools. Although Luc had contacts in Masonic and republican circles, he was nevertheless attacked for staying on the job under Vichy. In 1944 the Liberation government fired him and replaced him and his two assistants with Communists. His most notable achievements during his eleven years as director were the creation of the Centres de formation profession-nelle in 1938 and the conversion of the écoles pratiques into collèges techniques in 1941.

CONCLUSIONS ON THE INTERWAR YEARS

During the interwar period the technical education division was in charge of a relatively small but growing system of intermediate schools ranging from the écoles pratiques to the écoles d'arts et métiers. Thanks to the Astier law of 1919 it also supervised a national program of continuing education courses for workers. It was also re-sponsible for vocational orientation and manpower planning, tasks that often ran beyond its limited resources and personnel. As its func-tions increased, the division came in for increasing criticism as being a ghetto within the education system, despite its transfer in 1920 from the Ministry of Commerce to the Ministry of Public Instruction. Labbé and Luc tried to define a new technical humanism to enhance the position of technical studies in the education system. Caught be-tween the instrumentalism of employers and the superior attitudes of academics, they had limited success. Within the confines of their world, they did make definite improvements, streamlining adminis-tration, upgrading programs, and overseeing the expansion of the écoles nationales professionnelles and écoles pratiques, which em-phasized training highly skilled workers, foremen, and technicians.

Although the number of students in the schools under the techni-cal education division increased steadily, it was still not sufficient to meet the demands of French industry for skilled workers and techni-cians, and there is no doubt that the training of ordinary workers was neglected both by the education system and by industry itself. The *cours professionnels* called for in the Astier law were not always established, and many young workers avoided attending them. The introduction of the *centres de formation professionnelle* in 1938 and again under Vichy suggested that eventually the technical education division would be in charge of a large system of schools teaching a mass of skilled workers and technicians, paralleling the public edu-cation system. Critics questioned whether the division had the re-sources for such a large enterprise and whether it was in France's interests to allow parallel systems serving different social classes, economic interests, and world views.

Zay's project to establish a single école unique meant the integration of the écoles pratiques de commerce et d'industrie into a new middle school with the first cycle of the écoles nationales professionnelles, and eventually into a new system of lycées techniques. This assumed the end of the technical education division. It is not surprising therefore that the division, backed by AFDET, UIMM, and by political supporters in the Radical and other right-centre parties, helped to defeat the Zay bill and resisted all efforts to integrate the technical schools into the broader education system. In defending the status quo in a tacit alliance with the division of secondary education, the technical education division unwittingly found itself defending the privileges of classical secondary education. For some observers this emphasized the anomaly of its position in the education system and to others it underscored the absurdity of an education system that perpetuated such anomalies. Clearly the education system would have to be consolidated, but this meant the loss of a small but well-organized system in close contact with business and industry that had trained a good many skilled workers, technicians, and engineers. The prospect of absorption into a division that had never shown much sympathy for applied science and industrial technology was the source of yet further irony, but thanks to war and the immobility of the post-war years, the division of technical education survived another twenty years.

THE LIBERATION, 1944–46

During the Liberation period, Charles De Gaulle headed a provisional government as president-prime minister, composed of Free French and Resistance groups located mainly on the left, the Communists, Socialists and Christian Democrats (MRP). As seen in the Zay reforms and in various plans for reform that evolved toward the end of the war, the left was committed to increasing state intervention and to the consolidation, democratization, and expansion of secondary education.

The Langevin Commission, 1944–47

On 8 November 1944, with the war still going on, Education Minister René Capitant set up a new ministerial commission to reform the entire education system. The commission had the power to conduct a broad investigation, to set up its own sub-committees, call witnesses, and establish its own investigatory agencies and documentation centres.[53]

Although the limits to the commission's powers were poorly defined, it appeared for a time to be a semi-official body dictating educational policy to the government.

Capitant named the distinguished physicist Paul Langevin as chairman, and Henri Wallon and Henri Piéron, both professors of psychology at the Collège de France, as vice-chairmen.[54] The commission was composed of twenty members, plus the four divisional heads sitting ex officio.[55] All were *universitaires*, professors, teachers, and administrators from the various branches of the education system. Five were professors at the Collège de France: Langevin, Wallon, Piéron, Lucien Febvre, and Emile Coornaert. There were two schoolmasters, two women, and two representatives from the technical branch.[56]

Beginning its deliberations in late November 1944, the Langevin Commission had much material to draw on, from the report of the original Compagnons to the Zay reforms, various official and unofficial studies that took place during the war, and the reports of the three main parties, all of which endorsed educational reform.[57]

The commission rejected the traditional classical culture of the bourgeoisie, redefining it in terms of a new democratic and scientific culture based on respect for the individual and the realities of the modern world. Education was to make accessible to the many the high culture that had formerly been available only to the few. The commission believed that the gradual advance of culture and the benefits of modern science and technology would bring about increasing prosperity, social stability, and the creative use of leisure. The guiding principle was thus "educational equality for all children, regardless of their social or ethnic origin, in order to permit each child, in the interest of all, fully to develop his personality with no other limitation than that of his aptitudes."[58] Concrete intelligence, used by working people in the pursuit of practical objectives, was to be considered just as noble as formal intelligence. Educational psychologists of the time, notably Jean Piaget, defined the concrete operational period as a natural stage of human development coming prior to formal reasoning and reached only by a certain number of people. This led the commission to accept the streaming of young people into classical, modern, and technical streams after the common classes of the école unique. Streaming was to be done by "experts" on the basis of the scientific detection of "natural aptitudes" and not social class.[59]

The commission held sixty-eight sessions, concluding on 2 June 1947. It recommended consolidation of the primary and secondary systems and the introduction of compulsory education from ages six to eighteen, divided into the elementary cycle to age eleven, the orientation-observation cycle from eleven to fifteen, and the determination cycle from fifteen to eighteen. The two-year orientation cycle, to be taken by all students, would consist of a core curriculum of French, history, mathematics, and a modern language. In the following two-year observation cycle students would be oriented into literary, scientific, and technical streams within the middle school. In the determination cycle students would be directed into one of three branches: the lycée, leading to the baccalauréat and higher education; technical-artistic, for middle level careers in business, industry, agriculture, and artistic fields; and practical or apprenticeship programs for those engaged in manual work. The idea was to introduce a common middle school for all French young people from the age of eleven to fifteen, streaming them toward their vocational specialties but with continual guidance and the possibility of transfer from one stream to another. Those in the third stream, the practical program, would be free to go to work at sixteen but would be required to take a hundred hours of continuing education courses in their fields to the age of eighteen.[60]

For the system to work sound guidance and orientation procedures were crucial in order to assure social justice – that each person did the work for which nature had suited him or her. Guidance counsellors were to be trained in the new educational psychology that had developed during the interwar years.[61] Langevin, Wallon, and their colleagues placed great faith in the emerging social sciences; they believed that society could be organized along rational and scientific lines in which individual aptitudes could be accurately evaluated, justifying the streaming of students into various sectors of the economy. Once this was accepted and once wage inequities were redressed, society would come to acknowledge the value of all work, of manual "concrete" intelligence as well as theoretical learning. Guidance counsellors would be able to assign students to fields of study according to their abilities without being constrained by social prejudices and parental pressures.[62] The system of orientation and guidance would assure social justice and economic growth at the same time.

The Langevin-Wallon commission assumed that the technical education division would disappear into a consolidated and reformed education system.[63] The commission recommended merging the centres d'apprentissage and the collèges techniques into the new middle schools and the écoles nationales professionnelles into a new system of lycées techniques. Although they were against the continuing existence of the technical education division, most commission members were not opposed to technical education per se and foresaw a technical stream in both the observation cycle of the middle school and the creation of a national system of lycées techniques. They hoped that the modernization of the education system and the advance of science, technology, and the social sciences would foster the growth of a new technical humanism.[64]

The Communists, who participated in government during 1944 to 1947 and who were winning around 27 per cent of the vote in elections had a history of attacking the technical education division as linked to big business and as training only an elite of workers. But during the Liberation period the party adopted nationalist themes and, with its labour affiliate the Confédération générale du travail (CGT), proposed to fight "la bataille de la production."[65] The party abandoned its relative indifference toward educational improvement (it had concentrated on the class struggle during the interwar years) and came out in favour of an increased state role in education and bringing together working class and technical cultures. With the left in a powerful position in the provisional government, the chances for the survival of the technical education division seemed remote.

But as the debates of the Langevin Commission dragged on over two and a half years, the provisional government decided to replace Luc and his two assistants with Paul Le Rolland (1944 to 1948), a Communist who named two fellow Communists as his assistants, until the Langevin commission could produce a plan for the reorganization of the education system.[66] In 1944 the government also decided to maintain the centres de formation professionnelle despite their connection with Vichy, renamed them *centres d'apprentissage* and placed them under the division of technical education. Numbering around 900, with 65,000 students, these schools were designed to train skilled workers and employees. Le Rolland and his administration soon saw to it that the CGT organized the teachers who were mainly former primary school instructors and former workers. The centres d'apprentissage would remain a bastion of the CGT, in contrast to the other schools under the division of technical education that were affiliated with the Fédération de l'Éducation nationale and their mainly socialist teachers' unions. This led to the charge that the division was educating "deux jeunesses."

The Resistance coalition collapsed with De Gaulle's resignation in January 1946 and the expulsion of the Communist Party from the government in April 1947.[67] This meant that when the Langevin Commission finally reported on 2 June 1947, its recommendations went unheeded by the government. In the midst of a rebuilding program after the war, France lacked the resources to introduce the reforms recommended by the commission. Strong resistance to reform among the teaching corps and other interest groups had also emerged by 1947.

As part of the general move to the right of this period, Le Rolland and his assistants were fired from their posts in 1948. André Morice, a Radical deputy and businessman from the construction industry was named secretary of state for technical education in 1947 and served until 1951. He played a role in the replacement of Le Rolland by Albert Buisson, a senior bureaucrat who had risen through the ranks of the technical education administration and who had the confidence of businessmen.[68]

THE TECHNICAL EDUCATION DIVISION DURING THE 1950s AND 1960s

As a result of the reorganization of the post-war years, the technical education division by the 1950s was quite strong. With the addition of the centres d'apprentissage, it possessed a system running from the primary level to higher education. It had extensive teacher-training facilities in the Écoles normales nationales d'apprentissage (ENNA) to serve the centres d'apprentissage, and in the École normale supérieure de l'enseignement technique (ENSET) at Cachan near Paris training professors for the ENP, the écoles pratiques, and other technical schools.[69] ENSET prepared students for the certificat d'aptitude pour le professorat de l'enseignement technique (CAPET) and recruited its professors mainly from among graduates of the Écoles d'arts et métiers and other technical schools and as well from business and industry.[70]

During the 1960s the technical education department disappeared and ENSET became an école normale supérieure. The CAPET was overhauled to make it the equivalent of the lycée professor's certificate, the CAPES. Those holding the CAPET or better frequently taught in the new Sections de techniciens supérieurs established in 1952 and in the Instituts universitaires de technologie set up in 1966. Professors for the lycées techniques were trained in centres de formation des professeurs techniques created in 1965. The various schools and centres for teacher-training for technical and professional schools were merged in 1991 into the Instituts universitaires de formation des maîtres (IUFM). This coincided with the merging of the lycées techniques into the lycées généraux as lycées d'enseignement général et technologique (LEGT).

Whether at ENSET, ENNA, or in other professors training schools, technical education developed a unique pedagogy combining theory and practice, conception and execution. Schools had to find ways to reconcile general programs with technical ones and with practical exercises in labs and shops. They emphasized learning from experience, "active" methods, and cooperative learning, and they were the first to establish evaluation based on course assignments and projects rather than exams, allowing students to accumulate credits toward degrees and set their own pedagogical goals. They pioneered factory visits early in the century and later practicums in industry. The schools discussed the impact of technology on modern culture, the possibility of defining a technical humanism for the modern age, and new ideas in educational psychology. These questions were also taken up by the review *Technique, Art, Science,* published jointly by AFDET and the Ministry of National Education from 1946 to 1977.[71]

In addition to the administration of the schools under its jurisdiction, the division of technical education collected and centralized information about supply and demand for skilled workers, technicians, and engineers. It also established facilities for vocational guidance and orientation, and it did economic forecasting and planning.[72] Yet the division found itself in a relatively weak position to deal with growth. In the absence of any general reform of education during the Fourth Republic and faced with rapid population and industrial growth it had very limited resources; its share of the education budget actually fell from 17.7 per cent in 1947 to 11.4 per cent in 1952.[73] While the division managed to open many schools, it was unable to keep pace with demand. Between 1945 and 1960 the number of students in the écoles nationales professionnelles, the collèges techniques, the Paris schools, and other related institutions grew from 70,000 to 138,500 while the centres d'apprentissage expanded from 60,000 to 203,340.[74] The ENP grew to twenty-six schools (sixteen for boys, seven for girls and three mixed) with 16,000 students in 1957 and the collèges techniques (the old écoles pratiques) and affiliated schools swelled to 87,000 students, but the division of technical education still had to reject 60,000 students a year for lack of space.[75] These flooded into the secondary schools, which grew from 80,000 students in 1914 to over 600,000 in 1955 even though their archaic structures could not handle the numbers.[76] By the early 1950s it was more difficult to gain admission to the écoles nationales professionnelles and the collèges techniques than to the lycées and collèges, even though there was more demand for graduates of the former.

Clearly there was very little coordination within the education system and even less effort to develop a broader strategy linking education to the economy. This was left to an inadequately funded and isolated enclave within the system. France in the 1950s seemed to many observers to be undereducated and technologically backward: 40 per cent of fourteen-year-olds left school without vocational training (200,000); only twenty-two per cent attended secondary schools, lycées, or collèges modernes (the old écoles primaires supérieures); sixteen per cent enrolled in technical and vocational schools, including the centres d'apprentissage; nine per cent went to agricultural schools; and thirteen per cent were apprenticed.[77] The twenty-two per cent who managed to obtain a secondary education were frequently ill-prepared for modern economic life. Only a third of those entering secondary schools in the sixth class ever obtained a bac, less than half of those achieved a university credential, and most of these were in the arts rather than the sciences. In 1953 for example, the universities granted 4,700 *licences* in law and letters and only 1,100 in the sciences.[78] This resulted in a serious shortage of science teachers in the lycées, collèges, écoles nationales professionnelles, and collèges techniques.[79] By the end of the 1950s, France still spent less than one per cent of its gross national product on science and technology, far less than Great Britain, West Germany, the Soviet Union, and the United States.[80]

ATTACKS ON THE TECHNICAL
EDUCATION DIVISION

Academic critics of the technical education division have charged, with some justification, that behind the rhetoric the division was, in the words of Charlot, "très perméable aux exigences du patronat." It was the willing accomplice of big business and the tacit ally of the division of secondary education, the Société des Agrégés, and the Société Franco-Ancienne in opposing the école unique and in maintaining an elitist and segmented education system. They pointed out that schools under the technical education division were organized into a hierarchy that reproduced the social and professional stratification of French industry and society. They argued that the division concentrated on training an elite of highly skilled workers, technicians, and engineers, while providing the mass of young workers with only derisory apprenticeship training and continuing education under the Astier law.[81]

A number of observers who sympathized with many of the goals of the technical education division, in particular the need to teach more science and technology and to define a technical culture, also had doubts about the wisdom of confiding technical education to an enclave within the education system. Like Langevin, Wallon, and other reformers, the sociologist Georges Friedmann, a professor at the Conservatoire d'Arts et Métiers, advocated the reorganization and consolidation of the education system to make more room for science, technology, and the new social sciences. He saw it as part of a broader goal of defining a new technical humanism designed to heal the rift between culture and work ("le travail en miettes") that had characterized the evolution of modern industrial society.[82] Consequently, he advocated merging the technical education division into the education system generally, not because technical education was inferior to general studies but because it represented the wave of the future and belonged in the mainstream.

In response to Luc's charge that the integration of technical education into the education system would create an inferior technical track into which weaker students would be directed, Friedmann, Zay, Langevin, and others argued that a socialist state, enlightened by the new social sciences, could rationally evaluate its manpower needs and assign people to their tasks automatically and fairly. By the 1950s and 1960s, Pierre Naville and Serge Mallet among others were emphasizing that the high tech industries of the future would employ a much higher percentage of engineers and technicians than workers.[83] Because their education involved increasingly less practical work in lab and shop and more scientific content, they could be taught in modernized lycées and institutes for higher education rather than in special technical schools. In an economy characterized by steady growth, the state could predict manpower needs on a large scale and take over manpower planning and vocational training without the need for a separate technical education division.

THE FAILURE OF REFORM UNDER
THE FOURTH REPUBLIC

When the Langevin Commission finally submitted its recommendations for reform in June 1947 after two-and-a-half years of discussion, the reforming impetus that had led to its appointment had long since passed and the plan was shelved.[84] During the next decade, 1947 to 1958, no less than ten bills and projects, all more or less based on the recommendations of the Langevin commission, would fail to pass.[85] These bills called for some kind of observation period in the 6th and 5th classes (eleven and twelve years old) prior to streaming young people into classical, modern, or technical studies or into the workforce at fourteen. The more adventurous projects, especially the Billères bill of 1956 which was the most faithful to the Langevin reforms, called for the extension of the school-leaving age to sixteen, the abolition of the technical education division, and the establishment of a middle school for young people of all social classes aged eleven to fifteen. The divisions of technical education and secondary education favoured milder projects such as the Berthoin bill of 1954 that proposed a brief orientation cycle at the junior secondary level in existing schools rather than the creation of a consolidated junior secondary school.[86]

The Billères bill aroused a powerful education lobby to the defense of Latin and *culture générale*, drawn from the right and the left and ranging from professors' unions to the Société des Agrégés and the Société Franco-Ancienne.[87] In a country that tended to confuse moral issues with the defense of special interests, the education system had come to resemble, in the words of Billères, "a juxtaposition of fortresses." One sought allies on the basis of common enemies rather than genuine affinity.[88] Thus the four "feudalities" of the education system came together in a common defense of the status quo, represented in the national assembly as usual by Hippolyte Ducos, the perennial gravedigger of educational reform. Ducos, a Radical and former professor, always spoke eloquently in favour of the autonomy of the technical education department, not because he had any love for the manual and vocational, but because the defence of *technique* was a cover for the defence of *classique*, which also allowed him to appear to be a friend of the working people.[89]

The Billères bill disappeared with the fall of the Guy Mollet government in 1957. René Billères himself, who had shown great energy in mobilizing the ministry to open schools to accommodate the baby boomers of the post-war years, was retained by the remaining governments of the Fourth Republic, and he was still minister of education when the republic fell in May 1958.

THE COMING OF THE FIFTH REPUBLIC AND THE END OF THE TECHNICAL EDUCATION DIVISION

By the end of the Fourth Republic the technical education division had reached its apogee. It had survived a series of reform bills during the late 1940s and 1950s and enjoyed the support of powerful interest groups: AFDET (with 25,000 members), the UIMM, as well as the alumni associations of the École nationale d'arts et métiers (with 20,000 members) and the Écoles nationales professionnelles (which had 12,000 members). It directed a complete hierarchy of schools ranging from the centres d'apprentissage to the Écoles d'arts et métiers and the École centrale des arts et manufactures, training skilled workers, technicians, industrial engineers, and businessmen, with well over a half million students. The proportion of young people taking technical and vocational courses reached about a quarter of those enrolled in secondary institutions.

Having reached a peak at the end of the Fourth Republic, the division disappeared at the beginning of the Fifth. The new president-prime-minister, Charles De Gaulle, had three goals: to increase the power of the executive, to find a solution to the Algerian war, and to modernize the economy, which meant educational reform.[90] In order to achieve national unity and reform, he was determined to break the power of interest groups.

He moved cautiously at first. In 1959 he decreed the Berthoin bill of 1955. Though the law in itself was mild, it inaugurated thirty years of reform profoundly altering the nature of French education and thoroughly transforming technical and vocational instruction. In 1960 the Ministry of Education abolished the division of technical education, merging its schools into secondary and higher education institutions.

Initially the technical education division was merged into the newly established Direction générale de l'organisation et des programmes scolaires. When this agency was abolished in 1962, technical education was transferred to the department of programs and personnel (*Enseignements et Personnel*) with its own Conseiller permanent pour l'enseignement technique. This department was replaced in 1964 by two divisions, pedagogy and personnel, which supervised all types of schools and teachers. The technical education division disappeared as a distinct unit. A new law in December 1966 set up a *Conseil national de formation professionnelle* including representatives from the public sector, owners, and workers, which represented a growing preoccupation with vocational training in the education system. In 1969, Prime Minister Jacques Chaban-Delmas and his education minister Olivier Guichard named a secretary of state for technical education. A technical education department with its own head was established in the Direction of Elementary and Secondary Education. But two other departments, Educational Institutions and Personnel, also had jurisdiction over technical establishments, so that responsibility for technical education continued to be scattered among various departments. When Guichard ceased to be education minister in 1972, the secretariat disappeared and technical education was cast adrift again until the appearance of the Socialists in the 1980s. The Chevènement ministry of 1984 named a secretary of state.[91] Since then technical education has sometimes had its own secretary of state, sometimes not, but there has been no division of technical education and no single administration.

WHY WAS THE TECHNICAL EDUCATION
DIVISION ABOLISHED?

With the rapid economic growth in the 1950s and increasing social demand for secondary education, it was becoming obvious that the four feudalities could not manage a modern education system. The technical education division had almost a million students by 1960 and yet it had relatively few links with the rest of the education system. It had to supervise a disparate corps of employees and deal with their professional associations: professors, teachers, shop instructors, technologists, workers, employees, etc. There were splits among Taylorists and humanists, among those favoring the old autarky ("verticalists") and those calling for more cooperation with the other divisions ("horizontalists"), and among "elitists" favouring the training of technicians and engineers and "democrats" wanting to concentrate on centres d'apprentissage for the working classes.[92]

The division was attacked from all sides. The left saw it as the Trojan horse of business and industry in the education system and criticized it for standing in the way of the democratization and consolidation of secondary education. The right disliked its utilitarian approach to education. Most importantly, the technocrats who dominated the Fifth Republic of the 1960s and who were intent on modernization were concerned about its failure to meet the exploding demand for skilled personnel, especially technicians and production engineers. The tendency of the 1950s and 1960s was toward the consolidation of education under increasing state control, with an emphasis on instruction in schools rather than on the job. This meant the introduction of standardized programs and certification on a national scale, at the cost of local and industrial control and work-study approaches to vocational training. This coincided with the coming of the Common Market, centralized national planning, the appearance of the consumer society, and standardized mass production in the Taylorist-Fordist mode. This in turn led to two conclusions: in an economy characterized by steady growth it was possible to predict manpower needs on a large scale and therefore the state could take over manpower planning and vocational training; and in the high tech economy of the future, engineers and technicians rather than skilled workers would be most in demand and, because of the increasing scientific content of instruction, these could be trained in modernized high schools, universities, and higher technical schools rather than in specialized intermediate technical institutions.

Although the machine, metallurgical, and electrical industries re-gretted the disappearance of the technical education division in which they had great influence, they accepted centralized and consolidated state control over technical education because it assured augmented public funds, standardization and coordination, a steady source of skilled workers, engineers, and technicians, and the certainty that these would possess a good general background in science, math, French, and some of the vocational skills necessary in an age of rapid technological change.

But the real reason for industry's abandonment of the technical education division had to do with rapid economic change and a shift in the thinking of executive circles. In the late 1950s industry was moving toward a form of Fordism and Taylorism: long assembly lines, mass production, centralized control, and "scientific manage-ment" which required massive investment, technological develop-ment, and the training of a new managerial class (*cadres*) of middle-level managers and engineers, as well as technicians and other spe-cialists. The Gaullist planners and bureaucrats disliked the enclaves and blockages that had balkanized the education system and stifled progress in the country for so long. In a mass production, high tech society characterized by automobiles, consumer goods, and the mass media, they foresaw a fluid, open world in which everything commu-nicated. The old education system of compartmentalized feudalities, which was in reality no system at all, stood as a barrier to any real communication with the outside world. To the technocrats in Paris it appeared to be incapable of training the qualified scientists, engi-neers, and managers needed to rebuild the country along scientific lines and of training a workforce of disciplined operatives for the assembly lines of the future. In 1958, as the Gaullists came to power, most of the state technocrats subscribed to the human capital theory that posited a linear and automatic connection between skill develop-ment and economic performance. If state aid to big industry was to be successful, it would have to accompany a major overhaul of the rigid and dated structures of the education system.

3 Vocational Education and the Training of Workers from the Third to the Fifth Republics, 1900–1981

Après l'organisation de l'armée des fusils, il nous faut
l'organisation de l'armée des outils pour combattre la
concurrence étrangère.

Denis Poulot, *Le Sublime*, 1872

The period from 1900 to 1981 saw two world wars and a depression, the end of the Third and Fourth Republics and the appearance of the Fifth, the rise and decline of Fordism-Taylorism, and alternating periods of rapid growth and economic difficulty. Growth was rapid from 1900 to 1931 and during the "trente glorieuses" years (really twenty-five) from 1948 to 1973. Between 1958 and 1973, the French economy grew at the fastest rate of any country in the European Economic Community, averaging around five per cent a year.[1]

In vocational education the period from 1900 to the Second World War saw an experiment in part-time vocational training for young workers who left primary school at age thirteen (fourteen after 1936) until the age of eighteen. Confined mainly to the metallurgical, mechanical, and electrical industries, the program failed to provide sufficient skilled workers to solve a chronic shortage by the 1930s. By the late 1930s and early 1940s vocational-training schools established by the Third Republic and Vichy, the *centres de formation professionnelle* (renamed *centres d'apprentissage* in 1945) succeeded in attracting reasonably good students and grew to around 200,000 trainees by the end of the Fourth Republic.

The Fifth Republic, intent on the modernization of the economy and the education system during the 1960s, abolished the division of technical education, extended the school-leaving age to 16, and introduced a comprehensive junior high school or *collège*. This meant that the centres d'apprentissage, renamed *collèges d'enseignement technique* in the 1960s, became senior secondary trade schools, but in practice guidance counsellors steered young people aged thirteen or fourteen who were unable to succeed academically in the new collèges to the CET, which soon became dumping grounds for weaker students. This, combined with poor integration with business and industry and outdated equipment, confirmed the CET as low status schools. As a result employers tended to promote reliable workers on the job to skilled positions, even though over half of them did not possess even the certificat d'aptitude professionnelle or CAP. This, combined with the importation of thousands of unskilled workers to man the long assembly lines of the Fordist system, placed France in a low-skills economic regime.

APPRENTICESHIP AND CONTINUING EDUCATION: THE ORIGINS OF THE ASTIER LAW, 1901–19

The education of workers has been a controversial issue in France since the eighteenth century, and nothing like the German consensus on the importance of worker training emerged in France until recently. Apprenticeship in France was weakened by the French Revolution, notably by the Loi Le Chapelier of 1791 that outlawed working class organizations, and then by the Industrial Revolution which undermined traditional artisanal practices.[2] During the first half of the twentieth century, apprenticeship survived in certain sectors, usually in small companies and was associated with private *chambres de métiers*.

Between 1880 and 1900 the main preoccupation of the Ministry of Industry and Commerce was to train an elite of skilled workers who could operate the new machine tools and direct and teach other workers. Thus the écoles d'apprentissage of 1880 became the écoles pratiques d'industrie of 1892 training skilled workers, foremen, and shop supervisors. But the question of the training of ordinary workers and the decline of apprenticeship persisted. It was generally agreed that because of mechanization and generally poor conditions, the factory was no longer suitable for apprenticeship. This led to the idea of introducing a national system of part-time continuing instruction for young workers between the ages of thirteen and eighteen.

In 1901 as Minister of Commerce, Alexandre Millerand referred the question of apprenticeship to the Conseil supérieur du travail (created in 1891) and asked the Office du travail to launch a major investigation into the state of apprenticeship in France. It sent questionnaires to industrialists and to 229 professions in which apprenticeship was practised, of which three-quarters favoured the introduction of compulsory vocational instruction of young people during the workday in preparation for a skills certificate. In 1902 the Conseil supérieur du travail endorsed the establishment of a national system of vocational training for young workers. It also decided to launch a study of vocational education and apprenticeship, whose findings supporting improved apprenticeship instruction were published in 1905.[3]

Armed with the recommendation of this council, the division of technical education asked the Conseil supérieur de l'enseignement technique to prepare a law on apprenticeship. A commission established by the conseil supérieur then conducted its own study of vocational education and produced a preliminary bill in 1904.[4] The proposal called for the introduction of compulsory continuing education in France, with the cities responsible for organizing vocational courses and employers for assuring that workers attended them for two hours a day during the workday, for a total of eight hours a week. In the meantime, the city council of Paris and the Ligue de l'enseignement endorsed the principle of compulsory continuing vocational education.[5]

The Conseil du travail studied the proposed law and approved most of the provisions at the end of 1905. Fernand Dubief, minister of commerce, presented the bill to the Chamber of Deputies on 13 July 1905.[6] The parliamentary commission ratified it, and Placide Astier, Radical senator from the Ardèche and manufacturer of pharmaceutical products, presented a favourable report to parliament on 17 March 1906. Referring to the menace of military-industrial competition from the Germans and other rivals, Astier insisted that vocational education should not be limited to just the "sous-officiers de l'armée industrielle" but needed to be extended to the mass of foot soldiers as well. The costs of establishing compulsory vocational education for young workers would be repaid by greater productivity, prosperity and social peace. "A single battleship," he said, "costs more than the annual cost of providing technical education in France."[7]

Astier's arguments for compulsory vocational education paralleled those of a generation earlier for universal primary education. The state had the double obligation to assure the training of a working class elite in technical schools and the mass of workers in vocational courses. The result would be better quality production and increased national strength. According to Bernard Charlot and Madeleine Figeat, these arguments reflected the growing alliance between the modernizing bourgeoisie and Jacobin patriots advocating a more prominent role for the state in national economic development.[8]

Dubief's bill was essentially the same law that passed under Astier's name in 1919, fourteen years later. It obliged all young workers and employees between fourteen and eighteen years of age to take vocational courses during the workday. But the Fédération des industriels et des commerçants hesitated to support the bill in 1905. F. de Ribes-Christofle, its president, saw some merit in continuing vocational courses but argued that the state should stay out of the workshop, leaving employers to take the initiative to provide vocational instruction for their young employees as they saw fit. Insofar as vocational courses were to be established by private enterprise, the state was to bear most of the cost without having much control.[9] Not surprisingly, the government abandoned the bill.

In 1909 the Paris Chamber of Commerce reversed its earlier decision and came out in favour of compulsory vocational instruction. In October 1911 Commerce Minister Charles Couyba established departmental committees on vocational education composed mainly of businessmen, industrialists, and professionals in an effort to involve them more closely with technical education. These committees advised on the creation of écoles pratiques and vocational curriculum and the granting of subsidies to private schools. The government established a certificate of vocational aptitude (*certificat d'aptitude professionnelle* or CAP), which exists today, for each of the crafts. Examinations for the certificate were to be taken by young people after three years of apprenticeship and/or evening courses.

In the years before the war several other projects for compulsory continuing education were presented to parliament, all of which failed to pass. Henri Michel, deputy from the Bouches-du-Rhône, tried twice, in 1904 and 1907.[10] Gustave Dron, senator, presented a law in 1911 establishing a national network of vocational courses, and during the same year the industrialist Jules Siegfried put forth a bill calling upon cities of 20,000 or more to maintain vocational schools and those of 10,000 to offer courses. The Radical deputy Ferdinand Buisson presented bills in 1910, 1911, and 1913, which extended the school-leaving age to fourteen and established compulsory vocational courses for workers until the age of seventeen, but none were successful.[11]

Given the support of AFDET (Association pour le développement de l'enseignement technique) and UIMM (Union des Industries minières et métallurgiques) and of many prominent citizens for a law on apprenticeship, why did the various bills fail to pass during the decade before the war? The answer lies in the resistance of low-skill industries – building, textiles, and food processing in particular – and small artisanal firms, so numerous in France, that opposed compulsory continuing education classes on company time that would raise education and skills beyond the level they considered necessary. Technical schools and continuing education courses were of interest mainly to the machine, metallurgical, and electrical industries, which were more technologically advanced than other industries in France and had greater need for skilled workers. The Astier bill would pass immediately after World War I, under different conditions, but it stood little chance before the war.

Astier introduced his bill in the Senate on 4 March 1913. It passed on 30 June 1916 and moved on to the Chamber of Deputies, which passed it almost without debate in July 1919.[12] The law has been referred to as the "charter of technical education" in France, which is somewhat misleading because it was a failure in many respects. The preamble stated: "Because of the changing needs of industry and the role of business and industry as a source of national wealth, the state must take the place of private associations in providing vocational education for the sons of workers." Technical education was defined as "the theoretical and practical study of the sciences and the arts and crafts from the point of view of industry and commerce, including a complement of general education," a carefully crafted compromise formula between the Public Instruction and Commerce ministries.[13] The first four articles essentially codified existing legislation. Under Title V of the law the Minister of Industry and Commerce, on the advice of the departmental committees, designated cities that were obliged to create and finance vocational courses. The courses could be established by municipalities, departments, or private corporations and were compulsory for young workers under eighteen except those who were already in school or already possessed the certificat d'aptitude professionnelle or related diplomas. Companies were responsible for registering their young workers at city hall and were obliged to provide free time for the courses, assure their attendance and stamp their passbooks.

As the school leaving age was then set at thirteen, the young worker had to attend the courses from the age of fourteen to the age of eighteen for four hours per week and for a minimum of 100 hours per year. At the end of the four-year period the young person took examinations for the CAP. These examinations were organized by departmental commissions, which established juries composed of businessmen, manufacturers, and workers.[14] About fifty private schools (écoles de métiers) already in existence – usually run by the chambers of commerce – were provided legal status and state recognition.[15]

The law attempted to compensate for the pedagogical incapacity of factory and workshop and the decadence of apprenticeship by transferring instruction to continuing education.[16] Governments provided no financial aid to establish the courses, and manufacturers frequently failed to require their young workers to attend when such courses existed. The eight-hour law of 1919 weakened their willingness to allow young workers time off to take courses, and the latter frequently had to do so after hours or in the evening, which meant that they worked very long hours. The law applied only to larger companies, though it was revised in 1934 to include all companies with an annual payroll over 10,000 francs.[17] It applied only when municipalities or private organizations provided the necessary courses and the young person lived close enough to attend them.[18]

The law appears to have passed because Astier and other supporters implied that it would not be vigorously applied in the early years.[19] Provisions for inspection and compliance were weak: inspectors were volunteers who had little time for the task; and fines for non-compliance, whether on the part of the employer or employee, were minimal and some employers preferred to pay them rather than establish the courses.[20] The law was successfully implemented only where the mechanical, metallurgical, and electrical industries were well represented, and where municipal governments and local business associations were determined to introduce the program, as in the north, parts of the Paris region, and in Lyons under Mayor Edouard Herriot.[21]

THE 1920S

In an effort to strengthen the law of 1919, an apprenticeship tax was introduced in July 1925, fixed at 0.2 per cent of gross salaries. Companies that set up their own apprenticeship programs or vocational schools could be exempted from the tax. They could also be excused if they gave subsidies to other technical or vocational schools and programs, provided grants to students in such schools, or gave donations supporting vocational guidance, women's programs (*l'enseignement ménager*), or laboratories doing research in the applied sciences.[22] When they paid the tax, they could specify a preferred school or program, which led to complaints that businessmen abused this process by subsidizing schools and programs representing their philosophical views and having little to do with the training of young workers. Requests for exemptions took up an enormous amount of the department committee's time. The Department of the Seine alone had to deal with 20,000 requests annually in the Paris area in the mid-1930s. Still, the directors of the technical education division, Edmond Labbé and Hippolyte Luc, defended the exemptions as the only way to fund vocational guidance, women's programs, and applied research, for which the state provided few funds.[23] The main problem with the law was that employers paid the tax and then considered themselves free from the responsibility to concern themselves with apprenticeship and the education of their workers.[24]

Another law in 1925 strengthened the *chambres de métiers*, composed of businessmen, industrialists, and professionals, which were charged with the job of organizing the vocational courses and establishing the rules governing apprenticeship in the various professions and crafts in their regions. They also oversaw examinations, the drawing up of contracts, and the work and conduct of apprentices.[25] A new law passed on 20 March 1928. It required the employer to state in the apprenticeship contract the courses that the apprentice would take, assuring that he or she took the examination for the certificat d'aptitude professionnelle at the end of the three-year training period.[26] For the first time, inspecteurs du travail were designated to enforce the terms of the contract. Even then many companies evaded the law. Apprentices were frequently absent from their courses and the instructional level tended to be weak. Only 9,000 of 162,000 attending the courses in 1929 obtained the CAP.[27]

Nevertheless, during the interwar years a great many CAP programs were established, and many young workers had access to them. The legislation of 1911 establishing the CAP and regulating its application sought to decentralize programs, leaving the initiative to local and departmental committees composed of businessmen, industrialists, and officials, with only a cursory review on the part of the technical education division in Paris. The result was a proliferation of programs and certificates, which reached over 3,000 CAP during the interwar period, resulting in much fragmentation and overlapping from region to region.[28] By the late 1930s, as the lack of skilled workers became increasingly acute, the technical education division and many industrialists called for the introduction of national standards for programs and examinations, but such reforms were not introduced until Vichy and the post-war years.[29]

THE 1930s: THE CENTRES DE FORMATION PROFESSIONNELLE

The long period of prosperity from 1906 to 1930 in France gave way to depression and unemployment in the 1930s. Ironically, the high rate of unemployment among the unskilled (25 per cent in 1935) coincided with a shortage of skilled labour. Enrolment in vocational courses established as a result of the Astier law fell from 162,000 in 1929 to 133,572 in 1933.[30] In 1935 twelve retraining centres were established under the Ministry of Work to retrain unemployed workers in the skills for which there was a demand, but the 40 hour week passed by the Popular Front in 1936 rendered the shortage of skilled workers even more acute. The Walter-Paulin law of 10 March 1937 set standards for apprenticeship teachers and created a corps of salaried inspectors. A decree of 24 May 1938 required owners to hire and train a percentage of apprentices in relation to the number of employees generally and to assure their practical training in the workshop as well as attendance in the vocational courses prescribed by the Astier law. It also introduced vocational guidance (*l'orientation professionnelle*) for all young people in the public schools in their fourteenth year, and no youth under seventeen could be hired if he or she did not possess a certificate granted by an orientation centre. The law of 1938 was applied only in the metallurgical industry, which was required to engage apprentices at a ratio of nine per cent of the skilled workers employed in a firm (the industry reached seven per cent on the eve of the war).[31]

A series of decrees between September and December 1939 during the phony war organized *centres de formation professionnelle* training unemployed young people aged fourteen to twenty in skills required by defense industries. The centres were established for the most part in existing schools – in the technical sections in the higher primary schools and *cours complémentaires*, in the écoles pratiques and écoles nationales professionnelles, and in factory schools. Forty retraining centres (*centres de reclassement de la main-d'oeuvre*) were opened in the spring of 1940 and a hundred were in preparation.[32]

The training of apprentices in France during the 1930s was surprisingly lax considering the persistence of unemployment among unskilled and semi-skilled workers and the penury of qualified workers.[33] Some firms trained their own, notably in the automobile, machine construction and metallurgical industries. Several companies including the Peugeot automobile works at Sochaux (Doubs), the Parisian transport system (the RATP), and the national railway company (the SNCF) established factory schools.[34] Various industrial associations, chambres de métiers and even the CGT trained apprentices, but generally the results were inadequate. The lack of skilled workers, combined with a semi-military authority structure that placed emphasis on "leadership" and "the battle of production" meant that French companies remained centralized and rigid and were slow to introduce new ideas of factory organization, labour mobilization and management derived from the United States, Taylorism and Fordism. Efforts at rationalization and normalization were made, but slowly and selectively, mainly in the interchangeability of parts and labour discipline, but production lines remained relatively short and were devoted to the final stages of assembly. Output was diversified, contracting out (*sous-traitance*) was avoided, and old-fashioned authority structures only partly altered.[35] Workers were poorly paid and had low status, and the difference between the wages of skilled and unskilled workers was not very great. Thus the training of workers and the mobilization of labour were far from adequate in France on the eve of war.

VICHY

Vichy created the *centres de formation professionnelle et des centres de jeunesse* in December 1940 for young men aged fourteen to eighteen, with separate sections for young women. The three-year program involved a combination of skills training provided by ex-workers and classroom instruction taught mainly by former primary school teachers. The program took forty-six hours per week, and included twenty to twenty-four hours of shop training and two hours of technology and about twenty hours of general studies (French, science, math, physical education) as well as several hours of political indoctrination and outdoor activities.

The centres de formation professionnelle were placed under the Secretariate of Youth (*Secrétariat à la Jeunesse*) which was transferred to the Ministry of National Education in 1943 but not placed under the division of technical education. In July 1944 there were 897 centres with 56,000 students (36,000 boys and 20,000 girls). The centres survived the war and proved to be the most lasting educational achievement of the Vichy period.

The other key reform during the Vichy period was the conversion of the écoles pratiques, the various écoles de métiers, and the vocational sections of the higher primary schools into collèges techniques, and the conversion of the higher primary schools into collèges modernes. By 1944 there were 110,000 young people attending the technical schools (ENP, collèges techniques, etc.), 56,000 in the Centres de formation professionnelle, plus 190,000 in the vocational courses established by the Astier law, for a total of 356,000 receiving a vocational education out of a total of two million young people aged fourteen to eighteen. Under Vichy more young people had access to post-primary education and technical and vocational training than had been the case during the 1930s and during the Liberation period that followed.[36]

THE FOURTH REPUBLIC

During the Liberation in 1944, the provisional government decided to maintain the centres de formation professionnelle, renamed centres d'apprentissage (CA), despite their connection with Vichy, placing them under the division of technical education. With the Communist Party participating in the government, Luc was replaced by Paul

Le Rolland, a Communist, who brought in fellow party-members as his assistants. They saw to it that the communist-affiliated union, the CGT, represented the faculty. This led to constant inter-union squabbling with the teachers' union, the Syndicat national d'instituteurs, backed by the Fédération de l'éducation nationale to which it belonged, and to conflicts between unions and school officials backed by the technical education division. Moreover, the *cours complémentaires*, higher primary sections attached to the larger primary schools, set up their own industrial sections called *cours complémentaires industriels* in competition with the CA, which continued the old rivalry between the primary and technical education divisions, this time based on conflict between the teachers' union and the teachers of the centres d'apprentissage (CGT). Thus the CA developed in isolation, not only from the mainstream of public education but also from the other schools of the technical education division.

The centres d'appentissage also suffered during the post-war years from inadequate financing, dilapidated buildings, and outdated equipment.[37] For all their problems they grew rapidly during these years, from slightly less than 900 schools with 60,000 students in 1945 to 203,340 students in 1960 in about the same number of rebuilt and enlarged schools.[38] In 1954 sixty per cent of the students were the sons and daughters of workers and employees as opposed to 40 per cent in the collèges techniques (ex-EPCI) and 38.7 per cent in the écoles nationales professionnelles. In turn, 14 per cent of the students in the ENP were the sons of executives and managers, which was true of only 10 per cent in the collèges techniques and 4 per cent in the CA. In all, 84 per cent of students in the CA came directly from the *classes de fin d'études* in the primary schools, while 51 per cent of the students from the CT and only 12 per cent from the ENP did so (they had their own preparatory sections), with most of the remainder coming from the cours complémentaires industriels. All of these schools had a *concours* and were thus able to select good students, mainly from the skilled portions of the working classes. During the 1950s a million young people obtained the CAP, as opposed to only 168,000 in the 1930s.[39]

In the 1950s about a third of students in the centres d'apprentissage were girls studying fifty-six specialties: thirty-three in clothing and textiles, as well as home economics, secretarial, and medico-social work. Boys studied 113 specialties, of which 33 were in metallurgy and the remainder mainly in mechanics, electricity, woodworking, building, and automobile construction and repair. All female sections taught three hours per week of home economics in preparation for domestic duties. Young women who did obtain certification were less likely than their male counterparts to find jobs corresponding to their qualifications. Although women were numerous in the labour force (more so than in most other European countries), they were often found in low-level positions in the tertiary sector or in unskilled sectors of industry, mainly in the textile and food industries. The segregation of women in the labour force was reflected in horizontal segregation in all levels of the education system.[40]

In order to train teachers for the courses and shops of the centres d'apprentissage, five Écoles normales nationales d'apprentissage (ENNA) were established in 1946 in Paris, Lyon, and Nantes for men and in Paris and Toulouse for women. A sixth school opened at Lille in 1967. The ENNAs recruited mainly primary teachers as well as from teachers in the centres d'apprentissage. Until their disappearance in 1991 they were to play a key role in experimenting with new teaching techniques and seeking to define a technical culture.[41]

An inspectors' corps was established at the departmental level to oversee the centres d'apprentissage, replacing the old corps of volunteer inspectors – businessmen and industrialists for the most part – who now became *conseillers de l'enseignement technique*, drawn mainly from AFDET and concerned for the most part with administering local examinations for the CAP.[42]

In 1948 the vocational advisory boards (*commissions professionnelles consultatives*) were introduced, composed of businessmen, industrialists, local and government officials, and representatives from workers and teachers' associations. These were to play an important role in determining technical and vocational programs, examinations, and credentials for the CA and other technical schools in line with the changing manpower requirements of business and industry.[43] They worked in cooperation with the technical education inspectors, the departmental committees and with UIMM, AFDET, and other industrial associations.

The main task of the vocational advisory boards in the early years was the reform and standardization of the certificat d'aptitude professionnelle. Programs for the CAP had been established at local levels but they had proliferated to several thousand certificates and specialties, uneven in quality and frequently overlapping. The work of the boards led to a law in 1953 introducing national standards for the CAP and regulated examinations, juries, and programs. A national wage scale was introduced, applying the UIMM scale and employment classifications to all industries.[44]

The UIMM played a key role in the formulation and application of the 1949 law that gave the centres d'apprentissage their definitive organization and statute, establishing them as public schools for the

training of skilled workers. The cas were to provide practical, technical, and theoretical training for a particular occupation and a general
education directed toward the well-rounded development of the
young person. The statute of the teachers in the ca was regulated by
a law in 1954 that placed them below the collèges techniques, at the
same level as the *cours complémentaires* but with longer teaching hours
(forty hours per week for the shop teachers).

Gérard Noiriel describes 1954 as the year that France reached a
peak of workers as a portion of the industrial population: 87.2 per
cent compared with 5.1 per cent in management and 7.7 per cent salaried staff.[45] The proportion of males employed in the industrial
workforce grew from 64 percent in 1931 to 69 percent in 1954, while
the number of foreign workers dropped by 1.3 million between 1930
and 1954. Most of those who remained had been in France for some
time. The period was also marked by a very low rural exodus
(in 1946 46 per cent of the population lived in small towns while
38 per cent were farmers and agricultural workers).[46] Studies have
shown that this generations of workers, or at least the more skilled
elements within it, moved easily from blue to white collar supervisory positions. A cnrs survey showed that by the 1970s 41 per cent
of its subject group of workers' sons had moved into salaried staff
categories.[47]

The stability and homogeneity of the working class during the
1950s, the increasing number of those obtaining the cap, and the fact
that even the ca were relatively selective in their choice of students
helps explain why graduates of the ca of this generation did very
well in industry, often starting as skilled workers and ending up as
foremen, shop supervisors, and even plant managers. Even those
who did not possess the cap, but who had the certificate of primary
education (which only a minority of primary school leavers obtained), frequently managed to do well through promotion on the
job. Surveys of the education of middle-level managers, technicians,
and engineers thirty years later in the 1980s would reveal that as
many as half had no more education than a primary education certificate or cap.[48]

During the 1950s working class young people had few alternatives
to careers in industry. Only 6.5 per cent of university students in 1956
were the children of workers and peasants compared with 60 per cent
for civil servants, the liberal professions, and employers.[49] In 1958 the
proportion of sons of workers in post-primary education was 33 per
cent in the *cours complémentaires*, 19 per cent in modern sections of the
lycées, and 9 per cent in classical sections.[50] The upper levels of the
working class were in a much better position to build solid careers

through possession of the CAP and/or through promotion on the job in industry, but the middle level supervisors, technicians, and engineers who rose in this manner were not very well trained for functions that were becoming increasingly technical in content, and they were not allowed a great deal of initiative by senior management.

THE FIFTH REPUBLIC, THE CONSERVATIVE PERIOD, 1958–81

The first decade of the Fifth Republic, 1958–68, saw a series of reforms that laid the basis for the transformation of French education that has continued to the present day. Under the pressure of rapid industrialization, the old, rigid, segmented and compartmentalized system gave way to one that was more open, integrated, unified, and more oriented toward the economy. The years 1959 and 1960 saw the introduction of four key reforms:

1 the abolition of the division of technical education (chapter 2),
2 the extension of the school leaving age from fourteen to sixteen, and the strengthening of intermediate education for the entire youth population,
3 the transformation of the écoles nationales professionnelles and collèges techniques into lycées techniques (chapter 5),
4 the transformation of the centres d'apprentissage into collèges d'enseignement technique (CET).

A second wave of reforms began three years later under Christian Fouchet, education minister from 1962 to 1967, that prepared the way for the école unique. In 1963 he created the *collèges d'enseignement secondaire* (CES) for young people aged eleven to fifteen, which gradually brought together a plethora of junior secondary schools under a single roof: collèges d'enseignement général, collèges modernes, and cours complémentaires. The CES provided one year of common studies followed by orientation into one of three streams, classical, modern, and practical for the next three years. In 1975 Education Minister René Haby introduced a *collège unique*, a consolidated junior secondary school teaching a common program (*tronc commun*) during the first two years in the 6th and 5th classes before steering students into one of the three streams taught within the collège in the 4th and 3rd classes, classical-modern, technical, and vocational. At sixteen the student had four choices: he or she could go to work, enter a classical-modern or a technical lycée (l'enseignement secondaire long) to prepare for higher education, continue into a collège d'enseignement technique (l'enseignement secondaire court) to prepare for the job market, or be apprenticed.

The collèges d'enseignement technique (CET) recruited young people in the 3rd class, age fifteen, and offered them a "short" two-year vocational program leading to the CAP and the BEP (brevet de l'enseignement professionnel) leading to skilled jobs in business and industry. In theory students could cross over into the technical and even the classical streams of the lycées, but this seldom happened. Because their preparatory classes had been absorbed by the collèges, the CET were no longer able to select their own students, and because of the system of compulsory orientation students and their families had no say in the choice of a school. The CET were obliged to accept students deemed by counsellors to be incapable of continuing academic studies in the collèges, frequently at the end of the 5th class, at age thirteen, once they had completed the initial year in the common program. The CET soon came to be widely regarded as a *filière de relégation*, a dumping ground for the weaker students (*les exclus*) who were often the children of foreign workers who had to stay in school until the age of sixteen before seeking employment (30 per cent had gone to work at age fourteen in 1958). They grew very rapidly from 200,000 students in 1960 to 700,000 in the late 1970s, though many were not there of their own volition.[51]

The reforms of Fouchet and Haby from 1963 to 1975 modernized secondary education into a simplified 6/4/3 system (primary schools, collèges, lycées). This should have been a major step toward the democratization of secondary education, but it failed to happen because the CET emerged as inferior schools designed mainly for working class youth. The French could, and probably should, have opted for the successful German apprenticeship model, mixing learning on the job with part-time schooling for those not destined for senior high school and higher education. The choice of an inferior academic model over apprenticeship was made because republicans had always been suspicious of the factory as a place to learn, industrial workers had little standing in society, and because the state was playing an ever larger role in the economy generally. This corresponded to the human capital theories of the time that saw the education system as a gigantic sorting machine producing human capital for the economy.[52] The CET were a convenient means of taking the pressure off academic programs in the collèges and lycées and funneling young people of "concrete intelligence" into positions in the economy as skilled workers (level V) as envisioned by the Fourth and Fifth Plans 1962–1970. The Taylorist-Fordist organization of labour then being introduced into French factories called for a great majority of semi-skilled workers to man the assembly lines of the big new companies. This deskilling of the mass of factory workers, combined with the expulsion of working class populations (especially those of North African origin) from the centre of Paris and other cities to suburban ghettos increased the sense of exclusion among the working class populations.[53]

To make it worse, the abolition of the division of technical education in 1960 divorced the schools from their traditional connections with business and industry. This, and poor labour relations dating from the post-war period, the influence of Marxist ideas, and the unpopularity of capitalism among many students during the 1960s, added to the problem of low morale and indiscipline, especially in the vocational schools of the burgeoning industrial suburbs of Paris and other big cities.[54]

In an effort to improve the status of the CET and to enable it successfully to meet manpower demands for more adaptable workers, Fouchet created the *brevet de l'éducation professionnelle* in 1967. The BEP required concentration in a sector of activity rather than an individual specialty, introducing for example the field of machining (*usinage*), which brought together fitting (*ajustage*), lathing (*tournage*), and milling (*fraisage*). Though in theory it was the equal of the CAP, the BEP provided a broader education, which made it possible for the better students to obtain skilled jobs and/or continue their studies through a *classe d'adaptation* in one of the lycées techniques, usually for one of the new *baccalauréats de technicien* created by Fouchet in 1966 (chapter 5). This in turn could lead to a two-year technical-vocational program for senior technicians in the *sections de technicien supérieur* (1952), two-year programs in higher education in the lycées techniques, or to one of the new *instituts universitaires de technologie* located in the universities, another of Fouchet's creations in 1966 (chapter 6). In practice, however, very few with a BEP (12 per cent) continued their studies into higher education.

In the midst of introducing the collège unique in 1975, Haby transformed the CET into lycées d'enseignement professionnel (LEP) and envisaged (as Fouchet had done before him) doing away with the three year CAP (4th through 2nd classes) and turning it into a two year program in senior high school, but once again this plan was not implemented. Young people continued to be streamed into the LEP after the 5th class (roughly Grade Seven, children aged twelve). Despite the more prestigious title, the LEP still prepared students only for the "short program" and for vocational certificates, the CAP and BEP, and were intended mainly for working class families. The percentage of young people studying for a CAP who were the sons or daughters of workers was 53 per cent in 1960, 56 per cent in 1973, and 59 per cent in 1980, while the number of workers in France remained stable at 40 per cent during those years.[55]

Although the collèges introduced in the 1960s and 1970s were supposed to be democratic innovations, in fact they streamed young people into classical, modern, technical, and vocational studies. This is not surprising when one analyses the "liberal" ideas of educational reformers, from the Compagnons, Jean Zay, Paul Langevin, and Henri Wallon to René Haby. French academics were schooled in the classics and most espoused the Platonic idea of "justice," that young people should be oriented toward the professions to which nature had best suited them, as in the metaphor of the metals in the *Republic*.[56] This point of view was complemented by Jean Piaget's influential theory of cognitive development that defined childhood growth in terms of four stages: sensorimotor (to age two), pre-operational (ages two to six), concrete operational (ages seven to twelve), and formal operations. Piaget argued that many young people failed to reach the formal stage of abstract, logical thought, and so he favoured some streaming to assure that students learned at their own speed.[57] In referring to Piaget, René Haby argued that manual work was a natural, biological human function (as opposed to historical, social, or economic) and that roughly half of young people were incapable of moving from concrete to formal operations, hence the reason for (and fairness of) streaming into classical, modern, and vocational fields, so long as the means of selection were scientific and unbiased.[58]

Although these arguments were thought to represent the best educational theory of the time, by the 1960s and 1970s some sociologists were charging that the theories of biological development and "concrete intelligence" were being used as a smokescreen to justify the tracking of working class young people into inferior schools such as the CET, where they received a rigourously functionalist formation before being guided into industry as hopefully docile workers. In an important study in the mid-1950s, Alain Girard found that 55 per cent of elementary school children had been forced to repeat at least a year (40 per cent one year, 13 per cent two years, 2 per cent three years or more) before they had even finished primary school. He also found that 79 per cent of the children of agricultural workers and 64 per cent of the children of industrial workers had been obliged to repeat at least one year while only 24 per cent of the children of higher executives had done so.[59] Pierre Bourdieu and Jean-Claude Passeron pointed to the upper class monopoly over the elite sectors of the education system – and therefore over formal language and culture – that enabled their children to "reproduce" their social-cultural dominance while impeding working class advancement through education (chapter 6).[60]

While reformers on the left were locked into disagreements about how to remedy the inequality of educational opportunity, conservatives were united in bitterly opposing any reform that lessened "parental choice" and undermined the role of the classics in secondary education. Every time governments introduced reforms leading to the establishment of the collège unique, fierce conservative opposition particularly from professors' associations, parent groups, and other educational and vocational lobbies forced them to water down the reforms. Secondary professors especially disliked having lowly elementary schoolmasters teaching classes even in the early years of secondary education, and all of the groups feared a decline in standards with the introduction of modern programs and mixed ability classes. Once having retreated, the reformers particularly Haby, were bitterly criticized by left-wing intellectuals.[61] But as Charlot and Figeat point out, the real problem was that French society accepted the social hierarchy of work and placed too little value on productive functions, so that democratization and reforms of work organization remained difficult to achieve.[62]

INDUSTRY AND OCCUPATIONAL TRAINING, THE 1950s THROUGH THE 1970s

While failing to achieve democratic objectives, French secondary schools also fell short in training sufficient skilled workers for industry. Industry in turn did not utilize well the ones they had. There are several reasons for this. The rapid modernization and growth of the economy along Fordist lines during the 1950s and 60s led to haphazard practices of training of workers and actual deskilling. In order to keep costs down, the big companies relied upon unskilled labour, usually peasants, women, and immigrants who were mainly from North Africa. The number of immigrants rose from 1.7 million in 1954 to 4.1 million in 1975, by which time a third of workers in the automobile sector were of foreign origin.[63] Women also entered the economy in increasing numbers (up from 33.4 to 38.7 per cent between 1962 and 1975), especially in the service sector. Until the mid-1970s, workers, skilled and unskilled, managed to find jobs but the economic crisis that developed during that decade threw thousands out of work, especially the unskilled.

Second, the centralized and hierarchical organization of industry combined with a rigid system of job classification made it difficult to utilize existing skilled labour. Workers were frequently promoted on the basis of seniority and competence demonstrated on the job rather than acquired skills. Moreover, traditional hostility between management and labour undermined efforts to establish collaborative work that formed part of new forms of flexible or "lean" production which began to appear during the 1970s. The exclusion of labour unions from the making of industrial policy facilitated the deskilling of workers and inhibited technological innovation, so that companies hired large numbers of unskilled workers and middle level supervisors and technicians to supervise them and frequently purchased machinery and patents abroad. This explains the emphasis in government and industry on the education of engineers, technicians and middle management and their relative indifference to the training of skilled workers.

With increasing unemployment in the 1970s possibilities for professional advancement began to dry up. The opening up of the first cycle of secondary education to the working classes during the 1960s and 1970s and large increases in enrolments did not lead to increased professional mobility for workers. Indeed sociologists discovered in their studies that working class children were invariably relegated to the inferior vocational branches of study in the secondary schools, and that even those who managed to obtain credentials often failed to find jobs consistent with their level of training.[64]

Why was industry content to recruit a poorly-trained workforce, and why did it not give greater preference to the CAP and other technical and vocational certificates? The main reason for this lay in the rigid French job classification system. The impersonal wage scale originated in the French dislike of face to face conflict, which is reduced by the use of objective administrative criteria. This is why French labour and management alike preferred seniority to skills and productivity as the criterion for worker evaluation.[65] The reliance on seniority reflected a search for institutional guarantees of fairness and led to a highly formalized system of pay allocation, more legalistic than economic in character and poorly adapted to the market. All workers were treated in the same way by management, regardless of their training or professional capability. Skilled workers could be promoted to shift leader, foreman, and even production supervisor, but these individuals had limited initiative and technical competence, their functions having been mainly supervisory. Under the Fordist regime, real power rested with the engineers and technicians in the planning and personnel departments, and important decisions were normally passed up the line to management. Companies had a more or less free hand in managing their personnel, with the proviso that they abide by the strict hierarchical classification of jobs and the vested rights of each occupational category.[66]

Industrial wage scales were introduced in the interwar and Vichy periods. Post-war agreements dated to 1954 in which a series of agreements were made first with the UIMM and then in other industries, and in 1967 when the government introduced a nation-wide six-step hierarchy of employment categories.[67]

In the French system, each job was assigned a coefficient linked to educational level and was situated along a continuum running from the lowest worker to senior technicians. As the coefficient was attached to the job rather than to the worker, the system rated the skill requirement of the position rather than the skill of the worker. The classifications were arrived at by negotiation within each branch of industry, but each firm was free to assign coefficients to previously defined job categories in the light of the job content set forth by the collective bargaining agreement for the branch as a whole. The assignment of coefficients, reminiscent of the civil service, resulted in attributing considerable importance to the organizational structure of work as a bargaining issue and meant that grievances had to be referred to a higher level of authority.

As wages were associated with coefficients and coefficients with jobs, a worker could be awarded a raise only if he or she changed jobs and/or moved into a higher rated position. This normally required either that a job be created or, more commonly, that a post be vacated. Because promotion to a higher coefficient set a precedent, only senior management could make the decision, not the foreman or the production supervisor. Indeed the supervisors were deprived of all professional authority in a system in which job definition, pay classification and ultimately the attribution of status to the worker was determined by hierarchical structures.[68]

Rigid salary scales fit in well with French versions of mass production and Taylorism in the developing heavy industry of the 1950s and 1960s. Jobs were becoming increasingly deskilled and therefore were narrowly defined in terms of a specific function. By the 1970s with the appearance of the information revolution and new forms of production demanding greater autonomy and adaptability on the part of the worker, the agreements were clearly outdated. They were revised in the *Accord national* of July 1975 on the classifications of workers in metallurgy (further revised in 1980 and 1983) in line with changes in the nature of work. The accord was based on carefully negotiated agreements on qualifications between labour, business and government in which job levels were defined and a new salary scale established.

Table 3.1
National employment categories

Levels 1–2: Executives, liberal professions: second or third cycle of higher education, licence and higher, grande école diplomas.

Level 3: Higher technicians: first cycle higher education, BTS, DUT, DEUG, DEUST.

Level 4: Middle level supervisory, technicians: baccalauréat général, baccalauréat technique, baccalauréat professionnel (since 1987), brevet professionnel.

Level 5: Skilled workers: CAP, BEP.

Level 6: Unskilled or semi-skilled workers, no vocational certification.

Source: BEP = brevet de l'éducation professionnelle (brevet d'enseignement professionnel), BTS = brevet de technicien supérieur, CAP = certificat d'aptitude professionnelle, DEUG = diplôme d'études universitaires générales, DEUST = diplôme d'études universitaires scientifiques et techniques, DUT = diplôme universitaire de technologie.

Specifically, the accords of 1975 did away with the unskilled worker (*manoeuvre*) as an employment category and introduced a new position at the top of the scale, the factory technician (*technicien d'atelier* or TA). What remained then were two semi-skilled categories (OS, *ouvrier spécialisé*, 1 and 2), three skilled (OP, *ouvrier professionnel*, 1 to 3), and the factory technician organized into three levels, the top of which overlapped with supervisory positions (*la maîtrise*). The cut-off point between workers and executives came with senior technicians, who were considered workers in terms of pay scale, vacations, overtime, benefits, etc., even though in reality their functions overlapped with engineers, who were defined as executives (*cadres*). This led to many complaints and conflicts over the years.

The rigid job classification system and the habit of many companies of promoting mainly on the basis of seniority and good behaviour rather than skills, put little premium on formal certification. Although industries hired and promoted CAPs, they did not always make an effort to match them to specialties or to promote them according to their skills. Only 31 per cent of all workers in French industry during the 1970s held the CAP (45 per cent of skilled workers) and the programs for many of these certificates were dated and/or of low level. The majority (69 per cent) had received some general schooling, of whom 41 per cent had attended primary and/or secondary school but had no diplomas or possessed either a primary education certificate (the certificat de l'enseignement primaire) obtained by a minority of primary school leavers after taking a national examination or the *brevet d'études du premier cycle* (BEPC), a certificate stating that the student had completed the first cycle of secondary education. Neither of these credentials had any technical or vocational content.

THE EDUCATION OF SKILLED PERSONNEL IN GERMANY

The education of workers in Germany was far more developed than in France. It derived from a widespread system of apprenticeship within industries that developed in the nineteenth century. These programs were not standardized until the Second World War. After the war, with the devastation of industry and the discrediting of conservative elites, the government of the German Federal Republic, business, and labour cooperated to rebuild the economy along the most modern free market lines and to organize, as part of that effort, a high skills system of vocational training called the Dual System. This involved the cooperation of the German states, the länder, the Chambers of Commerce, and the labour unions. Since the same requirements were imposed on large, medium, and small industry of all sectors, they had a common interest in taking the long-term view of industrial development and career training and retraining.

At the end of four years of primary education the German education system was split into three branches:

1 the *Gymnasium*, a nine year program leading to the *abitur* (equivalent to the French baccalauréat) and university studies,
2 the *Realschule*, a six year program, intermediary, modern and vocational, for the training of technicians that led in some cases to engineering and higher technical schools,
3 the *Hauptschule*, the second cycle of primary education lasting five years, concluding at the end of the students' fourteenth year.

At fifteen the students from the Hauptschulen were oriented either into the *Berufschule* as part of the dual system (one quarter instruction, three-quarters on-the-job training) or into the *Berufsfachschule* for two years of further study before apprenticeship. In the early 1980s around 70 per cent of German youth followed the third route, 50 per cent through apprenticeship and 20 per cent via the vocational school (Berufsfachschule), while in France the approximate figures were 14 and 40 per cent.[69] The German programs provided skills training for around 375 professions designated by the state in consultation with business and industry.

This meant that skilled workers were well trained for their jobs and were granted a level of independence, autonomy, and salary above that of their counterparts in France. Maurice, Sellier and Silvestre found in their study in the early 1980s of French and German plants in the same field of production, that the unskilled German workers possessed roughly the same skills as the French skilled workers.[70] German workers also had a better chance of being promoted to positions as foremen, supervisors, and even engineers (with the aid of continuing education), positions that enjoyed real supervisory authority, unlike in France. Twenty-five per cent of German executives began their training as apprentices.[71] The strong point of the German system was that employees at all levels of the industrial hierarchy frequently shared a similar background and had a common interest in good product development.

A second strong point was that the system of vocational training involved a combination of on-the-job training (under the direction of the capable *meister* in the German firm) and school instruction combining theory and practice. This was closely tied to an extensive system of continuing education, which meant that German workers were kept abreast of technological change. When the third wave of industrialization came in the 1970s, involving a high value-added accumulation regime and the adaptation of advanced technology to rapidly evolving industrial demands, German workers (and those in Austria, Sweden, and Switzerland, which had similar systems) were in a far better position to adapt to change than low-skills regimes such as France, Great Britain, and to some extent the United States.[72]

In 1985 there were around 1,832,000 young people enrolled in apprenticeship programs, or about 70 per cent of the corresponding age group. This figure had fallen to 1,500,000 in 1990. During the 1990s the percentage of apprentices declined to about 40 because many young people preferred to continue their education in either a realschule or gymnasium in the hope of reaching higher education. This has accompanied a higher rate of unemployment among young people in recent years and the fear that early specialization might lead to outmoded credentials down the line.[73]

The greater autonomy of the German worker meant that German firms required about half the supervisory personnel as in France. In Germany in the 1970s one foreman supervised twenty-two workers; in France the figure was one to eleven.[74] In 1980 the French had 40 supervisory/managerial staff for 450 workers as opposed to the German ratio of 20 to 450. The French also had a higher percentage of technical personnel to workers: 31 per cent to 12.8 per cent.[75] Workers are better paid in Germany than in France, and the gap between the salaries of white and blue collar employees is less great.[76] The German firm has traditionally been functional and horizontal in organization, the French vertical and bureaucratic.

Such factors as these, combined with growing opportunities for horizontal and vertical mobility, caused many trained French workers to abandon the factory floor in favour of the tertiary sector, small firms, and/or middle level white collar positions. This mobility, though good for the individuals involved, tended to destabilize the workforce and accentuated poor manpower planning on the part of the state and industry.

MODERNIZATION AND MANPOWER POLICIES DURING THE 1960s AND 1970s

All sections of the French Resistance in the Second World War were united in their condemnation of the elites of the Third Republic and Vichy. They saw these regimes as having protected "retrograde France," a world of uneconomic small producers, pluralistic cultures, and a traditional way of life that had caused the divisions and inequities that had seriously weakened national unity by 1940 and had crippled the ability of the country to adapt to the modern world. Many planners, educators, civil servants, and politicians adopted the view that France must modernize at all costs. They seized upon the idea of state planning and *dirigisme* as the only way of achieving national unity, rejuvenating the country, and healing old political and social wounds. This meant industrial restructuring along Taylorist lines, mass production, and the consumer society. It also meant urban renewal, state-directed regional and local planning, and the recasting of the education system. The latter had to be integrated, unified, and updated so that it could provide scientists, engineers, and managers (*cadres*) as well as augmented industrial research facilities for the new mass production and consumer industries. Taylorist-Fordist methods of production coincided with traditional hierarchies, including academic ones. The grandes écoles produced an elite of highly educated senior managers while the petites grandes écoles educated a rapidly growing number of middle-level technicians and managers. The latter were clearly separated both from their superiors and from the mass of semi-skilled workers on the assembly lines whom they supervised and who were relegated to the lowest levels of the education system.[77]

Modernization also meant changes in the way people lived, notably the restructuring of national territory and the rebuilding of cities and regions to fit them into the high tech industrial world that was evolving. This restructuring had obvious implications for education, which would become less "disinterested" and increasingly geared to the needs of the economy. It meant also that central cities and certain suburbs would increasingly be reserved to the new middle class (the number of high-level managers increased by 51 per cent in twenty years), while downtown *quartiers populaires* composed of workers (particularly foreign ones) would be expelled to distant industrial suburbs that would eventually form into ghettos, again with obvious implications for education, especially vocational education. Between 1954 and 1973, Paris saw the demolition and reconstruction of a full 24 per cent of its buildable surface, Paris proper lost 550,000 people and the number of workers declined by 44 per cent, changes of the scope of the *Haussmannisation* of Paris a century earlier. Similar alterations and demolitions took place in provincial cities. As Kristin Ross pointed out, "the logic of exclusion had its roots in capitalist modernization."[78]

In the field of industrial development, Charles De Gaulle favoured *grands projets* in each industrial sector in order to achieve national independence and prestige. French companies were thought to be too small to compete on the international scale (few figured in the Fortune 500 polls), so the government directed its planning efforts toward augmenting the "critical mass" of big business, advancing technology and promoting mergers while leaving middle-sized and smaller firms to the vagaries of the market. The "national champions" receiving massive public investment were located particularly in the aerospace, computer, electronic, nuclear, and telecommunications industries, but state-directed plans for rationalization were also introduced in the more traditional automobile, textile, steel, and shipbuilding sectors. The weakness of this grand approach was that too much emphasis was placed on production and not enough on market and cost considerations. This was particularly evident in such projects as the Concorde, the ocean liner La France, Roissy Airport, the big steel complex at Fos-sur-Mer, the New Towns, computers and information technology (Plan Calcul 1966). It was more successful with Airbus (passenger aircraft), Ariane (satellite launcher) and the TGV (trains à grande vitesse). As Storper and Salais point out, the modernizing state did not intervene to promote market dynamics but instead projected the will of key groups of technocrats and private interests and worked to preserve industrial patrimony and employment by installing modern technologies.[79] This meant that many companies came to rely on large state contracts and protection in order to survive.

The close alliance of the state and big business, solidified by the grandes écoles and grand corps background of high-level civil servants, planners, and businessmen, excluded small- and medium-sized firms, labour, farmers, and women. It focused almost exclusively on firm size, which tended to produce industrial groups that were little more than diversified financial conglomerates. The argument was that the wealth created by "national champions" would trickle down into the rest of the economy, but in reality the economy was only partly modernized and the new mass production techniques were imperfectly realized. In this vulnerable situation, the spectacular oil price hikes of 1973 hit France very hard, particularly as it imported more oil than any other European country and provided for only 22 per cent of its own energy needs. In the years between 1974 and 1985, French industrial output fell by 13.6 per cent.[80] Initially many firms and policy-makers tried to cut costs by carrying Fordism to an extreme, the usual reaction when the old technology is challenged by a new one.[81] French governments pushed for the merger of companies in difficulty into larger companies in even greater difficulty, favouring long runs of low-cost, standardized products with little innovation and with massive layoffs of workers, particularly in the automobile, metallurgical, mining, and textile industries. Companies closed plants and mechanized systems. But mechanization failed to compensate for other defects in the system: arms-length relations with suppliers, an excess of white-collar personnel, labour problems, poor research and development, and a lack of skilled workers and technicians. Faced with competition from advanced economies – Japan, Germany, the United States – on the one hand, and low-wage Third World countries on the other, most companies proved unable to compete and relied increasingly on state contracts and protection from imports to survive.[82]

Jacques Chirac, the first prime minister (1974–76) under the presidency of Valéry Giscard d'Estaing (1974–81), rushed to the rescue of lame ducks in the steel and shipbuilding industries and tried to stimulate the economy by encouraging industrial production and modernization, but this led to renewed inflation and a steep deficit in the balance of payments, as the French used their increased purchasing power to buy mainly German and Japanese imports rather than French consumer goods. His successor Raymond Barre (1976–81) tried deflation and austerity, with only mediocre results because such policies were not accompanied by the restructuring of French industry. The industrial *politique de créneaux* (niche strategy) favoured by governments provided state encouragement to key industries in key sectors with the result that by 1976 six large companies received 50 per cent of public subsidies to industry.[83] None of these policies worked in the face of chronic inflation, trade deficits, corporate indebtedness, and low investment, all of which were compounded by increased payroll taxes on companies that rendered them less competitive in a saturated world market. Government reluctance to allow massive layoffs further undermined austerity policies. By the late 1970s some of France's largest firms were verging on bankruptcy, notably in the automobile, computer, and metallurgical industries, and the country was beginning to deindustrialize.[84]

The oil crises of the 1970s and the collapse of traditional domestic markets accompanied rapid changes in work organization. Such changes, usually called "lean production," developed in the Toyota automobile works after the Second World War, enabled the Japanese to produce automobiles, electronic appliances, and other consumer items more efficiently and cheaply than the Americans or Europeans. The new method favoured smaller more flexible companies with shorter production runs and highly skilled workers. It was based on two organizational features: the transfer of the maximum number of tasks and responsibilities to those workers actually adding value to the car on the line; and a system for detecting defects that quickly traces the cause of the problem (workers are allowed to stop the assembly line if they spot a defect).[85] The system made possible rapid product development, just-in-time supply of parts, and a close working association between assemblers and suppliers. It gradually replaced the long assembly line producing standardized products and introduced shorter production runs of more specialized goods, which committed less capital and freed the company from dependence on large markets. Computer-controlled machinery made possible manufacture in small batches and/or customized items for increasingly sophisticated tastes, facilitating rapid adjustments of machinery to changing market demands and greater precision and quality. Changes in production accompanied changes in the nature of work. The worker needed to assume more responsibility, cooperate with others, have an understanding of the production process, and be better trained technically.

In discussing "flexible production" in the early 1980s, Michael Piore and Charles Sabel predicted that those countries having a surviving craft tradition (Germany, Sweden, and Japan) would adapt better to changing technology than those in which that tradition had disappeared (France, the US).[86] During the economic crisis that lasted from 1974 to 1986, Germany and Sweden were in fact more successful than the French in implementing new technologies and more flexible work organization, mainly because they had educated managers steeped in the production process, a workforce that enjoyed considerable autonomy, a tradition of cooperation with management, an excellent system of vocational training, and relatively good labour relations.[87] French industry, with its rigid, bureaucratic and Colbertist traditions, augmented by an immature Fordism, relied too heavily on unskilled labour supervised by too many middle-level managers who referred too many decisions to their superiors up the line.[88] Adversarial labour relations and inadequate technical and vocational education discouraged independent initiative on the part of the worker and collaboration with management.

The failure to restructure industry in the 1970s accompanied an equal failure to reform technical and vocational education. The new emphasis on the autonomy of the worker meant that the programs in technical and vocational education had to become less specialized, more flexible and more technically demanding. Flexibile production also placed great emphasis on the quality of management, which had to be well versed in the technical side of production, have good communication skills, and the ability to make important decisions rapidly and collaboratively. All this required basic changes in the French command structure as well as the restructuring of industry and the education system.

Most of the educational reforms during the 1970s were inadequate to deal with the crisis. The apprenticeship law of 1971 was a step in the right direction in bringing education and business closer together, but relatively few apprentices were trained in France during the 1970s and 1980s (the number of apprentices averaged about 200,000), and these were usually employed in small artisanal firms or in the food industry. Other laws in 1971 laid the basis for improved continuing education and work study programs, but they were only implemented later in the decade, and the large-scale introduction of work-study programs and continuing education had to await the 1980s and 1990s (chapter 4). Governments also failed to reform the programs of the CAP, which were overly specialized in traditional skills (e.g., filing, fitting, lathing, or milling). Haby's promotion of the collèges d'enseignement technique into lycées d'enseignement professionnel was an empty gesture because little but the name changed. The CET-LEP did not possess sufficient computer controlled and other modern equipment. Such equipment was expensive and in any case many of the teachers, schooled in the old trades, were unfamiliar with the new processes. Moreover, too much emphasis was placed on vocational training in schools with no provision for on-the-job training. This was unfortunate because advanced industrial skills are very hard to teach in schools without reference to the workplace.[89]

CONCLUSION

In one generation France experienced Fordist industrialization, the automobile age and the consumer society, the rise of a new middle class, and rapid urbanization. In education the slow pace of change of the interwar and postwar years gave way to considerable reform during the 1960s and 1970s. These years saw the dismantling of the compartmentalized and fragmented structures of education and the building of a consolidated and integrated education system, the first genuine "system" of education that the French had known. The period saw the introduction of the école unique and the opening of secondary (and therefore higher) education to the average person, the creation of a lycée technique and a technician's baccalauréat, and the establishment of two-year technical and vocational schools in higher education.

The modernization of the education system responded to capitalist rather than democratic logic. The emphasis was on the education of a new professional middle class of *cadres* who could be managers, employees, and technicians at the same time, managing workers but punching a time clock too. For this reason the old education hierarchies and tracks remained, but these were updated, broadened, and modernized according to the manpower requirements of the emerging Fordist regime that sharply differentiated the training of managers and engineers on the one hand, and low-skilled assembly-line workers on the other. In the 1960s the new middle class, possessing the qualifications necessary for the high tech society of the future, was the focus of education while the working classes, especially those of foreign origin, plus the petite bourgeoisie and peasantry, all considered *en voie de disparition*, were relegated to the lower ranks of the education system.

A hybrid system of production, partly traditional, partly Fordist, accompanied a poorly coordinated system of training. The relative unity and coherence of technical education under the old Division of Technical Education, closely linked to the machine, mechanical, metallurgical, and electrical industries and recruiting and training good students, gave way to a mass system in which mainly working-class young people were tracked into vocational schools possessing little prestige, where they were taught often outmoded skills and were increasingly marginalized. Thus the French workforce was hardly prepared for the sudden transition from the Fordist accumulation regime of the 1950s and 60s to a high technology one of the late 1970s and 1980s. Moreover, about half of technicians and almost as many engineers were poorly educated for their positions, having been promoted on the job. The education system was too segmented and balkanized to be easily adapted to economic change. Although governments attempted to develop industrial strategies, their policies were based on grandiose and uneconomic projects, on an immature and yet increasingly outmoded Fordist system, and on inadequate vocational training, so that it was very difficult for industry to move toward a system of flexible production and high-skill policies.

4 Vocational Education and the Training of Workers since 1981

Changez tout, mais ne touchez à rien: telle pourrait être la consigne des Français à leurs ministres de l'éducation nationale.

Lionel Jospin, Minister of Education, 1988–92

THE SOCIALIST ECONOMIC REFORMS OF THE 1980s

In 1981 the newly elected Socialists, blaming the economic crisis on Raymond Barre's deflationary monetarist policies, returned to a full employment policy as the instrument for economic renewal. In 1982 they nationalized numerous companies and banks and reorganized them into vertically integrated firms, recapitalizing them and streamlining their operations, eliminating jobs and closing obsolete plants. The state ended up owning thirteen of the twenty largest firms in France and thirty-six banks.[1]

In addition, the government of Prime Minister Pierre Mauroy raised wages, ran deliberate budget deficits, hired 100,000 civil servants over three years, raised the education budget, and decentralized government. It also reduced the work week from forty to thirty-nine hours, added a fifth week of vacation, and reduced the retirement age to sixty. By 1982 government spending was up 27.6 per cent and inflation was running at fourteen per cent. Such measures came just as other countries in the developed world were introducing tight monetarist policies in order to attack the inflation stemming from the second oil price shock of 1979. The weak competitiveness of French industry, rising wage costs, and the reduction of the work week led to declining profit margins. Industrial production went up but imports outdistanced exports as foreign competitors undersold inefficient French consumer industries. Private investment fell 12 per cent in 1981, and the economy declined in 1982.[2] Between 1981 and 1985, French industry lost 200,000 jobs a year, posting an 11.5 per cent fall in its labour force.[3] This led to the first of three devaluations of the franc.

In early 1983 a battle took place within the government between those who wanted to withdraw from the European monetary system and retreat into protectionism, led by Jean-Pierre Chevènement (Minister of Industry), and those who wanted to keep free trade and abandon Fordist policies, led by Mauroy, Jacques Delors (Minister of Finance) and Laurent Fabius (Budget Minister). The victory of the Mauroy group led to the great U-turn of March 1983 that introduced a *politique de rigueur*: cutting back spending and social policies, bringing trade accounts into balance, and reducing wages in order to dampen inflation. The government introduced financial reforms that enabled business to gain new sources of financing thus diminishing their dependence on government for subsidies and on the banks for loans. As industry minister in 1983–84 and prime minister from 1984 to 1986, Fabius took a new approach to restructuring that targeted companies to cut losses, reduce excess capacity, improve productivity, and produce profits. While using state power to bring about modernization, he gave nationalized companies greater autonomy and allowed some informal privatization. He offered incentives to all firms rather than a special few and refused to rescue failing enterprises, allowing the metallurgical company Schneider-Creusot to go under, the biggest bankruptcy in French history.[4]

As a result of such measures, inflation dropped from 14 per cent in 1981 to 2.7 per cent in 1987, buying power improved and the deficit in foreign balance of payments was stabilized. Steel and automobiles, the recipient of half of government subsidies in the early 1980s, were turning a profit by 1988. If textiles and machine tools continued to languish, the aviation, aerospace, nuclear energy, and telecommunications industries forged ahead.[5] The top ten nationalized companies, which lost more than 13 billion francs in 1981, made over 26 billion in profits in 1990, about the same as the top ten private companies, which had been barely breaking even in 1981.[6] In 1988 and 1989 the economy grew by 3.6 per cent each year.[7] Nationalization made it possible for industries to do what they had not been able to do so easily before: to restructure, close obsolete plants, and eliminate jobs. This accompanied the installation of highly automated, computer-controlled equipment and the gradual adoption of Japanese-style practices emphasizing teamwork and improved union-management relations.[8] In the belief that high skills promote technological innovation, great emphasis was placed on the improved education and upgrading of qualifications of the workforce.

The victory of the right in the parliamentary elections of 1986 saw the formation of a neo-liberal right-centre government under Jacques Chirac, backed by his finance minister, Edouard Balladur, both of whom favoured a policy of liberalism and deregulation. Chirac and Balladur declared their intention to privatize sixty-five companies. The profits of these companies had increased over the two previous years to such an extent that privatization was a success: 1.35 million individual shareholders were drawn into the stock market in the 1986–88 privatizations, and in the Balladur government of 1993–95 (Chirac was President of the Republic by that time) 2.5 million more first-time shareholders invested in shares disposed of by the government.[9]

With the re-election of the socialists in 1988, Mitterrand declared a policy of "ni ni," neither nationalization nor privatization. In fact, the socialists were comfortable with privatization and made no effort to renationalize. This policy has continued under the government of Lionel Jospin since 1997. Having begun with *dirigisme*, the socialists ended up embracing a moderate form of economic liberalism, and promoting the disengagement of the state from the economy. The result has been the creation of a mixed economy in which cross-shareholdings and interlocking directorships involve banking-industry partnerships and affinity groups of industries, banks, insurers, and other service providers and suppliers. Private and public firms formally control one another, with the state assuming an increasingly indirect role, even in state-controlled companies.[10]

EDUCATIONAL REFORMS
DURING THE 1980s

The 1970s and 1980s saw the decline of bureaucratic and Taylorist industrial models and the appearance of new industrial systems and manufacturing techniques. It had become clear that investments in automated technology could only succeed if allied with investments in human resources, especially in updating skills and increasing worker autonomy. Put another way, companies were more likely to opt for high-skill forms of production given an adequate supply of skilled workers from the education system. The right-centre governments of the 1960s and 1970s introduced the école unique, opened secondary and higher education to the common person, created the lycée technique and the lycée d'enseignement professionnel at the secondary level and the Sections de technicien supérieur and the

Instituts universitaires de technologie in the first (two-year) cycle of higher education. They introduced technical baccalaureates and the brevet de l'enseignement professionnel. But the system that they established was essentially geared to Fordist production hierarchies, emphasizing the training of engineers, technicians, and a certain number of highly skilled workers for technical functions, plus a mass of semi-skilled and unskilled workers for assembly lines.

Despite their quasi-Marxist ideology and the fact that they were a party composed mainly of teachers, professors, and civil servants, the Socialists came to power in 1981 with no coherent plan for educational reform. Pierre Mauroy, prime minister until 1984, named Alain Savary as his education minister. Savary quickly moved away from the confrontationist, anti-capitalist approach of the party education platform, defining his approach as one of decentralization, debureaucratization and of "cooperation rather than confrontation."[11] He moved toward change on a very broad front, planning the reform of higher education, private education, the democratization of the collèges, and the restructuring of technical and vocational training. To lay the groundwork he named a series of commissions to study the key sectors of the education system: the collèges (Louis Legrand),[12] the lycées (Antoine Prost),[13] and the teaching profession (André De Peretti).[14] He also launched studies of primary and higher education. He increased spending by 17 per cent in the 1982 budget and created 34,000 jobs in the education system.[15]

As part of his study of secondary education, Prost was asked to analyse intermediate technical and vocational education. Savary considered merging the lycées d'enseignement professionnel and the lycées techniques into a unified general lycée, but Prost recommended retaining the vocational schools because of their proven capacity for pedagogical innovation, providing they remained flexible and adaptable to technological change and not just repositories for weaker students.[16]

Armed with the recommendations of the Prost commission, Savary ordered the modernization of all technical and vocational programs by the vocational advisory boards (commissions professionnelles consultatives) and an improved technical course in the collèges, the 4e and 3e technologiques. He put an end to compulsory orientation in the 5th class, at age twelve or thirteen, deferring the key decision as to whether the child was to be oriented into general or vocational studies to the 3rd class, at age fourteen or fifteen. The purpose was to place vocational education at the senior high school level in order to establish some semblance of equality with general studies. But this proved difficult because the BEP (brevet d'enseignement professionnel) and

CAP were mainly terminal diplomas that led directly to the workforce at level V. Only 12 per cent of the holders of the BEP for example continued their studies in the early 1980s.[17]

Jean-Pierre Chevènement replaced Savary as minister of education in 1984 under the government of Laurent Fabius (1984–86).[18] At this time, spokesmen for industry led by the UIMM were pointing to changes in work away from the repetitious and parcelized gestures of the assembly line in favour of the ability to operate and repair the new automated machine tools and computer operated machinery. Since the nineteenth century the UIMM had played a key role in vocational planning and training. It included not only the machine, metallurgical, and mining industries, but also the automobile, aviation, electronic, electrical, and various related industries. It now complained of the scarcity of middle-level factory technicians possessing an understanding of industrial processes and capable of taking greater initiative.[19] In theory the *bacheliers de technicien* were supposed to fill such posts, but the great majority of them especially in the industrial sections (F) continued their studies into higher education, mostly in the sections de techniciens supérieurs, leaving a void at level IV of the employment hierarchy between skilled workers possessing the CAP-BEP (level V) and senior technicians (level III).

The question then arose whether industry should retrain its skilled workers or depend on the education system to train a whole new category of worker-technicians. The UIMM favoured the latter position, partly because more than half (53 per cent) of skilled workers had no formal training or certification for their posts, having been promoted on the job, and were considered difficult to retrain.[20] Following the lead of the UIMM, the great majority of companies polled in other industries took the same position, except for the chemical sector, which decided to reskill its existing workers. They favoured the large-scale training of factory technicians (*techniciens d'atelier*), a category created in the *Plan national* of 1975 at about the same level as *la maîtrise* (foremen, workshop supervisors – lesser supervisors situated between workers and technicians) but which had failed to develop in sufficient numbers.

The position of the UIMM was supported by the conclusions of the Haut comité éducation-économie, which had been recently set up to study ways of cooperation between the education ministry and business and industry.[21] In collaboration with the Bloch commission named by Chevènement, the Bureau d'information et de prévision économique (BIPE), and the Centre d'études et de recherche sur les qualifications (CEREQ), the committee reported that by the year 2000 the number of un- or semi-skilled jobs (levels VI & V) would decline dramatically (56 to 32 per cent), while the demand for technicians (level IV), senior technicians (level III), and engineers and managers (levels I-II) would rise sharply.[22]

Chevènement saw the advantage of creating a *baccalauréat professionnel* to train factory technicians at level IV at a time when only 30 per cent of young people were obtaining the baccalauréat.[23] There was considerable discussion however whether preparation for the new diploma should take place in the lycées techniques, which were designed to prepare for level IV, or the lycées professionnels, which trained skilled workers for level V. The CGT and the secondary teachers' unions (SGEN, SNES, and SNPES) preferred the former option arguing for the unity of secondary programs, while proponents of the lycées professionnels argued that the lycées de technicien prepared students mainly for higher education, while industry was demanding factory technicians that were immediately employable in factory and shop. Moreover, the chance to offer a baccalauréat would raise the status of the lycées professionnels and provide opportunities for advancement for working-class young people. References were made to Japanese and American worker-technicians who possessed high school diplomas.[24]

Chevènement decided in favour of the lycée professionnel. With considerable fanfare, he announced in 1985 the policy of achieving 80 per cent baccalauréats (or the equivalent) by the year 2000, which would be made possible by the introduction of the baccalauréat professionnel. Once in possession of its bac, vocational education would become a stream of "success" rather than one associated with academic failure. To that end, he announced the conversion of the lycées d'enseignement professionnel into lycées professionnels (law of 23 December 1985).

There is no doubt that a consensus had developed in industry in favour of the lycée professionnel and its "bac pro" and that generally they have been well received since their implementation in 1987. But these creations, and the conversion of the BEP from a diploma for workers into a preparatory program for the bac pro, involved the devaluation of the CAP and the rejection of the proposal to retrain existing workers in the new industrial technology. As a result, many workers were laid off or were retired early, and consequently France has the lowest percentage of workers over 55 (47.5 per cent in 1988) in the developed world.[25] Many of those who remained were assigned to traditional machines while the techniciens d'atelier operated the new automated equipment. Older workers frequently remained isolated and poorly paid compared to their younger, better-educated counterparts who were generally able to establish good working relations with senior technicians and engineers.[26] On the other hand, in some fields young bacheliers professionnels were hired as ordinary workers and found that prospects for promotion were limited by the tendency of senior managers to reduce the number of middle-management categories in line with new "lean-management" techniques.[27]

THE BACCALAURÉAT PROFESSIONNEL

The bac pro programs were designed by the vocational advisory boards, which carefully set out frames of reference linking programs to industrial requirements. Programs avoided the usual sequential approach, regrouping the twenty-seven-week courses (in each of two years) into three areas: vocational training and technology (industrial sciences and techniques, mathematics and physical sciences, economics and business); general studies (French, foreign languages, communication); and applied arts, sports, etc. The schools rely mainly on graded exercises rather than on examinations.

For the first time vocational studies had its own bac designed from the outset to include work placements in industry; the company and firm were considered legitimate places of instruction.[28] The work placements of sixteen to twenty-four weeks were considered learning experiences and were assessed and graded by the company *tuteur* in collaboration with professors from the schools.[29] The work terms had been established in laws in 1971 and 1979 in the CAP and BEP programs but had not been fully integrated into regular programs. A law in July 1989 required work-study for all programs in the vocational schools (CAP, BEP, and bac pro) as part of their learning experience and preparation for diplomas.

In 1996 the lycées professionnels offered fifty-four baccalauréats professionnels, forty-five BEP (seventy-three in 1990) and 250 CAP (300 in 1990). The number of diplomas has been reduced at all levels in favour of flexible instruction opening up a family of skills. This transversal approach, cutting across traditional skills, allows more adaptability. However there is always the danger that the vocational advisory boards will miss the mark and that a new diploma will not provide sufficient employment. Most *bacheliers professionnels* in industry get jobs in production, maintenance, and repair. In hiring practices, companies do not always distinguish between the bac pro and the BEP (levels IV and V), especially in manufacturing where bacheliers professionnels often end up as skilled workers, overqualified for their jobs. Around a quarter of bacheliers professionnels continue their studies, depending on the field, mostly in the sections de technicien supérieur.[30] This compares to over 90 per cent of general bacheliers and 80 per cent of technical bacheliers who do so.[31]

The comparatively small number of professional bacheliers who continue on to higher education has sparked debate between those who want to keep the program specialized and oriented toward the workplace, and those who favour a more general program providing students with a better chance of reaching higher education and offering social advancement for a largely working class clientele. Many in this group would like to see the assimilation of the professional lycées into the LEGT, lycées d'enseignement général et technologique, just as the modern and technical lycées had been integrated earlier into the general ones (1963 and 1985). This group argues that the baccalauréat has always been a secondary-leaving diploma and the first university credential, enabling holders to register automatically in university faculties, and that the professional bacheliers should have the same options as the general and technical ones.

Industrialists frequently express annoyance with such views, noting that both the BEP and the baccalauréat de technicien began as diplomas that prepared young people for careers in business and industry and ended up preparing them for higher diplomas. They complain that *universitaires* constantly push to increase the general content of programs to prepare young people for "life in a democratic society," which deprives industry of the skilled specialists it needs.[32] They point out that the presence of factory technicians on the production line has established better links between the shop floor and the planning department and reduced the need for supervision.[33] This has proved effective in the use of computer assisted manufacturing and in the more recent implementation of high-performance ceramic and metal materials that make new levels of machining possible.[34] For this reason, industrialists do not want to see the bac pro become just another academic diploma.

The academic side acknowledges the contributions of factory technicians in industry, especially in such fields as computers, electronics and telecommunications. However about 60 per cent of students in lycées professionnels today prepare for jobs in the rapidly growing service sector (the reverse of a decade ago) of which 40 per cent study office and secretarial studies (*bureautique*) alone. These young people must compete with general and technical bacheliers on unequal grounds, not to mention those holding the brevet d'enseignement professionel and brevet de technicien supérieur. This problem is particularly serious for young women who tend to enroll (or be streamed into) several overcrowded tertiary fields – secretarial, accounting, hairdressing, hotels, and health services. Competition is so intense that it is an advantage to obtain further credentials, especially the brevet de technicien supérieur.[35]

The number of candidates presenting themselves for the bac pro exam rose from 31,525 in 1990 to 83,607 in 1999. Over three-quarters of students in the program obtain the bac (77.6 per cent in 1999 as opposed to 78.5 per cent for the general and technical bacs).[36] In all, professional bacheliers constitute 16 per cent of bacheliers as compared to 56 per cent of general bacheliers and 28 per cent of technical bacheliers.[37] The number earning the bac pro is continuing to grow at a rate of 4 to 6 per cent a year, whereas those obtaining the general and technical bacs have been declining 1 or 2 per cent a year.[38] One reason for this is that professional bacheliers get jobs at about the same rate as university graduates. In 1996 for example 7.2 per cent of graduates of the bac pro class of 1992 were unemployed as opposed to 7.8 per cent of graduates in higher education, second cycle and higher (l'enseignement supérieur long).[39]

THE CERTIFICAT D'APTITUDE PROFESSIONNELLE (CAP)

Prior to 1971 the CAP were local certificates that gave students specific vocational skills. By the end of the 1970s there were too many of them (over 500), often overlapping and preparing for a plethora of specialties, not all of which were well adapted to a changing technology. Between 1984 and 1987, 80 CAP programs were created or restructured and 130 abolished by the vocational advisory boards so that by the end of the decade most young people in the program were studying for certificates that had been updated during the past five years in line with the requirements of business and industry.[40]

The decision in the 1980s to abolish the three-year CAP program in the collèges and lycées professionnels (5th through 3rd classes) and turn it into a two-year senior high school program in the LP in direct competition with the brevet d'enseignement professionnel caused a serious decline in enrolments – from 475,000 students in 1970 to 63,000 in 1993. The BEP, more broadly defined and leading to the bac pro, was the sought-after diploma and grew rapidly, from 170,000 students in 1970 to 487,000 in 1990.[41] The fall of enrolments in the CAP programs led to a decline in enrolments in the lycées professionnels, which fell from 805,000 students in 1986 to 726,000 in 1992. These have since recovered with the advance of the BEP and bac pro, rising to 825,000 students in 1997.[42]

The CAP survived in the lycées professionnels partly because students studying for the BEP frequently acquire CAP specialties as well, particularly the overlapping ones, and also because businessmen continue to hire CAP, mainly in manufacture and assembly in larger companies as well as in smaller, artisanal and/or specialized industries.[43] During the 1990s the CAP has become the certificate closely associated with apprenticeship and continuing education programs, in other words with the weaker students at level V only 3 per cent of whom were able to make it to the long cycle of secondary studies.[44] Nevertheless, those in possession of the CAP and BEP are much more likely to obtain and keep jobs than those without; in 1998 the unemployment rate among the former stood at 10.7 per cent, among the latter 17.4 per cent. Indeed their rate was slightly better than that of regular or technical bacheliers (11 per cent).[45]

THE BREVET D'ENSEIGNEMENT PROFESSIONNEL (BEP)

In the early 1980s the BEP had roughly the same prestige as the CAP, but by the end of the decade it was considered superior to it, even though officially both still trained for level V (skilled workers). The program lasts two years, beginning in the second class. Like the CAP, the vocational advisory boards began in 1984 to revise and update BEP programs in line with changing industrial technology, the number of programs falling from seventy-six in 1970 to thirty-six in 1993.[46] The general programs, however, remained untouched from 1973 until 1993 when the courses in French, history-geography, mathematics, and the physical sciences were revised to create a core of subjects common with the technical and general lycées. Students must also study modern languages, technology and vocational subjects, plus practical work. All this extended the time spent on general courses from 28 per cent in 1973 to 37 per cent in the industrial division in 1993 (in the tertiary division 38 to 40 per cent). This provides students with an opportunity to gain a general culture and to continue their studies but leads to overloaded programs. Vocational and technical programs vary from sixteen to twenty-two hours, and general instruction ranges from eleven to eighteen hours a week depending on the sector.[47] The programs reach as high as forty hours per week.

As the general courses are the most difficult for students, the long haul through high school is lengthened further. Over half (53 per cent) of students in BEP programs have repeated one year in secondary school and nine per cent have repeated two years. They spend two years working for the BEP starting in *seconde* and (in the case of three-quarters of them) another two for the bac pro. The result is that the average age of those earning the baccalauréat is one or two years higher than in the general lycées, around age 20 as opposed to 18.[48]

There has been considerable discussion in recent years of abolishing the BEP. Because three-quarters of students in the program continue their studies to obtain a bac pro, it is argued that an expanded CAP, supplemented by a year of specific vocational training, would suffice for the quarter who enter the labour force. This is the position of the Kastler report on vocational certification in 1998, which argued in favour of a single vocational diploma at each level of the secondary system (at level V the CAP, at level IV the bac pro, at level III the BTS).[49] The problem is that the BEP has more prestige than the CAP, and the quarter entering the labour force after obtaining the certificate, frequently young women of migrant and working-class origin, would face even greater obstacles in obtaining a job (about 40 per cent are unemployed in the years after leaving the lycée).[50]

APPRENTICESHIP

A new law on 16 July 1971 clearly defined the role of the state and the private sector in providing apprenticeship programs, continuing education, and work placements in business and industry. The law stated that "apprenticeship is a form of education. Its purpose is to provide young workers who have completed their compulsory schooling with general, theoretical and practical training with a view to obtaining a vocational qualification ... Such training, enshrined in a contract, is partly provided within a business, partly in an apprenticeship training centre."[51] Apprenticeship is a form of vocational training that alternates classroom instruction with experience in the workplace. Unlike pupils at vocational lycées for whom work experience constitutes part of their training, apprentices have a contract governed by the labour code and are paid a wage. They are enrolled in apprentice training centres, *centre de formation d'apprentis* (CFA) usually run by chambers of commerce, which replaced the old vocational courses instituted by the law of 1919.[52] The apprentice is paid a small salary, a percentage of the minimum wage, which increases over the two or three year term. The employer provides instruction in the workplace and assures that the apprentice is attending the training centre and is studying for the CAP. The state ensures that the terms of the contract are being fulfilled, while employer and employee organizations coordinate at the national and regional levels and provide input into the establishment of programs and certificates.[53] The law of 1971 stipulated 360 hours per year in courses in the CFA, two-thirds in general and technical education and a third in practical training.

Training on the job takes place mainly in the building, mechanical, food, and craft trades, usually in small firms – 93 per cent in companies with fewer than 50 employees and 79 per cent less than ten.[54] The CFA was part of the move by French apprenticeship toward the German model, involving schooling as well as learning on the job and industrial as well as artisanal apprenticeship.[55]

A ministerial circular of 3 July 1972 established pre-vocational sections, the *classes préprofessionnelles de niveau* (CPPN), in the collèges and in the collèges d'enseignement technique. The CPPN received young people in academic difficulty streamed in the 5th class and provided a work-study program for one or two years in the 4th and 3rd classes. The law also created pre-apprenticeship sections, the *classes préparatoires à l'apprentissage* (CPA) in the collèges, the CET and the vocational training centres. The pre-apprenticeship class recruited at age fifteen and provided a year's preparation for those destined to begin full apprenticeship at sixteen.

The CPPN and CPA programs were seen by many as undemocratic, defeating the purpose of the école unique. In the early 1970s about half of the students in the program left school at age sixteen with no certification. Around 200,000 per year or 20 per cent of young people between the ages of sixteen and twenty-five had quit school without certification.[56] As unemployment became a chronic problem in the 1970s, young people without skills formed a high percentage of the age group unable to find work.[57] For them apprenticeship constituted a viable option. Between 1977 and 1984 around 39 per cent of apprentices came from a CPA, 22 per cent from the collèges, 11 per cent from CAP or BEP programs, and 7.6 per cent from a CPPN.[58] Because of the modest nature of these programs, apprenticeship did not enjoy much prestige. It was also a male preserve, for young women constituted only about a fifth of apprentices in the 1970s and a quarter in the 1980s. In 1984 Alain Savary, the education minister, transformed the CPA and CPPN into a technical program in the collèges, the *4ᵉ et 3ᵉ technologiques*.[59]

The law decentralizing some aspects of public education on 7 January 1983, transferred jurisdiction over apprenticeship and the vocational training centres to the regions, which have the power to enter into agreements establishing apprentice training centres (*centres de formation d'apprentis*) and to finance them. The academy rector, representing the state, is responsible for programs and inspection. Another law on 23 July 1987, made it possible for an apprentice to pursue diplomas above the CAP, technicians and even engineering credentials. The law also established an interministerial council bringing together the ministries of Education, Work, and Agriculture to coordinate national policy and to clarify the role of the state and the regions in the management of apprenticeship.[60]

Another law in 1992 increased government participation in apprenticeship programs, defined the roles of state, region, profession, and firm, revised pay scales for apprentices and improved the training of teaching personnel in the firm (*tuteurs* and *maîtres d'apprentissage*) and in the apprentice training centres (*formateurs*). It ordered the renovation of the vocational training centres, enlarging them and improving their programs. The law extended apprenticeship into higher education, providing for the part-time training of engineers, and introducing large-scale state support for apprenticeship programs at all levels. In the mid 1980s all of the 212,000 apprentices were studying for the CAP (level V). In 1995, 69 per cent were working for the CAP, 11 per cent the BEP, 13 per cent the baccalauréat professionnel and 7 per cent the brevet de technicien supérieur, the diplôme universitaire de technologie and various engineering credentials.[61]

In terms of the number of apprentices, there were around 400,000 until the mid-1960s, but raising the school leaving age to sixteen during the 1960s and the expansion of the collèges d'enseignement technique caused enrolments to fall from 429,000 in 1967–68 to 302,940 in 1972–73. They leveled off to around 150,000 during the 1980s.[62] Growth began again, particularly with government encouragement under the Jospin ministry (1988–92), and have since risen from 205,000 in 1992 to 300,000 in 1998.[63]

The CAP is the key credential of apprenticeship, continuing education and special needs programs for young workers and employees. In 1992, 60 per cent of those obtaining the CAP were apprentices.[64] Ten per cent manage to reach level IV (technicians), mainly via the professional baccalauréat. However, their success rate at passing the CAP is considerably lower than that of the students from the lycées professionnels: 49 per cent versus 70 per cent.[65] Many apprentices study in pre-apprenticeship programs, once located in the collèges and lycées professionnels but now situated mostly in the apprentice training centres. In 1992 over half of those apprenticed were over sixteen and two thirds had no certification. The CAP still remains the best chance for most apprentices and an alternative for young people in academic difficulty, though the rate of joblessness remains higher among holders of this certificate than of any other. The *loi quinquennale* of 1993 requires all young people leaving secondary school to possess a certified skill and/or an academic diploma. This means that the weaker students will obtain a CAP, which provides no certitude of employment. In 1993, a year in which unemployment was particularly severe, 40.3 per cent of apprentices possessing the CAP could not find work as opposed to 17.5 per cent for those having the bac pro, though on the average about three-quarters find employment during the first year.[66]

CONTINUING EDUCATION

A 1971 law gave all salaried employees a right to training leave. As a result of subsequent legislation it is now possible to accumulate credits toward virtually any diploma. In 1990, 2.9 million workers and employees spent 140 hours upgrading their skills, one employee in three as opposed to one in ten in 1972.[67] In 1993, five million adults were enrolled in continuing education courses.[68] These, however, tend to benefit better educated employees more than workers. Fifty-five per cent of those in the workforce at levels I through IV (executive, engineer, technician) have received at least some continuing education as opposed to 18 per cent at levels V and VI (skilled and unskilled workers).[69]

Apprenticeship, job-training and retraining programs are financed by payroll taxes (*taxe d'apprentissage* and *taxe de formation professionnelle*) that come to 0.6 and 1.5 per cent of gross salaries respectively. Larger, more technically advanced companies (over 2,000 employees) whose employees need to be constantly abreast of technical changes spend an average 3.5 per cent, and some companies (air transport, energy, electronics, electricity, information, telecommunications) spend up to 13 per cent of total salaries on job training and retraining.[70] For each employee a company trains, it receives a reduction in the payroll tax.[71] If the company spends 1.5 per cent of its sales on training, it pays no tax. The same is true of apprenticeship training (0.6 per cent). This provides the company with an obvious incentive to set up training programs, which is necessary because companies are otherwise not particularly interested in getting involved in such schemes. Since all have to do so, no one gets a free ride. This assures long-term planning for training and retraining at the company level.

WORK-STUDY PROGRAMS

In France there are three forms of work-study:
1) apprenticeship, in which the young person learns mainly on the job, attending classes one day a week in the apprentice training centres (*centres de formation d'apprentis*).
2) work contracts for unemployed young people aged sixteen to twenty-five who finished their studies or left school without a diploma. They work four days and take courses on the fifth in training

Table 4.1
Diplomas awarded in technical and vocational education, 1980 to 1996

Year	1980	1990	1996
BEP	78,905	156,543	192,436
CAP	235,046	274,981	213,325
Bac. Technol.	62,660	112,621	132,300
Bac pro	—	24,116	72,156
BP and BT	19,168	20,576	14,929
BTS	17,442	52,667	76,490
DUT	19,769	27,825	37,433
Total	432,990	669,329	739,069

Source: BP, brevet professionnel, BT, brevet technologique. L'Enseignement technique, 176
(Oct.–Dec. 1997), 4–13. Ministère de l'Éducation nationale, direction de l'évaluation et de la
prospective, Repères et Références statistiques sur les enseignements et la formation, Paris, 1992.

centres in order to obtain a vocational certificate, usually the CAP. Work contracts are similar to apprenticeship but usually involve shorter periods of time, a greater variety of occupations, and more flexibility.

3) work placements or practicums in factory and firm by students from technical and vocational schools, the lycées professionnels, the sections de technicien supérieur and the instituts universitaires de technologie. These are negotiated by school and business and are considered part of the learning experience to assure that work and study are mutually reinforcing and contribute to the young person's training and employability.

The Astier Law of 1919 and the Berthoin Law of 1959 touched on the idea of work-study terms in business and industry, and there was a brief period of experimentation with agreements between schools and industry in the 1950s and again by Fouchet in 1965 and 1966, but it was really the law of July 1971 and growing unemployment among young people during the 1970s that established the principle that business and industry could play a role in the education of its labour force and laid the basis for work-study programs that developed in the 1980s.[72]

In response to the law of 1971, the National Council of French Employers (Conseil national du patronat français, CNPF) declared its interest in becoming involved in vocational training. Experimental work terms were introduced in 1975 for unemployed young people between the ages of seventeen and twenty-five, which soon led to the introduction of *contrats emploi-formation* for a fixed term of nine or ten months in industry. These were set up under the Ministry of Work rather than Education and grew from 4,500 contracts in 1975 to 18,250 in 1976. In 1977 they were replaced by six-month *pactes nationaux pour l'emploi*. These were not well financed and often went to those who already possessed a diploma and who sometimes ended up doing tasks below their qualifications.[73] Deciding to strike out on their own, the national employers council stated that industry would organize its own work terms.[74]

The prospect of industry moving into the field of vocational training alarmed the Education ministry, the labour unions (the CGT especially), and the teachers' federation (Fédération de l'éducation nationale). Education Minister Christian Beullac who replaced Haby in April 1978, was a *polytechnicien*, a former director of the Renault Auto Works and later Minister of Work, and was open to a variety of possibilities involving the cooperation of school and business in the educational process. Early in 1979, he and the State Secretary for Vocational Training, Jacques Legendre, initiated talks between industry (the CNPF), labour unions, and the government that led to a Pacte pour l'emploi (1979–81). The CNPF renounced its plan to build its own vocational institutes and obtained in exchange an acknowledgment of its right to cooperate with the state in vocational training.[75]

Beullac and Legendre also drew up a law on work study programs for technical and vocational schools. The FEN and the CGT strongly opposed this as weakening public education by placing too much power over students in the hands of the bosses. After complex negotiations, a ministerial circular of 16 July 1979 introduced compulsory work periods (*séquences éducatives en entreprise*) for ten weeks for students in the lycées d'enseignement professionnel (the old collèges d'enseignement technique) in the CAP and BEP programs. Finally, a law on 12 July 1980, diverted a portion of the apprenticeship tax for work-study programs and gave business and industry increased influence over programs.[76]

When the Socialists came to power in 1981 they hesitated to continue Beullac's policies. They and their Communist allies had traditionally argued that young people needed to be protected from the bad influence of factory and firm. But the Pactes pour l'emploi had already grown from 30,000 to 60,000 young people. Moreover with the collapse or near-collapse of many industries in the early 1980s, hundreds and thousands of workers and employees especially the unskilled lost their jobs and were in need of retraining, a daunting prospect in view of the fact that 63 per cent of the workforce had no formal qualifications or skills.[77]

Work Study for the Unemployed

In 1981, Savary and Marcel Rigout, the head of the Ministry of Vocational Training (*Formation professionnelle*) asked Bertrand Schwartz, an eminent mathematician, to report on work-study programs for unemployed young people. In his 1982 report, Schwartz argued that the government should make the struggle against youth unemployment "a national priority," ensuring that no young person leave school without professional qualifications. He proposed that the government introduce work-study programs in the private and public sectors and establish local centres drawing on a cross section of community resources to provide job counselling and assistance to unemployed young people.[78]

The government moved cautiously to implement the Schwartz recommendations, maneuvering between the teachers, labour unions, and the national employers council (CNPF), which was suspicious of socialist ministers particularly Marcel Rigout who was a communist. The CNPF feared that the government was trying to shift expenses and burdens onto the company. The Schwartz recommendations were implemented in a decree on 26 March 1982, describing the occupational training and placement of young people as a "national obligation." This meant the introduction of regular work terms in business and industry for students in technical and professional schools, plus a program of work contracts for specified periods of time for unemployed young people over sixteen who lacked vocational skills. These involved periods of practical training on the job and study in training centres leading to a CAP or other certificates.[79]

The all-party accord of late 1983 was significant in that it represented a consensus between government, business, and most teaching and labour unions. It led to a law on vocational training on 24 February 1984, establishing employment contracts for further training on the job while taking courses. These included the *contrats de qualification*; the *contrats d'adaptation*, ranging from six to twenty-four months; and a three to six month program called the SIVP (*stages d'initiation à la vie professionnelle*) designed to familiarize young people with factory and firm.[80] These programs grew rapidly from 30,000 students in 1979 to 195,000 in 1984, and 800,000 in 1987.[81] By 1993, 2.5 million young people had obtained an employment contract over the previous decade.[82]

The Schwartz recommendations also led to the creation of the Missions locales and permanences d'accueil, d'information et d'orientation (PAIO), which are centres for young people sixteen to twenty-five providing vocational guidance and orientation, assistance in defining professional objectives, help in finding employment, as well as counselling, housing, and cultural services. These agencies were designed to cooperate with local branches of the national employment agency (Agence national pour l'emploi) but were to be more flexible and personal, helping in a variety of ways that a national agency could not manage. In 1994, there were 411 PAIO and 257 missions locales.[83]

Gradually the state and industry began to build better relations, but the way was sometimes difficult. Businesses received state subsidies and tax exemptions for hiring young people, usually paying the minimum wage (SMIC) or below. The larger industries, with the exception of building and public works, were underrepresented, ranging between 17 and 25 per cent of employment contracts, except for the contrat d'adaptation (30.4 per cent), but the latter appealed to older, better-certified young people.[84] When big industry did get involved in large-scale work-study programs it usually preferred to hire unemployed graduates coming out of the schools on a fixed term contract (*contrat de durée déterminée*), and was often accused of trying to procure skilled labour at a low price. This was the case in 1994 at the time of the Balladur government when the National Employers Council proposed a "contrat d'insertion professionnelle," quickly dubbed the "SMIC-jeunes," to accept large numbers of students mainly from technical and vocational schools (including senior technicians from the IUT and STS) at less than the SMIC. This proposal combined with other discontents (chapter 6) led to student riots in the universities and IUT.[85]

Today about three quarters of young people involved in various employment programs work in firms employing under 50 persons, many in firms of under ten employees, mainly in building and public works, retail, commercial services, restaurant-hotel-food, and automobile dealerships.[86] Critics argue that the work is often repetitive and simplistic with little learning value, and sometimes involves seasonal employment or filling in for employees on vacation. Some companies pocket the subsidy or tax break, pay the young person less than the minimum wage, and employ those whom they might have hired anyway.[87]

The government has created a number of programs in the public sector designed for unemployed young people. These included Travaux d'utilité collective (TUC), which was replaced by the Contrat emploi-solidarité. The latter embraced about 400,000 in 1994 (of

720,000 looking for a job that year) of whom only about a fifth ever found a permanent job.[88] More recently, Claude Allègre, the education minister, and Martine Aubry, minister of work in the government of Lionel Jospin, set up *Emplois-Jeunes*, designed to provide 350,000 jobs in the school system and public services for unemployed young people possessing at least the baccalauréat. They are paid the minimum wage, mainly as teacher-aids in ghetto schools in or near Paris and other big cities. Though the employees provide valuable assistance in schools where learning and discipline are problems, the jobs, poorly paid over a five-year term, lead nowhere. The growing resentment among students and teacher-aids in the lycées that the government is using the program to provide cheap labour to cope with rising enrollments played a role in sparking the student riots of March 2000.[89]

A hierarchy has developed among the various agencies and programs. The more effective programs involve genuine work contracts, especially the contrat d'apprentissage or the contrat de qualification, because once a firm has been involved in training young people over a two- or three-year period they are more likely to hire them at the end. But it is generally those who already possess skills, the CAP, BEP, or bac pro, who obtain these contracts.[90] On the lower end, such programs as the TUC or the Contrat Emploi-Solidarité and their successors were designed to provide temporary employment in the public sector for those at the bottom of the heap, usually of working class and immigrant backgrounds who have experienced chronic academic failure, coming up from the "filières de relégation" in the ghettos.[91] The pattern of academic failure carries over into the workplace (la sélection par l'échec); those without credentials, or with minimal ones, drift from program to program barely avoiding *la galère* of permanent unemployment.[92]

The various programs introduced by governments as a panacea for unemployment have not always realized the high hopes invested in them. Governments, under pressure to find solutions to youth unemployment, constantly invoke *l'alternance* (alternating between work and school) and develop programs that usually provide only temporary relief. There are clearly too many gimmicky and expensive programs, work terms, and contracts, overlapping, overly administered, and competing with each other. Most studies show that these programs are no more likely to lead to full-time employment than personal and family connections, individual searches, employment agencies, classified advertisements, etc. The mere fact of having worked part-time while attending school increases one's chance of finding a job later. The ability to get a job, and the quality of that job, are closely linked to the diploma obtained.[93] Nevertheless without the placement programs and various manpower agencies, youth unemployment would certainly be worse. In 1976–78, for example, three-quarters of young people coming out of secondary school had a steady job nine months later; in 1988 only 30 per cent did.[94] The worst effects of unemployment among the young were probably attenuated by the various *mesures jeunes*, state aid in the training and placement of young people in difficulty. About two-thirds of young people were enrolled in or had gone through at least one of the programs discussed above (TUC, SIVP, Contrat d'adaptation, Contrat de qualification, etc.).[95]

Is youth unemployment in France really serious enough to involve such an extensive effort on the part of government and business? Generally, French unemployment is not much worse than the average in the European Union, 11 to 12 per cent in the late 1990s, as opposed to 10 to 11 per cent in the EU.[96] What is exceptional is the number of young people between sixteen and twenty-five who are not working, who are unemployed, who are students (41 per cent), or who are doing military service or something else. In 1995 only 29 per cent in that age group were employed as opposed to 48 per cent in the European Union. The French unemployment rate among young people sixteen to twenty-five in the labour market was around 26 per cent in 1997 as opposed to 20 per cent in the EU.[97] France is about average in terms of GDP spent on education and in terms of economic growth (above average in growth 1997–99), yet French industry does not produce jobs as rapidly as do neighbouring countries.[98] It is difficult to state exactly why this is true, but several reasons are frequently given. The policy of national champions of the 1960s and 1970s provided aid to big companies and neglected the small and medium ones that create more jobs. The response to technical and economic problems since 1973 has frequently been mechanization and robotization rather than job creation. The tendency of large companies to invest abroad meant that fewer jobs were created at home. Deflationary socialist policies (strong franc, high interest rates) beginning in 1983 and carrying through the Bérégovoy government in 1993 favoured industry over consumers and labour, lowered living standards, and dampened job creation. The budget balancing and cutbacks by the right-centre Balladur and Juppé governments that followed did little to change this. Although many European workers have lost their jobs since the 1970s, the number was particularly high in France because of the massive importation of unskilled workers from the 1950s to the 1970s, and the very high number of layoffs beginning in the 1970s and continuing into the 1990s (steel lost 60 per cent of its employees in the ten years between the early 1980s and the early 1990s) as companies restructured. This created an unusually large backlog of unemployed people competing with the young for jobs. High payroll taxes, a fairly high minimum wage, credentialism, and the inelastic wage classification scale are also blamed for high rates of youthful unemployment.

Given the declining number of career opportunities offered by business and industry, young people in the labour market must compete with workers changing jobs or older unemployed people looking for jobs who tend to get hired over young people just entering the market.[99] The various arrangements made by employers and labour unions have tended to protect existing employees with the result that precarious employment (part-time work, short-term fixed contracts, dead-end jobs) becomes the problem particularly of the young, but also of women and older people. The standard retirement age is now sixty, but in some fields it has been lowered to 55: the public services, the RATP (Paris transportation system), SNCF (national railway company), and trucking. This means that able-bodied people at both ends of the scale are frequently not working. The rate of activity of people over fifty years of age has dropped from 65.5 per cent in 1970 to 27.1 per cent in 1996. Women in particular are frequently found in part-time and precarious employment, especially in low-end tertiary sectors; 25 per cent of women in the labour force have part-time jobs as opposed to 5 per cent of men.[100] A study of young people going into the labour force in 1992 revealed that by 1997 83 per cent of men and 71 per cent of women were working, while 12 per cent of men and 18 per cent of women were unemployed.[101]

Today jobs are closely tied to credentials, which makes the scale quite rigid. The French codify the rights and privileges of occupational groups in much greater detail than in most other countries, defining courses, diplomas, and entrance tests an individual must pass to be admitted to various occupational levels. Because credentials seldom correspond perfectly to a changing job market, considerable training takes place in the firm. As Michael Storper and Robert Salais point out, credentials do not encourage labour mobility within an occupation, but instead define positions and privileges for those who possess them.[102] Because of the large number of young people possessing a credential of some sort, employers tend to hire at higher levels of qualification than are required for the vacant position. This makes advancement difficult, unless one acquires further credentials, and means that the first job may be decisive for the young person's career. Students thus tend to stay in school longer to acquire as many diplomas as possible before entering the job market. It is not surprising that the unemployment rate declines as one accumulates diplomas, depending to some extent on the specialty. In all EU and OECD countries employers tend to accept academic credentials as suitable criteria for hiring, but many French employers go a step further in defining their manpower requirements by using the categories and classifications of the education system rather than by the organization of work and job content.[103]

Work Study in Schools

The work-study programs involving technical and vocational schools have been generally successful, though it is not always possible for the school to satisfy the skill requirements of business and industry. Educational programs are by their very nature slow to change while industry is in constant flux. No two firms are alike in their recruitment and management of personnel, and there are major differences in terms of size, sector, and technological development among companies and industries. The high degree of demarcation in French companies (vertical, between supervisory and operative staff; horizontal; between different operatives; and functional, between production and services) makes learning on the job more difficult.[104] As Antonio Monaco has pointed out, work study does more than centre on questions of integration; it must be analysed in the larger context of the politics of employment and of practices involving the organization and management of labour. Employment is not just a given but is rather a social construction involving the study of the politics of promotion, the sources of professional mobility, the conditions governing the allocation and implementation of youth labour, and the changing working conditions in the business, industrial and service sectors.[105]

Some businessmen and educators criticize the school as being inadequately adapted to the productive system and its personnel needs, but in reality industries do not always have a clear idea of their own requirements. As Monaco notes, the education system is somehow expected to penetrate the "mysteries" of the system of work and find a way to conform to its rules and methods, and the failure to do so is seen incorrectly as the result of inept pedagogy rather than of problems in the production system.[106] Simple institutional arrangements are not likely to solve problems of unemployment, which have to do with the social system, technical factors of production, the allocation of resources, downsizing, technological innovation, and the flight of industry abroad, all factors that have changed the demand for skills and employment in all industrial societies. Such uncertainties make it difficult for the individual employee, and the business, to plan educational training in advance, especially in view of the fact that career ladders are hard to establish in a constantly changing economy in which even skilled workers and technicians in a prosperous industry might suddenly find their skills obsolete and have to move on.

It is difficult therefore to develop a coherent pedagogy for work placements; the student obviously has a well-defined place in the school, but his learning role in the firm is much less clear, especially as he or she has to move abruptly from learning to action. Teachers visit the factory or firm and work closely with the company *tuteur* who supervises students during their practicums, but the tuteurs are seldom trained or paid for their work and have no particular status, so that coordination with the teacher is difficult.[107] Supervising a number of students, the tuteurs are not always well-versed in grading and evaluation for academic purposes. The evaluation of the student is based on his or her ability to acquire professional skills; competence; knowledge of techniques; skill with computers, machines or tools; clarity of expression; and ability to get along with others – qualities that are not always easy to assess.

Despite these problems, work-study programs are now well-established, and the relatively long work terms of the lycées professionnels, the STS and IUT, that last from sixteen to twenty-four weeks are considered to be part of the students' overall instruction for which they are evaluated and graded. After twenty years of experience many problems have been ironed out and the experiment in work study in France is widely accepted today as part of the curriculum of technical and vocational schools. Recent studies on the value of technical and vocational education suggest that in-school vocational training is of little value unless it is supplemented by work terms and on-the-job training.[108] The 1989 law foresaw the extension of work-study programs to all secondary and higher schools, but this has proved impossible in view of the fact that of 1.2 million firms in France only 200,000 have more than ten employees and not all are capable of taking on large numbers of students and unemployed youth.[109] Most secondary students at least visit factory or firm during the course of their studies, but they do not spend work terms there.

THE 1990s: THE JOSPIN MINISTRY, 1988–92, THE ORIENTATION LAW OF 1989 TO THE LOI QUINQUENNALE OF 1993

In 1988 prime minister Michel Rocard named Lionel Jospin to the education ministry, where he remained for four years. With a considerably augmented education budget (55 billion francs or 23.7 per cent) and the teachers' unions generally on side, Jospin clearly had a mandate for change.[110] During his term in office, Jospin was to reform the lycées and universities, improve teachers' salaries, consolidate teacher-training, and reform technical and vocational education, which the government saw as a means of improving economic performance, dealing with youth unemployment, and achieving social justice.

In the 1989 law Jospin declared that every young person has the right to finish high school with a diploma and/or vocational qualification. He revised Chevènement's projection of 80 per cent obtaining a secondary credential (bac, BEP, CAP) to 80 per cent obtaining the bac and 20 per cent earning a credential at level V (CAP, BEP). He restructured the second cycle as an ensemble of three tracks of "equal dignity" – general, technical and vocational – and moved to integrate the programs of the second class (seconde) in the general and technical lycées with the BEP program.

Jospin was particularly alarmed by the persistence of high unemployment among young people and their growing marginalization, and by the concerns expressed by many businessmen and industrialists over the education system's neglect of training at the CAP and BEP level in favour of technicians. Clearly it made no sense that in the midst of youth unemployment, linked to lack of skills in many cases, that industry should be complaining of a shortage of certain categories of skilled workers while the education system was cutting back on the number of CAP options and generally devaluing that certificate. In December 1990, Jospin and his secretary of state for technical education, Robert Chapuis, called upon Lucie Tanguy, a sociologist and director of research in the CNRS, to study the best way to provide for vocational skills at level 5 (skilled workers and employees), in other words to study the quality of the programs for the CAP and BEP and their effectiveness in preparing students for skilled positions in business and industry.

Lucie Tanguy argued that the 1985 decision to train 80 per cent of high school students as bacheliers or the equivalent was based on an exaggerated estimate of rising demand for technicians and falling demand for skilled workers. This had led to the downgrading of the CAP without a careful examination of the nature of demand for skilled work in the French economy. Although demand had declined in the high tech industries, in others such as automobiles, machine manufacture, construction, food, and entertainment, and smaller artisanal type firms demand for skilled workers and the CAP remained constant. Tanguy provided a survey of the industries and sectors in which skilled workers were still being hired.[111]

Tanguy also criticized the government for neglecting the needs of 100,000 young people who left school each year without certification, excluded from employment on the basis of academic failure rather than demonstrated incapacity for work.[112] She criticized the tendency to confine females to the tertiary sector (producing, for example, far too many hairdressers, medical aides, and secretaries) as another example of dysfunctional employment planning. She criticized the tendency of politicians to solve all problems with work-study programs, which in practice were all too frequently beyond the capacity of business and industry to accommodate on a mass scale.

Tanguy saw that the essential error in the 80 per cent baccalauréat goal lay in trying to solve problems by raising the level of studies rather than in improving the content of existing programs. It made little sense, she argued, to continually produce more technicians when the workers with whom they had to work possessed inadequate skills; it made more sense to raise the skills of workers generally so that they would require less supervision.[113] She favoured a radical departure along the lines of the German system by creating a revitalized system of work-study emphasizing apprenticeship, continuing education, and other creative forms of cooperative learning at the secondary and even higher education levels.[114] She argued that young people in vocational programs might learn more readily by moving from factory to school rather than from school to factory and that the firm needed to play a larger role in vocational training.[115]

Legislation in 1989 requiring all young people leaving secondary school to have either a baccalauréat or the CAP-BEP involved considerable diversification of the education system.[116] The 1991 law sought increased ways of expanding apprenticeship and work study. In 1993 legislation begun by Jospin was introduced by his successor Jack Lang as the *loi quinquennal sur l'enseignement*, which increased decentralization and diversification, especially in apprenticeship and continuing education, and reaffirmed the 1989 law that every young person had the right to acquire a skill by the end of high school.

THE GROWTH OF TECHNICAL AND VOCATIONAL EDUCATION SINCE 1981

The decade 1985 to 1995 saw tremendous growth in all branches of secondary education with technical-vocational education comprising over half of senior secondary students.[117] In the thirty years from 1960 to 1990 the number of students in the education system rose from 9.8 million to 14.2 million and today stands at about 14.5 million, with enrolments staying even in the mid to late 1990s mainly for general demographic reasons.[118] In 1940 there were just 70,000 students in the various schools under the Division of Technical Education. In 1966 the number of students in technical and vocational schools had risen to 800,000, of whom 350,000 female.[119] In 1998 this number came to over 1.5 million in 2,600 schools, out of a population of 2.6 million lycée students (60 per cent). Of these, around 800,000 attended 1,250 lycées professionnels studying for the CAP, the BEP, or the bac pro; 500,000 students were studying for the baccalauréat technologique in lycées polyvalents, and 250,000 the BTS. In addition, there were 300,000 apprentices enrolled in various programs, plus 137,000 *sta-giaires* who had signed *contrats de qualification,* 45,000 with *contrats d'adaptation* and 2,300 with *contrats d'orientation.*[120]

In the early 1990s the technical lycées (formerly the lycées techniques) were integrated into general schools as lycées d'enseigne-ment général et technologique (LEGT). Eighty per cent of the students in technical programs continue their studies, mainly into the STS. They no longer prepare directly for the work place and practical work-shop exercises have been drastically reduced. A gulf has opened between the technical and vocational schools, and it is not at all clear whether one can equate the two as in the time of the Division of Technical Education before 1960.

Between 1980 and 1995 the number of students obtaining general and technical baccalauréats rose from 226,000 to 425,000.[121] Since then the number has declined every year. Enrolment in the lycées profes-sionnels on the other hand, which had fallen from 740,000 in 1989 to 716,000 in 1992 mainly because of a decline in CAP programs, began to grow rapidly, reaching around 800,000 in the late 1990s. Appren-ticeship figures have risen also, from 212,000 in 1992 to 300,000 young people in 1998.[122] The trend seems to be away from general and tech-nical studies and toward vocational programs and apprenticeship.

REFORMS IN FRENCH VOCATIONAL EDUCATION SINCE THE MID-1980s

The most important creations of the period were the lycée profes-sionnel and baccalauréat professionnel introduced by Jean-Pierre Chevènement in 1985. The introduction of the professional baccalau-réat marks the first time in the history of French education that the bac was associated with the vulgar term vocational and was awarded to workers; it was also the first time that a major diploma was conceived involving periods of training in factory and firm. The company was designated as a place of education at roughly the same level as the school, symbolizing the end of a century of distrust between educators and businessmen and facilitating the evolution toward a high skills economy.

The lycée professionnel, training skilled workers and factory technicians in the CAP, BEP, and bac pro, assures a well-trained and highly skilled workforce capable of adapting to the new, more flexible forms of production.[123] At the same time the bac pro was superimposed on other vocational credentials and on the work hierarchy without any genuine retraining of existing skilled workers in many sectors. This has resulted in parallel hierarchies of workers, in which certain high tech sectors employ highly trained and skilled workers, while other more traditional ones continue to use Taylorist or hybrid methods and employ workers with more conventional skills. Young workers holding a CAP/BEP frequently find the way to employment and promotion blocked by older workers or by an elite of workers with a bac pro who are classified as factory technicians but are often hired as skilled workers. Unemployment among holders of the CAP combined with even more severe problems among young people who leave school with no diplomas led to the realization that academic weakness automatically condemned one to unemployment, regardless of one's capacity to do the job.

To counter this, the government has tried to improve the prestige of vocational programs by updating CAP and BEP programs, discontinuing the practice of streaming students in the 5th class in favour of the 3rd, and introducing a technology course in the collèges to increase understanding of modern industrial society. It has also provided a number of bridges back into academic streams for better students. Weaker students have been moved from the collèges and lycées professionnels to apprentice training and, in the case of young people with learning disabilities, into special education sections (sections d'éducation spécialisée). Determined government efforts to present the CAP, BEP, and bac pro as diplomas of "success" and the growing importance of credentials in obtaining jobs at all levels have led to some improvement in the status of vocational schools in the 1990s. But the fact remains that most students in the LPs are there because guidance counsellors and school boards have placed them there. The LP marks its students as academic failures while providing them the hope of achieving a job in a rapidly changing economy.

The CAP has become the diploma of updated apprenticeship and continuing education programs, which can now lead to more advanced credentials as well. Students are allowed to establish their own programs, accumulate credits gradually, and advance at their own pace (crédit formation individualisée). The result was that the number leaving school without diplomas dropped over the decade 1988 to 1998 from 100,000 to 40,000, just 5 per cent of the age group as opposed to 16 per cent in 1980 and 27 per cent in 1973, an important achievement.[124] By decentralizing and diversifying apprenticeship and work-study programs (now reaching 680,000 young people), governments hoped to increase the prestige of vocational education and to create two parallel streams: general-technical and vocational-apprenticeship, the former leading to higher education and the latter allowing the possibility of further education while leading mainly to the workforce.

Savary, Jospin and other ministers attempted to diversify programs and introduced alternatives to standard classroom instruction in the form of apprenticeship and continuing education. They also introduced a more open and decentralized approach to educational organization called "steering" (*pilotage*), which emphasized cooperation between the school and its partners in the community (parents, local officials, businesses), better teaching methods, small classes (*modules*), program evaluation. Finally, they created a variety of manpower placement programs for unemployed youth, paying subsidies to employers to hire trainees, and established various agencies providing vocational counselling, placement facilities, and social services. The make-work programs have been described by Stanley Hoffmann as "fiascoes, despite a bewildering variety of gimmicks, 'contracts,' and incentives, all weighing heavily on the budget."[125]

Despite the pessimism of such observers, the balance sheet of French education during the past two decades has been generally positive. French governments have integrated technical and general lycées and upgraded the lycées professionnels to some degree of equality with them. Governments have succeeded in opening up secondary and higher education to the mass of young people, and industry has responded by increasingly hiring those in possession of diplomas. The percentage of *bacheliers* rose from 5 per cent in 1950 to 30 per cent in 1984 to 61 per cent in 1998, plus around 20 per cent obtaining the BEP-CAP, so that the 1985 goal of 80 per cent bacs or the equivalent by the year 2000 has been realized several years early. The increasing tendency of the young to stay in school longer is evident even in the vocational stream: among young people obtaining the brevet d'enseignement professionnel, 81 per cent went to work in 1984 and in 1998, three-quarters continued their studies, usually for the professional baccalauréat.[126]

Observers note that in various boards and commissions at all levels, whether regional committees or vocational advisory boards that bring together representatives from all sectors of national life, there is a spirit of cooperation and problem-solving that did not always mark the early years. Technological change and the demands of international competition have bred a new flexibility that has made cooperation possible between old adversaries. Opinion polls indicate that popular hostility toward the education system, business, and industry has weakened and that people generally have a positive view of these institutions as providers of jobs, careers, and self-identity.[127] The rapprochement of school and company have accompanied changing conceptions of work brought about by automation, shorter hours, rising skill levels, and better working conditions. Improved relations can also be attributed to the decline of Marxism, the popularity of the Japanese consensual model and American management techniques, the decline in positions involving manual work from 39 to 30 per cent, and the greater attractiveness and autonomy of jobs today than in the preceding period of Taylorism and Fordism. This change in mentality is probably best exemplified by the creation of the Haut comité éducation-économie in 1987 designed to encourage cooperation between the education and production sectors.[128]

Although much progress has been made in improving relations between education and industry, some misunderstandings persist. Business and industry still do not believe that the education system is as well attuned to their needs as they would like, and they fear the unrealistic expectations of politicians and their tendency to want to extend work-study programs beyond industry's capacity to absorb them.[129] French educators argue on the other hand that French industrialists overestimate the importance of technical factors of production and underestimate human and organizational issues.[130]

For all the pace of change, the Socialists failed to achieve their goal of democratization. This is by no means unique to France because as Andrew Feenberg has noted, "the difficulty lies in the contradiction of participation and expertise, the two foundations of the system."[131] Recent studies indicate that despite significantly increased access to secondary and higher education over the past thirty years, there is no more advancement for the underprivileged to the universities and grandes écoles than there was a generation ago.[132] The introduction of more utilitarian objectives in education still accompanies the streaming of students and thus does not favour democratization, nor have increased enrolments led to better job opportunities because of credential inflation and high rates of youthful unemployment. This is not entirely the fault of the education system, and certainly many enterprising individuals from the working classes have done well by acquiring credentials, especially technical ones. But deindustrialization, the rise of major suburban ghettos, the persistence of racism and gender inequality, and student awareness that the consequence of academic failure is chronic unemployment, result in low morale and make teaching difficult. While industry has shown an increasing willingness to hire graduates from the education system, the growing emphasis on diplomas and certificates for access to the job market at every level of the economy benefits the middle and upper classes, who are in a better position to accumulate diplomas than are working class people. Even the bac pro benefits the elite sector of the working and lower middle class anxious to get ahead, leaving the rest behind with fewer opportunities. Even if one hundred per cent of the population manages to obtain a skill by the year 2000, which seems unlikely, many of those possessing lower-level certificates will continue to face serious problems procuring employment.

The policy of reaching 80 per cent bacheliers and 100 per cent certificate holders by the year 2000 came partially in response to social demand, but to some extent anticipated it. This has greatly increased the pressure on secondary and higher education and on young people, who now seek to stay in school as long as possible in order to protect themselves from technological unemployment. French governments have played a more active role than most other western governments in pushing public schools as a means of vocational training and upward social mobility, raising expectations and making themselves a target for discontent. And yet aside from a few select areas in the electronic and information fields, business, industry, and the public sector cannot create enough rewarding positions to accommodate young people and their families, who have often made great sacrifices to obtain further education. It has been estimated that 250,000 graduates seek 100,000 posts annually in managerial and white collar positions appropriate to their qualifications.[133] Moreover, skilled workers and technicians who have jobs cannot be certain that technological change will not render their skills obsolete in the future.

Although unemployment continues to be a problem, France has a well-educated and adaptable workforce. Governments of the left and right centre during 1980s and 1990s have been firmly committed to restructuring the system of production in line with the requirements of flexible specialization and a high value-added accumulation regime. This has accompanied the realization that such restructuring had to accompany a thorough reform of the education system in order to assure a good system of vocational training at all levels. It was first necessary to provide solid intermediate instruction in core subjects of language, science, maths, and information technology. This was accomplished in the 1960s and 1970s with the expansion of secondary education and the introduction of more utilitarian objectives in educational programs. Such a foundation was necessary, for companies are more likely to choose high-skill forms of production when they are assured that the labour force receives a solid education. Lacking this, they will tend to automate, using the new technology to deskill workers.[134]

During the 1980s the Socialists moved away from educational centralism in favour of "steering" that brought better cooperation between educational authorities, parents, local officials, and the business community. This accompanied more teaching of social as well as cognitive skills in line with increased emphasis on cooperation and participation on the job. After a century of mutual hostility, business, labour, and the state began to cooperate in developing work-study programs. The origins of this cooperation dated to the apprenticeship and vocational education payroll taxes introduced in 1925 and 1984, which apply to all firms employing over ten employees, and three laws in 1971 laying the foundation for work-study and enhanced apprenticeship and continuing education. The requirement of all companies, large and small, to participate in education and training assured long-term commitment by both employers and employees to training. Work study programs also brought to an end the narrowly academic approach to vocational training established after the dissolution of the technical education division in 1960. This misguided experiment demonstrated that skill training can not be adequately imparted solely in the classroom. Work-study in the professional lycées, the STS and IUT made possible a combination of in-school and on-the-job training combining theory and practice, which has proved very effective in training skilled workers, factory technicians, and senior technicians. This, along with expanded programs of apprenticeship, continuing education, and retraining, have made possible a much better educated and flexible workforce based essentially on the German model, and this has facilitated the adaptation of many French industries to a rapidly evolving high tech economy. As we will see in chapter 6, the restructuring of the economy and education over the past two decades appears to be bearing fruit in enhanced economic activity in the late 1990s.

5 Training Technicians in France since the First World War

À chaque fois qu'il y a fusion, le modèle pédagogique de
l'enseignement le plus prestigieux s'impose et supprime celui de
l'enseignement dominé.

Antoine Prost

THE INTERWAR PERIOD

Technicians exist in an intermediary category between skilled workers and engineers, usually supervising the first and assisting the second.[1] In Yves Legoux's words, technicians were "a new race of men"
situated between engineers and workers, formed "at the crossroads of
school and factory."[2] Although they had their precursors before the
First World War in the *sous-ingénieurs*, draftsmen, and shop and works
supervisors of various sorts, they emerged during the interwar period
as a clearly defined occupational group associated with the rapid
mechanization of industry.[3] During the 1920s universal machine tools
still required considerable manual dexterity and precision, but they
were gradually replaced during the 1930s by specialized machines organized into integrated, automatic systems that required a shift from
"reasoned manual skills" to "reasoned technical imagination."[4] In
other words the technician had to understand the logic of new kinds
of work, the nature of mass production, and the interaction of machines. In industry he played a particularly important role in the research and planning departments putting into practice the projects of
engineers and, on the production line, in the maintenance, repair, and
coordination of machines.[5]

Such functions required formal education at the secondary and
even higher level, especially in applied math and science, and so the
technician could not be easily trained on the factory floor.[6] The gap between technicians and skilled workers tended to increase as it became

more difficult to promote skilled workers to technical positions solely on the basis of job performance or a few evening courses. The low-skill profile of most French workers also favoured the use of large numbers of technicians for supervisory and planning functions.

There are three types of technicians in France; in reverse order of prestige they are: *agents techniques* (factory technicians) who are essentially highly skilled workers (chapter 4); regular technicians and draftsmen; and senior technicians (chapter 6). The category "technicien supérieur" did not appear officially until 1952 with the introduction of the *brevet de technicien*, renamed *brevet de technicien supérieur* in 1962. In all three groups technicians are frequently recruited from among skilled workers anxious to get ahead. Their value in the job market is therefore closely linked to the diplomas they possess. There is a major cultural gap between them, limited as they are to application and execution, and for example the *polytechnicien*, who has a broad general technical and scientific education. They rank just below the lesser engineers graduating from the *petites grandes écoles*, for example the École nationale supérieure de tannerie de Lyon, the École Breguet (École supérieure d'électrotechnique et d'électronique), and the École nationale des Arts et Industries textiles de Roubaix.[7]

During the interwar years the diploma of the écoles nationales professionnelles came to be recognized as a technician's certificate at roughly the level of the baccalauréat. The *brevet d'enseignement industriel et commercial* was introduced in 1931 for which students at the écoles pratiques studied at around age sixteen. This diploma prepared students for the *maîtrise* and jobs as section leaders (*chefs d'équipe*), foremen, and shop supervisors, which in turn led readily to promotion on the job to positions as technicians and middle-level managers. *The brevet professionnel*, introduced in 1926, taken two years after the CAP (*certificat d'aptitude professionnelle*), roughly at the baccalauréat level, frequently led to positions as senior technicians through promotion on the job to positions as technicians and middle-level managers.[8]

In France there were chronic shortages of skilled workers and technicians during the interwar years, even though the number of technicians increased substantially, from an estimated 76,138 in 1926 to 126,414 in 1936. This accompanied general growth in the number of senior executives and professionals (doctors, lawyers etc.), from 657,000 in 1926 to 821,000 in 1936.[9] The écoles nationales professionnelles, the écoles pratiques, and the Paris vocational schools grew in number but could not meet the demand for graduates, even during the Depression. This meant that many technicians were actually skilled workers who had been promoted on the job.

The extent of the shortage of skilled personnel is unknown, for there were no manpower studies done by the government during the interwar period. The alumni society of the Écoles d'arts et métiers did its own study of the relationship between vocational training and occupations based on the census of 1936. Published in 1942 the report estimated that around a quarter of the labour force should be made up of skilled workers and technicians, a higher percentage than had actually acquired such skills.[10] The Écoles d'arts et métiers had become engineering schools in 1907, leaving only the écoles nationales professionnelles and to some extent the écoles pratiques and Paris vocational schools to train technicians, and though the schools grew steadily during the interwar period they were unable to meet the demand.

In view of the steady economic growth that took place from the beginning of the century to 1930 and the extraordinary advances in industrial technology between 1900 and 1940, why was France so deficient in skilled workers and technicians? The reasons are complex. Post-war inflation followed by the depression undermined middle-class property before salaried white collar positions had expanded enough to compensate for the loss. Salaried positions linked to the possession of diplomas, including technicians and even industrial engineers, were associated with people who sold their labour on the market for whatever return they could get and thus were poorly remunerated.[11] Middle-level technical schools were unable to recruit in the bourgeoisie and even among certain upwardly mobile elements in the lower middle classes, hence they recruited mainly from the working classes. With the introduction of free secondary education in the early 1930s, attendance in secondary and higher education grew steadily between 1925–26 and 1935–36, from 6.8 per cent to 12.4 per cent and 0.68 per cent to 1.21 per cent, but still did not reach a high percentage of the population.[12] The elevation of the higher primary schools into secondary education by Jean Zay, education minister from 1936 to 1939, encouraged capable young people of working class origin who had formally attended technical and vocational schools to move into the arts and sciences, to obtain the baccalauréat moderne, and even to continue their studies in higher education. Many majored in the liberal arts, for whom there were few employment prospects. This did not help the recruitment of skilled workers, technicians, and engineers. Labour unions tended to focus on class struggle rather than the educational improvement of workers and, when they did take a stand, often preferred opening classical education to workers rather than increasing access to the socially inferior technical stream.

Finally, the technical schools were sometimes their own worst enemies, because, in imitation of the grandes écoles, they lobbied educational administrators and politicians, frequently through their alumni
associations, to limit growth and to obtain improvements in programs and diplomas, i.e., less manual and more intellectual content.
In this the well-organized and wealthy alumni society of the Écoles
d'arts et métiers had set the pace around the turn of the century. Their
signal success came with the upgrading of the five schools, originally
intended to train foremen and shop supervisors, to engineering institutions in 1907. After the Second World War they were advanced to
university level. With the coming of the Depression, the association
persuaded the administration to lower the intake of new students by
one-half, which contributed to the serious deficit of industrial engineers during the war preparations after 1936.[13]

The écoles nationales professionnelles were closely linked to the
Écoles d'arts et métiers, and the alumni association of these schools
pursued a similarly restrictive policy during the interwar period in
seeking to prevent the creation of additional schools. Although they
were not always successful in these efforts, their dogged resistance
may have limited the number of new institutions. Finally, the constant
comings and goings of governments, useless ideological struggles,
politicians with little comprehension of economic and technological
change, and chronic financial and budgetary constraints, stood in the
way of educational reform and the creation of new technical schools.

The écoles nationales professionnelles numbered eight in the
years after the First World War: the "quatre vieilles" at Armentières,
Vierzon, Voiron, and Nantes; a school planned at Tarbes on the eve
of the war but not opened until 1925; a school in Epinal converted
from an école pratique in 1918; and the écoles d'horlogerie at Besançon and Cluses. The eight schools grew to twenty-five during the
interwar period (including six for girls) with over 13,000 students.
The ENP were boarding schools that recruited by national examination (the *concours* was introduced in 1901). Students attended school
for three years plus a preparatory year until reform in the 1930s rede-
fined the purpose of the ENP as training technicians rather than
skilled workers and foremen. The program was extended to four
years, from the 4th class, age thirteen, to the first, around age seventeen, plus a two year preparatory program (6th and 5th classes).[14] In
the regular four-year program all students attended the same classes
for the first two years then began to specialize during the third and
completed their specialization in the fourth year. About half the students during the last two years were enrolled in a special section
studying for the entrance examinations for the Écoles d'arts et

métiers (about 40 per cent) or other technical schools (10 per cent), of whom more than half were accepted. Those who did not continue their studies prepared for the school diploma, the *diplôme d'élève breveté*, awarded by the division of technical education, and then went to work mainly in industry.

The programs of the ENP included chemistry, physics, mechanics, applied mathematics, technology, history, French, modern languages, and industrial drawing. Shop programs trained machinists, mechanics, fitters, assemblymen, lathers, metal workers, and electricians, mainly for the machine, metallurgical, and electrical industries (72 per cent).[15] The schools also provided some regional specialization. Armentières and Voiron for example, located in textile areas, had programs in the technology of spinning and weaving while Vierzon specialized in electricity and precision instruments and Tarbes had a program in hotel management.[16]

The students were mainly the sons of skilled workers, artisans, and employees, with about 20 per cent the sons of businessmen and executives (*cadres moyens ou supérieurs*).[17] Most graduates who obtained the school diploma began their careers as skilled workers and draftsmen, but within a few years three-quarters were promoted to foremen, shop supervisors, and technicians, and about 20 per cent reached positions as department supervisors, factory managers, engineers, industrialists and businessmen. Of 12,500 members of the alumni association in 1947, 500 were factory managers or industrialists and 2,000 were engineers (frequently with the help of continuing education in the Conservatoire d'arts et métiers and other institutions).[18] If one adds to this figure the 30 per cent of students who continued their studies at the Écoles d'arts et métiers or other technical schools, most of whom became industrial engineers, it is obvious that graduates did very well as a result of their training in the ENP.

Because of the growing demand for technicians after the First World War, the technical education division began to establish new schools – in 1925 at Corte (Corse) and at Bourges for women. It also provided for the conversion of the écoles pratiques at Lyon (the École La Martinière), Thiers, Morez, and Saint-Étienne into ENPs.[19] Suddenly, there were twelve schools (fourteen counting the écoles d'horlogerie at Besançon and Cluses). This awakened fears in the alumni association that the ENPs would be swamped by the less prestigious écoles pratiques, with the attendant decline in prestige of the schools and their diplomas. The association formally opposed the creation of further schools, but the technical education division replied by announcing plans to open even more institutions in Creil near Paris, Châlons-sur-Saône, Egletons, Limoges, Metz, and Saint-Ouen, mainly through the conversion of écoles pratiques. The association decided in 1930 to accept members only from the eight original schools, refusing to send representatives to the councils and boards of the new schools. It asked the division of technical education to rename the original eight schools *écoles nationales techniques* which would have created an intermediary set of institutions between the ENP and the Écoles d'arts et métiers.

Edmond Labbé, the director of the technical education division, considered implementing this idea but in 1933 his successor, Hippolyte Luc, refused to create any hierarchies among schools for technicians. Indeed he moved to create even more ENP.[20] By 1936 there were sixteen such schools and several more planned. The newer schools unrecognized by the alumni association began to discuss the possibility of creating a rival society.

The alumni association decided to hold a referendum on the issue in 1936.[21] Many members were having second thoughts, particularly in regard to the school at Creil because this was a modern, up-to-date institution with the latest in machinery, labs, and shops, and many members were sending their sons there. The membership voted to accept the graduates of all schools. By 1939 there were twenty-seven ENP.[22]

The alumni association's objection to the creation of new ENP was typical of the Malthusianism of the depression years. France badly needed technicians and the ENP were the only schools training them, yet the association did all it could to prevent the creation of more schools.[23] Its failure to do so was probably the result of the relatively low status of the schools and the high demand for technicians, and the fact that a third of the students continued their studies at an École d'arts et métiers or other technical schools. Whereas 80 to 90 per cent of graduates of the Arts et Métiers belonged to their alumni association, less than half of the ENP graduates joined theirs.[24] Had the alumni association of the ENP succeeded in limiting the creation of new schools, the shortage of trained technicians in France would have been even worse on the eve of the Second World War.

The proposal to create higher-level écoles nationales techniques, though self-serving had some merit and anticipated the creation of advanced sections in many of the ENP in 1952 and lycées techniques in 1962, the Sections de technicien supérieur, and the *Instituts universitaires de technologie* (IUT) in 1966 to meet the growing demand for senior technicians.

The students in the Écoles nationales professionnelles were similar to the *gadzarts* of the Écoles d'arts et métiers in many other ways, in their mainly upper working class backgrounds, their elaborate ceremonies, traditions, hazing, pranks, and their habit of collective resistance to the school administration.[25] For most young men of working class background with a technical bent, admission to the Écoles d'arts et métiers was the highest achievement possible. The arts et métiers were the École polytechnique of the common man, and the ENP most successfully prepared for them. The school at Vierzon for example began to prepare students for the arts et métiers in 1895 – between then and 1924, 786 of 1,044 of its candidates were accepted.[26] Yet by 1923 the graduates of the ENPs were no longer the most numerous in the Écoles d'arts et métiers because by then the 279 higher primary schools for boys, many of which had vocational sections, were contributing about half the students.

THE FOURTH REPUBLIC

The Écoles Nationales Professionnelles

As the Écoles d'arts et métiers were upgraded to university-level engineering schools in 1947 (reaching grande école status in 1974), the ENP also moved up a notch. The base for their advancement was laid in 1946 with the introduction of the technical bac, the *baccalauréat mathématique et technique,* and the *baccalauréat techniques économiques* in 1954. In 1952 the programs of the ENP were extended from four to five years, in addition to two preparatory years in the 6th and 5th classes, so that they became technical high schools at the same level as the lycées, instructing young men and women from the age of eleven to seventeen or eighteen. In the same year, the brevet de techniciens was introduced at the baccalauréat level.[27] About half of the students in the ENP continued to study for the *concours* of the Écoles d'arts et métiers or related schools. Those who failed (about 40 per cent) could present themselves for one of the technical bacs or the brevet de technicien and continue their studies toward the senior technicians' certificate, the *brevet de technicien supérieur.* Graduates of the ENP also had access to the new national system of engineering schools established in 1947, the *écoles nationales supérieures d'ingénieurs* (ENSI), composed of the old applied science institutes in the science faculties and various individual technical and engineering schools. Most graduates entered the workplace as technicians after obtaining the school diploma, but many continued their studies into higher education.

All this required an enormous amount of work in classroom and shop. The *concours* for the Écoles d'arts et métiers was difficult and competitive, and the new technical bac was one of the hardest bacs to

Table 5.1
Students accepted into the Écoles d'Arts et Métiers, 1925

School	Applied	Accepted	Percent
ENP	178	99	55.61
EPI	468	157	33.55
EPS	970	290	29.89
Lycées & collèges	89	17	19.10
Misc. private	162	37	22.84
Total	1,867	600	32.14

Source: Les Écoles Nationales Professionnelles, 1926, 24–7.

obtain. It combined all the science and mathematics requirements of the baccalauréat moderne and the technical requirements of the brevet d'enseignement industriel (BEI). Although *moderne* dispensed with Greek and Latin, it emphasized the French classics, mathematics and science. The result was that the technical bac attracted far fewer students than the liberal arts and scientific baccalauréats. In a country that awarded almost 40,000 baccalauréats per year by 1955, the bac technique was obtained by only 1,600, mainly from the ENP.[28]

Not surprisingly, the programs and workload of the ENP were described in the *conseil de l'enseignement technique* as "inhuman for children so young." During the first year of the program, the 4th class (students aged thirteen or fourteen) spent over forty hours a week in class and workshop (plus homework) and that figure rose to fifty hours a week in the following three years.[29] Substantial improvements in the rapid machining and filing of pieces made possible shorter hours in the machine shop to accommodate a much increased workload in mathematics, science, and technology.[30]

Thanks to its *concours*, the écoles nationales professionnelles were assured good students. In 1954 they accepted only 43 per cent of applicants (the collèges techniques accepted 58 per cent and the CA 68 per cent). In 1956 they accepted 1,599 male candidates and refused 3,808 (of a total of 5,407) or 30 per cent. They accepted 472 female candidates and refused 713 (of 1,185) or 40 per cent.[31] Most were trained in their own preparatory sections in the 6th and 5th classes (46.2 per cent), or were accepted from the primary schools among those holding the certificate of primary instruction (11.8 per cent), from the cours complémentaires (1.9 per cent), from the lycées and collèges (14.2 per cent), and the remainder, about a quarter, from the collèges techniques (former EPCI) and other technical-vocational schools and programs.[32]

At the moment of their disappearance in 1960, the ENP numbered forty-three (of which six were for young women) with 23,000 students, up about 10,000 in a decade.[33] After 1960, the "quatres vieilles" retained the title "lycées techniques d'état." As lycées techniques the ENP have gradually lost their separate identity and their alumni association has merged into a general association of technicians.[34]

About a quarter of the students in the ENP were young women.[35] The technical education division established six ENP for women starting in Bourges in 1929 and followed by Creil, Lyon, Poligny, Vizille, and Strasbourg.[36] Although they organized these schools, the views on female education of Edmond Labbé and Hippolyte Luc, the directors of the technical education division during the interwar years, were traditionalist. Luc believed that it was the "natural mission" of women to defend and maintain traditional institutions and to avoid "the slavery of work": "Il faut défendre la femme contre le despotisme matériel et moral du métier ... Aussi l'éducation professionnelle doit-elle doubler d'une éducation ménagère très largement conçue qui permette à la femme de jouer son rôle d'animatrice du foyer et son rôle d'éducatrice."[37] This meant that young women were confined to "female occupations," defined in the nineteenth century mainly in terms of needlework (cutting, sewing, dressmaking, corsetmaking, embroidery) and home-making (hygiene, child care, cooking, home economics), and in the twentieth century in terms of secretarial and office work, hotels and restaurants, and social or medical services, as well as teaching. The ENP and collèges techniques for women only slowly adapted to the new professions introduced by changing industrial technology. In the years after the Second World War there were 2.5 million women in the labour force, from business, banks, and insurance to automobiles and machine construction, and few of them had any professional training.[38]

On the eve of the conversion of the ENP into lycées techniques in 1959, there were 20,000 females enrolled, about a quarter of the number of males. In 1955 only 4.3 per cent of male graduates of the ENP had not found jobs compared to to 18.4 per cent of young women. The main reason for this was that women were concentrated in a few overcrowded fields. It was also difficult for them to study for the bac technique (baccalauréat mathématique et technique) and to obtain skilled positions, especially in the new fields of electricity, electronics, and information technology.[39] Even today one finds relatively few women in the industrial professions.[40]

From Écoles Pratiques to Collèges Techniques

The écoles pratiques de commerce et d'industrie trained what the French call "le personnel de la maîtrise," or group leaders, foremen, and shop supervisors. The schools were established on the initiative of municipalities and supported and run by them under the general direction of the division of technical education and with subsidies from the state. Their boards (*conseils de perfectionnement*) included municipal officials, local businessmen and industrialists, and representatives from the school administration and faculty. Businessmen had considerable input into programs, which were oriented toward their requirements.[41]

The EPCI accepted pupils possessing the primary certificate who were at least twelve years of age and who had successfully passed entry examinations (*concours d'entrée*). All schools were required to teach a core curriculum set by the technical education division composed of science, mathematics, history, geography, French and modern languages, technology, and industrial drawing, plus additional courses and practical work conforming to local economic needs. The schools prepared students for a brevet d'enseignement commercial and brevet d'enseignement industriel (BEC and BEI).

The programs of the écoles pratiques were terribly overloaded, with forty-six-and-a-half hours of classes per week (fifty-one in the third year) in 1927 for boys in their early teens. Courses were heavily weighted toward the practical: thirty hours of shop per week (thirty-three in the third year) with little attention paid to theories of work and technology.[42] Some of the schools offered an extra year to prepare for the Écoles d'arts et métiers for those who finished the BEI.

The écoles pratiques grew steadily during the interwar years, from eighty-two schools in 1919 to 176 (139 for boys and 37 for girls) in 1938. In 1914 they had 15,000 students; in 1938 they had around 60,000. Some of the growth came from the absorption of the vocational sections of higher primary schools.[43] In addition there were twenty-five écoles de métiers for boys and girls (usually private) plus various ateliers-écoles, technical sections in the higher primary schools, and the thirteen Paris vocational schools.

In 1941 the education minister, Jérôme Carcopino, converted the EPCI into collèges techniques as part of his policy of upgrading the various schools of the first cycle of secondary education into collèges. The higher primary schools (écoles primaires supérieures) became collèges modernes and the normal schools for teachers were abolished, leaving teachers to be trained in the lycées.

The reform of 1952 extended programs from three to four years, preparing students for the brevet d'enseignement industriel which became the certificate of factory technicians and *agents de maîtrise*. The schools had preparatory sections for students aged twelve, but recruited the majority of their students directly from among those possessing the certificate of primary education (51.2 per cent) and from the cours complémentaires. In 1960 when they were assimilated into the lycées techniques, the collèges techniques had around 120,000 students in 269 schools. In addition, 150 or so technical sections in lycées and collèges had about 63,000 students.[44] In 1956, 11,486 boys were accepted and 9,705 were refused (of 21,191 candidates), or 54 per cent. Among girls 8,710 were accepted and 4,640 were refused (of 13,350), or 65 per cent.[45] In terms of social origins, the collèges techniques drew upon the sons and daughters of skilled workers and small employees in business and industry and artisans (59 per cent of students), government employees (19 per cent), middle and high level managers (10 per cent), and farmers (7 per cent).[46]

The Shortage of Technicians in France

Together, the écoles nationales professionnelles, collèges techniques, the Paris municipal vocational schools, the technical sections in the lycées and collèges, and factory and other private schools produced only a part of France's needs in technicians. The ENP graduated 1,500 per year and the collèges techniques and related schools produced around 4,000 (not all technicians), while the demand for technicians was estimated at between 10,000 and 30,000 annually.[47]

The sudden growth of the economy in the early 1950s took many by surprise and made them aware of the impact of technological developments on industry and the nature of work. A series of surveys into the training of skilled workers, technicians, and engineers, most of which were organized by the UIMM, were conducted between 1955 and 1965 and revealed that three-quarters of middle-level executives (*cadres moyens*), about half of technicians, and a third of engineers did not hold diplomas suitable to their posts, most of whom were *autodidactes* promoted on the job. Moreover, for every three engineers there were only two technicians, instead of the usual figure of two to five technicians per engineer.[48] A 1963 study showed that 44.7 per cent of the 120,000 technicians in the machine and metallurgical industries aged 25 to 29 were uncertified.[49] Younger employees were more likely to be certified than the older ones in the more traditional industries, while in the high tech industries (aerospace, aeronautics, electronics, energy, and information), most technical personnel possessed diplomas.[50]

The Organization of Labour

Sociology and economics were in their fledgling state in the 1950s, and although several sociologists and economists had shown an interest in the study of industry and economic development, few had analysed the nature of work. An exception was Georges Friedmann, a professor at the Conservatoire national d'arts et métiers. In *Problèmes humains du machinisme industriel*, written during the war, he argued that technology was bringing about changes so revolutionary that they were transforming the human environment from a traditional natural milieu in which Western man had always lived into a technical milieu characterized by a complexity and rapidity beyond human comprehension. Friedmann likened technology to a body of water into which humans had fallen – in order to survive in this unnatural environment one had to learn the technique of swimming.

In *Où va le travail humain*, written just after the war, Friedmann predicted the disappearance of traditional forms of work and the replacement of skilled workers by technicians better prepared to "swim" in the constantly changing sea of industrial technology.[51] He foresaw in the post-war years an increase in white collar workers, first defined as a professional category of salaried managers or *cadres* in the 1930s, and that technicians would replace assembly line workers. This prospect of "job enlargement" brought with it the possibility that work might become more interesting, more democratic, and social than in previous stages of industrial development. But Friedmann also warned of growing disfunctions within the workforce. For a minority of the highly skilled he predicted increased opportunities for creative work and advancement, but for the unskilled and semiskilled, he foresaw increasing dequalification (*le travail en miettes*).

Friedmann advocated educational reform at once to satisfy increased social demand for education, to produce the technical personnel needed in a science-based economy, and to provide a means of culture and civic responsibility that had declined as society evolved from un *milieu naturel* to a *milieu technique*, especially for that portion of the population reduced to increasingly specialized and routine work. For Friedmann a reformed and consolidated education system teaching a new technical humanism was to be part of the Socialist reorganization of society, closing the gap between culture and work that had become increasingly acute during the previous century of industrialization.[52] For this reason Friedmann sided with reformers like

Jean Zay and Paul Langevin, and disagreed with Hippolyte Luc, in favouring the integration of the technical education division into the education system, the better to transform it.[53]

In response to the scarcity of technicians and skilled workers, governments under the Fourth Republic did make efforts to increase training facilities. The number of students in technical and vocational education quadrupled from 1939 to 1956, but they represented a minority of the two million young people aged fourteen to eighteen.[54] In 1939 the technical education division had somewhere between 66,000 and 70,000 students in the écoles nationales professionnelles, écoles pratiques, and affiliated schools – up from 15,000 in 1919 – plus around 60,000 students in the centres de formation professionnelle (not then a part of the technical education division).[55] Counting apprenticeship, private schools, and schools under other ministries, France probably had 200,000 young people attending vocational-technical schools, programs, and courses in the late 1930s. By 1956, Albert Buisson, the director of the technical education division, estimated that this figure had grown to around 850,000: 330,000 in the schools directly under the technical education division (ENP, collèges techniques, centres d'apprentissage), 170,000 in continuing education courses for young people aged fourteen and eighteen working in business and industry, 51,000 in *cours de promotion du travail*, 10,000 in correspondence courses, and 130,000 in private schools, for a total of 691,000. Including students attending vocational sections in the cours complémentaires (under the primary division), lycées and collèges, and apprenticeship, Buisson estimated 850,000.[56]

THE FIFTH REPUBLIC, 1958 TO THE PRESENT: THE LYCÉES TECHNIQUES

The Fifth Republic placed a high priority on the training of technicians. The Berthoin law in 1959 created the lycées techniques by merging the ENP, collèges techniques, technical sections in the secondary schools, the écoles de métiers and the Paris vocational schools into a single system. The early years of the lycée technique proved difficult, as a disparate set of schools had to be integrated into a uniform set of lycées techniques on a national level. The process did not go particularly smoothly because of bureaucratic mix-ups and the fact that the administration, faculty, and alumni associations of many of these schools, especially the ENP and the École Diderot of Paris, resisted the loss of their schools' identity. Then in 1963 they had to adjust to Christian Fouchet's new collèges d'enseignement secondaire, which combined the collèges modernes and collèges d'enseignement général into a single junior secondary school that streamed students into three sections under the same roof, the technical stream being less attractive than the classical and modern ones. This problem was exacerbated by the fact that the more prestigious general lycées were allowed to keep their "first cycle" (i.e. junior secondary divisions) on the condition that they introduce the programs and the three tracks of the CES. The lycées techniques had no such influence, and they lost their first cycle. This meant that they were heavily dependent on guidance counsellors in the CES for their recruitment. Students coming out of the first cycle in the general lycées were rarely tempted to transfer to a less prestigious lycée technique, particularly as this involved a change of school and, more often than not, a less attractive neighbourhood. Guidance counselors frequently had students repeat a year rather than orient them into "tech."

The result was a decline in enrolments in the lycées techniques during the 1960s. At the beginning of the decade the ratio of students in the lycées techniques compared to the lycées classiques et modernes was one to two; by the end of the decade it was one to three. By 1967 there were 15,000 empty places in the lycées techniques, which stood in stark contrast to the 1950s, when the ENP had accepted less than half of applicants. The administration had made the error of introducing a national system of lycées techniques, greater in number than the ENP and collèges techniques, without providing adequately for their recruitment. Moreover, the lycées techniques had to prepare students either for the baccalauréat technique (bac E), which was extremely difficult, or for the brevet professionnel, of uncertain status.

When in 1966 the government created the Instituts universitaires de technologie in the universities as a two-year program leading to the senior technician's credential, it announced that the Sections de techniciens supérieurs in the lycées techniques would be transferred to the IUT, thus amputating the most prestigious sections of the lycées techniques. This meant the loss of many senior professors as well as the better students. In the climate of uncertainty that resulted, enrolments in both the lycées techniques and the IUT suffered. By 1970 the latter had only 30,000 students, where they had room for 45,000.[57] France's supply of technicians was apparently drying up just at the time of greatest demand. It appeared as if Fouchet's reforms in technical and vocational education, combined with the disappearance of the technical education division in the early 1960s, constituted a serious perhaps fatal blow to French technical education, confirming the century-old fear among supporters of technical education that French academic administrators would destroy the system once in control of it.

Fouchet responded to these problems in his reform of the baccalauréat on 10 June 1965. He introduced three new semi-professional bacs, B in the economic and social sciences, C in mathematics and sciences, and E in the industrial sciences. The bac C in mathematics and sciences became the new *voie royale* to the grandes écoles, replacing Latin and the humanities and reflecting the increased importance of the high tech age in student strategies. But in reality the math content of the program was theoretical and was not well adapted to the computer age.

A: Literature, linguistics, philosophy
B: Economics and social sciences
C: Mathematics and physical sciences
D: Natural sciences
E: Science and industry

In 1966 Fouchet tried to deal with flagging enrolments and low morale in the lycées techniques by creating the *baccalauréat de technicien*, a reform that scandalized purists. But if technical education was to advance to the lycée level, it made sense that it should have its own baccalauréat so that students could continue into higher education. The new bac combined general studies with technical specialization in three fields, F (industry), G (tertiary: administration, business, secretarial), and H (information technology), each of which was divided into further specializations. In 1969 examinations were held successfully for fourteen technicians' bacs.[58]

The introduction of the baccalauréat de technicien in 1966 helped meet the demand for technicians and brought the bac closer to the working classes. Most graduates were expected to go into the workplace, but it was possible to continue one's studies into higher education, particularly into the Sections de technicien supérieur, but also into the new Instituts universitaires de technologie. Created by Fouchet in 1966, the IUT opened higher education to the technical stream for the first time.

Students in the collèges d'enseignement technique (lycées d'enseignement professionnel or LEP in 1976) continued to study for the CAP and/or BEP (brevet d'études professionnelles) in two or three years, but the more successful students could continue their studies for the bac de technicien by transferring to a lycée technique and enrolling in a "classe d'adaptation" that readied them to study for either the technician's bac or the technical bac E. This facilitated the access of at least some working-class students to positions as technicians and to higher education as senior technicians and engineers.

The introduction of the new technicians' baccalauréat and the reversal of an earlier decision to transfer the Sections de technicien supérieur to the IUT assured the success of the lycées techniques. During the 1970s and 1980s the scientific content of the baccalauréats de technicien grew steadily, and the number of hours spent in shop and lab declined by a third, reflecting the increasing importance of science in the instruction of technicians and the tendency of students to continue their education into an STS or IUT.

As a result the lycées techniques lost their uniqueness as schools that prepare for the workplace and began increasingly to be amalgamated to the general lycées. By 1980 there were 174 lycées techniques offering the baccalauréats de technicien F, G, and H and 723 general lycées with both general and technical programs. With the introduction of the lycées professionnels to grant the baccalauréat professionnel in 1985, the lycées techniques ceased to prepare for the workplace and were renamed lycées technologiques, which accentuated the scientific and academic content of their programs. In the early 1990s they were amalgamated with the general lycées as lycées d'enseignement général et technologique (LEGT).[59]

Eighty percent of bacheliers technologiques continue their education, over half to the STS, which tripled enrolments between 1980 and 1992, from 68,000 to 235,000.[60] Most graduates of the STS go into the workplace (about 30 percent continue their education into the second cycle of higher education). If the lycées technologiques have ceased to be a good source of technicians in their own right, they produce numerous senior technicians via the STS.

THE GROWTH OF TECHNICAL-VOCATIONAL EDUCATION SINCE THE 1980s

The decade 1985 to 1995 saw tremendous growth in all branches of secondary education (average growth was 9 per cent per year between 1987 and 1991), with technical-vocational education comprising 54 per cent of senior secondary students and over 40 per cent of the bacs.[61] In 1996 the total number of students in these programs came to 1.5 million in 2,600 schools, out of about 2.5 million lycée students. Of these, 725,000 attended the lycées professionnels studying for the CAP, BEP, or bac pro, and 527,800 students were studying for the baccalauréat technologique in general lycées. There were also about 300,000 apprentices.[62]

Between 1980 and 1995 the number of students obtaining general and technical baccalauréats rose from 226,000 to 425,000 and has since leveled off along with enrolments in general studies. The percentage of secondary students working toward the bac technologique was 27.5 per cent in 1996, 57 per cent for the general bac and 15.5 per cent for the professional bac. Of bacs awarded in 1996, the bac technologique constituted 28 per cent, the bac pro 13 per cent, and the bac général 59 per cent.[63]

Females have participated fully in this growth. They reached equality in primary education in the 1880s and were admitted to male lycées in 1925. By 1970 they were obtaining more baccalauréats than males and by the 1990s they comprised 54 per cent of lycée students and 56 per cent of university students. In the lycées they were overrepresented in literary studies (80 per cent of the students in terminale L) and in tertiary fields (64 per cent in terminale STT, sciences et technologies tertiaires), but in science and technology they made up only 40 per cent in terminale S (sciences) and 7 per cent in terminale STI (sciences et technologies industrielles).[64] They are very numerous in secretarial studies (60 to 90 per cent depending on the field) and in paramedical fields (over 90 per cent in many fields), almost non-existent in industrial technology.[65]

As the lycées technologiques have amalgamated with the general lycées since 1985, a new prestige gap has opened up between the lycée général et technologique and the lycée professionnel. Chevènement's decision in 1985 to award the new baccalauréat professionnel to the lycée professionnel rather than to the lycée technique did not come without considerable debate. Supporters of the latter, including most of the education unions, wanted preparation for the new bac to be placed in the lycées techniques. This, they argued, would further democratic objectives by providing students, mostly of working class background, enhanced opportunities to continue their studies into higher education, especially to the STS and IUT. They also pointed to the decline of Taylorism and the growing responsibility and autonomy of workers and technicians, which favoured general, less-specialized studies and increased scientific content.

The lycée professionnel's defenders in industry prefer a concrete practical program that meets the need of business and industry for specialists. They (AFDET, UIMM, etc.) have not been happy with the assimilation of the lycées techniques to the general lycées, the decline of practical work, the lack of work-study programs, and the streaming toward higher education. Even though most bacheliers technologiques end up in the STS and become senior technicians, the system as it now stands produces relatively few middle-level technicians situated between the factory technicians coming from the lycées professionnels, who are essentially highly skilled workers, and the senior technicians. The result is that many of the latter end up in jobs as ordinary technicians and sometimes even as skilled workers, clearly over-qualified for their posts.

DECENTRALIZATION AND DEMOCRATIZATION, 1981–98

In 1981 the Socialists inherited a system of education that had been considerably integrated and consolidated by right-centre governments since 1958. Indeed, one can argue that it was the latter who created the education system, hitherto too compartmentalized and fragmented to deserve the name. However a series of commissions set up to study the reform of secondary education during the 1980s found that administration was still too rigid, classes were overcrowded (34 per class on average), programs were too formal and encyclopedic, buildings were rundown, and extra-curricular activities were rare.[66] In the laws of 1983 and 1989 governments moved to decentralize the system. Lycées ceased to be "national" and were transferred to the regions, the collèges were transferred to the departments, and the primary schools remained under the municipalities. The lycées and collèges now answer to local boards (*établissement public local d'enseignement*) composed of a state official (the chair), usually a delegate of the rector or academy inspector, teaching and non-teaching staff, students and parents, and elected members from the community. While the state retained control over programs, diplomas, and personnel, the boards have jurisdiction over the organization of courses, time-tables, supplementary programs and continuing education, discipline, and extra-curricular activities. They vote the operating budget and draw up a five-year master plan stating goals and objectives.

The idea of steering (*pilotage*) gradually replaced top-down administration as the dominant principle governing the system. This approach emphasizes cooperative relations among various partners in education, openness to the community, evaluation, and participation. Teaching has been improved, small classes introduced with individualized instruction for those in need, and programs lightened. Students in all bac programs spend three hours a week in workshops engaged in concrete activities such as art, regional languages and cultures, sports, and computer and communications technology. In some fields, subjects once included in the bac examinations are covered by grading and professors' evaluations. Students who fail the bac (28 per cent) are obliged to retake only the parts they had failed and not the entire exam.

A directorate of evaluation and planning (DEP) was established in the education ministry in 1987 to provide statistical information on the state of the education system, short and medium-term forecasting, and student evaluation. It works closely with the central inspectorate, now oriented toward forecasting and the implementation of programs rather than control. Using advanced computer systems and databases established during the past twenty years, the DEP does national testing of student progress at the elementary level, CE 2 (age eight), the 6th class (first year of collège, at age twelve), and *seconde* in the lycée (age sixteen). [67] The directorate helps coordinate the system by facilitating better communication, assesses quality of teaching and student performance, evaluates program innovations, provides information on the number of schools, students, and resources, and periodically surveys the overall condition of the system. [68]

The baccalauréat has remained the secondary school-leaving credential and the first university diploma but has been thoroughly reorganized. In 1992 the seven general baccalauréat options were reduced to three by merging science, applied science, and math bacs C, D, D' and E into one baccalauréat scientifique (S); the conversion of bac A (letters) into the bac littéraire (L) and of B (economics and social sciences) into the bac économique et sociale (ES). The latter (ES) teaches more mathematics as applied to economics and the social sciences. Courses have become more statistical and less closely related to the humanities.

Although students in the programs L, ES, S may take up to three options, they may take only one in their major. This is to prevent them from specializing too narrowly. Despite efforts to raise the prestige of bacs L and ES by injecting more mathematics and science into them, clearly bac S in sciences is the elite diploma. Unlike North America where it is difficult to get native-born young people to major in math and science, the French still promote these subjects as the way into the grandes écoles.

In the science series all students take math, physics, and chemistry, plus French and foreign languages. They then specialize in the field of math, science, or applied science they prefer. Students take five to six hours of math a week, which is less than under the old bac C. They must also take courses in either biology-geology (five hours) or industrial technology (eight hours). The former prepare students to specialize in geology, medicine, etc., while industrial technology links up with technical programs in higher education, notably the STS, IUT, the DEUST, the technical DEUG and the preparatory programs for engineering schools. The purpose of this requirement is to centre the new program on the old bacs D (natural sciences) and E (industrial technology) rather than bac C, to avoid too much theory and the reconstitution of the "royal way." [69]

The sixteen technical bacs were regrouped under four headings: sciences et technologies industrielles (STI), which encompassed the old industrial F 1–4, 9–10, devoted to industrial technology; sciences et technologies de laboratoire (STL), regrouping the old F 5–7 and F7'; sciences médico-sociales (SMS), the old F8; and sciences et technologies tertiaires (STT) the old G 1–3 and H.[70]

The reforms of Savary, Jospin and others of secondary education, particularly of the lycées, have not proved to be particularly successful. A questionnaire sent to four million lycée students in 1997 revealed widespread disaffection among them concerning all aspects of the lycée: teaching, examinations, organization, and so forth, but especially concerning the unwillingness or inability of teachers and administrators to communicate with students. Jospin's education minister, Claude Allègre (1997–2000), antagonized professors and teachers by insisting on decentralizing and restructuring the educational system particularly at the secondary and university levels in return for pay increases and expansion in enrolments. He reduced teaching hours in the lycée from eighteen to fifteen hours while adding four hours per week for individual tutoring and small group learning. He offended professors and their unions by decentralizing job assignments and by criticizing academics for misuse of research and leave time. This, combined with a wage freeze in the public sector and the employment of poorly-paid part time teachers to deal with growing enrolments, plus a vague unease about the watering down of standards, the confusion of massification with democratization, and the replacement of cultural with utilitarian objectives, caused growing discontent. In March 2000 large-scale strikes and demonstrations erupted across the country among students and faculty alike, particularly at the lycée level, led by a united front of the five teachers unions. In early April 2000 this led to the replacement of Claude Allègre, a close friend and associate of Jospin, with Jack Lang, Jospin's replacement as education minister in 1993.[71]

CONCLUSION

The education system that has developed in France since the 1960s has transformed the old *système cloisonné* into a unified and partially decentralized system characterized by degrees and cycles running from primary to higher education, in which prestige lies more in the program and diploma than in the name of the school itself. General programs have more prestige than technical ones which, in turn, have more prestige than vocational ones. This, however, can be partly reversed by specialization in sought-after high tech fields: electronics, computer sciences, and telecommunications. In many crowded tertiary fields on the other hand few of the bacs provide easy entry into the job market.

The period since the Second World War has seen the gradual integration of technical and vocational studies into secondary education. The turning point came during the early 1960s with the extension of the school leaving age to sixteen, the abolition of the technical education division, and the introduction of the collège d'enseignement secondaire at the junior secondary level. The technical lycées were gradually assimilated into the general lycées during the 1980s and largely ceased to produce technicians directly for the workplace. The vocational schools were upgraded to lycée status and received their bac between 1975 and 1985, but they remained dependent on guidance counselors in the collèges for their recruitment, and they did not hesitate to assign them the worst students. They were thus left isolated as a low-status stream. The bacheliers professionnels, though supposedly technicians, were often glorified workers. One of Fouchet's principal advisors during the 1960s, Jean Capelle, repeatedly warned of the dangers of such a course and eventually resigned when it became obvious that technical-vocational studies were being relegated to an inferior position in the secondary system. He was only partly right; technical studies were upgraded but lost their uniqueness, while vocational schools became the *filière de relégation*.

In an age in which a knowledge of science and mathematics is increasingly important, the technical lycées provide a solid education in general studies and sciences with professional specialization, while preparing most of their students for higher education. As Yves Legoux pointed out, the modern technical school evolved from the *école-atelier* of the late nineteenth century to the *école-entreprise* of the first two decades of the twentieth, and finally to the *école-services techniques* in the advanced sectors of the economy during the 1930s.[72] Today they could be described as an *école-études technologiques*, opening the way to higher education and preparing highly skilled technicians for the various sectors of the economy.

Figure 5.1
Development of technical and vocational education in France

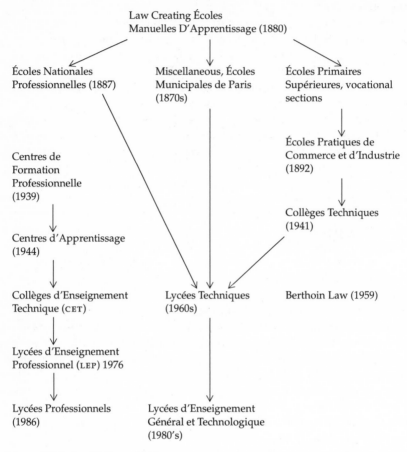

Law Creating Écoles
Manuelles D'Apprentissage (1880)

Écoles Nationales
Professionnelles (1887)

Miscellaneous, Écoles
Municipales de Paris
(1870s)

Écoles Primaires
Supérieures, vocational
sections

Écoles Pratiques de
Commerce et d'Industrie
(1892)

Centres de
Formation
Professionnelle
(1939)

Collèges Techniques
(1941)

Centres d'Apprentissage
(1944)

Collèges d'Enseignement
Technique (CET)

Lycées Techniques
(1960s)

Berthoin Law (1959)

Lycées d'Enseignement
Professionnel (LEP) 1976

Lycées Professionnels
(1986)

Lycées d'Enseignement
Général et Technologique
(1980's)

Source: P. Pelpel and V. Troger, *Histoire*, p. 155.

6 Advanced Education and the Training of Senior Technicians, Engineers, and Managers in France since 1981

French higher education is like a shipwreck organized in such a way as to pick out the best swimmers.

Alain Peyrefitte, Minister of Education, 1967

Higher education in France is divided into three types of institutions: the universities, the technical schools, and the grandes écoles. They are poorly integrated. In this chapter I discuss the evolution of the universities and the increasing practical content of their programs. I will also discuss the development of technical schools since the 1960s notably the STS, IUT, Instituts universitaires professionnalisés and the technological universities. Finally, I will discuss the grandes écoles, most of which are high level technical schools training executives for business, industry and government. I will pay particular attention to efforts to modernize and consolidate higher education and the relationship of the schools to business and industry since the 1960s.

THE UNIVERSITIES

University enrolments rose very rapidly during the 1950s and 1960s. This placed great strain on the overly-centralized and outdated structures, which had not been reformed since 1896, creating conditions that contributed to the student uprisings of 1968. Reform began in 1966 with Christian Fouchet's introduction of three degrees or *cycles* at the post-secondary level: the first, consisting of two years of study (bac + 2) leading to the DEUG (Diplôme d'études universitaires générales); the second leading to the *licence* and *maîtrise* (bac + 3 and 4); and the third to the doctorate. That year also saw the creation of the Instituts universitaires de technologie (IUT), introducing a professional element into the first cycle of the university for the first time.

In reaction to the *événements* of 1968, Edgar Faure, the education minister from July 1968 to June 1969, introduced a law for higher education that broke up the twenty-three universities. The old faculties were abolished and replaced by 700 *Unités d'enseignement et de recherche* composed of departments or groups of departments governed by councils elected by junior faculty, students, and staff as well as professors. The *unités* were then invited to group themselves into smaller new universities. The seventy-six universities that emerged enjoyed augmented power over budget, programs, research, and instructional methods. Although the Faure law easily passed, its application during the following years was weakened by the unwillingness of governments to relax their control, especially over finances, and the politicization of university politics. Growing communist influence on university councils in many urban universities provoked a conservative reaction. Alice Saunier-Seïté, the outspoken secretary of state and minister for universities from 1976 to 1981 under the government of Raymond Barre, curbed autonomy and returned the majority on university councils to senior academics. The 1970s saw the introduction of a series of professional diplomas at the master's level and higher: the maîtrise de méthodes informatiques appliquées à la gestion (MIAGE, 1970), the maîtrise de sciences et techniques (MST, 1973), the diplôme d'études supérieures spécialisées (DESS, 1974), and the diplôme d'études approfondies (DEA) in 1984.[1]

Alain Savary, the first socialist education minister, 1981–84, introduced a law in 1983 reforming higher education in the spirit of the Faure law. His bill restored democratic representation on university councils and granted the universities increased autonomy and more power to conduct research and to make contracts with industry.[2] Savary also proposed to transfer the *cours préparatoires* for the *grandes écoles* from the advanced sections of the major lycées to the first cycle of the universities and to transfer the STS (sections de technicien supérieur) from the lycées techniques to the IUT in the universities. This meant the consolidation of general and technical programs in the first (two-year) university cycle. The universities were to be allowed to impose entrance requirements at the end of this cycle (the DEUG) to continue into the second cycle (*licence* and *maîtrise*), placing them at last in a position to compete with the grandes écoles, which now had to select their students from the first university cycle. To complete the consolidation of higher education, all the grandes écoles were to be placed under the Ministry of National Education (almost half came under other ministries: Agriculture, Defense, Public Works, Industry, Telecommunications, etc.).

Had it passed in its entirety, the Savary reform would have solved many of the problems of higher education in France. Unfortunately it came at a time of intense and divisive national debate over the future of private (Catholic) schools. Moreover, any discussion of the introduction of admission requirements to the universities arouses enormous hostility among students and many professors. Student riots erupted in the spring of 1983, which played into the hands of the powerful interest groups associated with the *Conférence des grandes écoles*, alumni associations, and other groups opposed to the transfer of the *cours préparatoires* and the consolidation of the grandes écoles.[3]

The bill that finally passed in January 1984 was much amended and watered down. Although the measures reforming university councils and decentralizing the universities were retained, the transfer of the cours préparatoires and the idea of the grandes écoles recruiting from the first university cycle was abandoned. This confirmed the inferiority of the universities, because the grandes écoles, the IUT and the STS, whose students comprised around 40 per cent of those enrolled in higher education, retained the right to set their own entrance requirements.[4] In 1986 Alain Devaquet, the minister of higher education, sought to introduce admission standards for the universities and was met by massive student demonstrations that led the Chirac government to withdraw the bill. Any legislation eliminating the right of *bacheliers* to register in the university faculty of their choice meets with enormous resistance in France.

Lionel Jospin, education minister from 1988 to 1992, increased the power of universities to make contracts with business and industry and generally allowed them more autonomy, but the state continued to control finances, programs, and the assignment of personnel, so higher education still remains centralized, bureaucratic and ill-coordinated. Following Jospin, every government of the 1990s tried, and failed, to reform higher education. François Bayrou, education minister under the Balladur and Juppé governments, and François Fillon, higher education minister under Balladur, sought to reform the universities and the IUT in 1995 and were met with major student riots and had to withdraw their reforms. In response, Bayrou established the *États généraux de l'Université* in 1995–96 to try to find a consensus for reform, but he promised no additional funding should a consensus be found. Bayrou also named a commission to study reform of higher education, as did his successor Claude Allègre 1997–2000 (the Attali commission) but few of the recommendations were put into effect.

Between 1980 and 1997 the number of students in the universities went from 858,085 to 1,469,423.[5] The number in higher education generally grew from 1,181,108 to 2,155,950 during the same years, about 60 per cent of whom attend the universities.[6] The rapid rate of growth in higher education (8 per cent increase in students annually between 1987 and 1995) resulted from the policy of 80 per cent baccalauréat, the creation of the Instituts universitaires de formations des maîtres and the Instituts universitaires professionnalisés in 1991. Since 1995 enrolments have begun to level off, especially in the universities (down 22,000 in 1996–97 and 25,385 in 1997–98 or a 2.8 per cent overall decline), mainly because of improvements in the job market, demographic changes, and because more students are enrolling in two-year programs, the IUT, STS and the cours préparatoires.[7] In 1998 about half of French young people graduating from secondary school went on to higher education (up from 23.5 per cent in 1973), with one-third earning diplomas. But the number failing to obtain higher education diplomas doubled from 60,000 (7 per cent) to 125,000 (15 per cent), while those terminating their education at the end of high school declined from almost three-quarters to about half (table 6.2).

Almost half of university students in the faculties of arts, sciences, and law have fathers who range from middle managers to senior executives (47.5 per cent) and only 26 per cent have fathers who are workers and employees. The proportion of children of workers declines as students continue their studies: they make up 15 per cent in the first cycle, 9 per cent in the second, and only 6 per cent in the third. The children of senior executives, in contrast, represent 22 per cent of students in the first cycle and 31 per cent in the third, and they tend to be concentrated in the prestigious Paris universities in programs leading to the liberal professions, while working-class young people are frequently found in general programs in the arts and sciences in provincial universities in regions that are in economic difficulty.[8] Only the IUT and especially the STS have a significant percentage of children of workers and employees.[9] Ironically, a generation ago the social composition of the universities was considerably more modest, particularly compared to the grandes écoles. Today the difference is less marked, especially in the second and third cycles of university studies.[10]

At 56 per cent of the student population, women are more numerous than men in university and are found overwhelmingly in literature, law and, economics (70%), less so in science. By the third cycle they have become decidedly less numerous. Still fewer women study engineering in France, though the number has risen from 5 per cent in 1972 to 15 per cent in 1983 and 21.5 per cent in 1992 but has remained stable since then (22% in 1999).[11]

Table 6.1
Technical diplomas in higher education

First cycle: BTS, DUT, cours préparatoires, DEUG technologique, DEUST

Second cycle: Licences technologiques, MST (Maîtrises de sciences et techniques), MIAGE (Maîtrise d'informatique appliquée à la gestion). Diplomas of the grandes écoles, three-year diplomas awarded by the IUT and the diplomas of the Instituts universitaires professionnalisés (IUP), notably the DEUP (diplôme d'études universitaires professionnalisées).

Third cycle: DESS (Diplômes d'études supérieures spécialisées), DEA (diplômes d'études approfondies), Doctorate.

TECHNICAL EDUCATION

The technical schools date to the 1950s and 1960s and were designed to elevate technican training into higher education. The Sections de techniciens supérieurs (established in 1952) were situated in the advanced division of the écoles nationales professionnelles and, after 1960, the technical lycées, and belonged to the first cycle of higher education. The Instituts universitaires de technologie training senior technicians were introduced in 1966 in the first cycle of the universities (bac + 2). In 1991, Jospin created the Instituts universitaires professionnalisés (IUP) to educate technical engineers in the second cycle of higher education (bac + 4).

The Sections de Techniciens Supérieurs

The STS have enjoyed very rapid growth over the years which continues to this day (table 6.2).[12] Entrance decisions are made on the basis of the student's academic record rather than by examination or *concours*. Students possessing the technical, vocational, or general baccalauréats, or the brevet de technicien are eligible to apply.[13] Fifty-five per cent of first year students in the STS possess the baccalauréat technologique (baccalauréat de technicien), 20 per cent have the general bac and 6 per cent the bac pro. Around 11 per cent come from the universities, frequently from an IUT.[14]

Programs are introduced and modified after the input of regional *commissions professionnelles consultatives*. The two year STS program is heavily loaded. In the 1990s students spend thirty-two to thirty-seven hours a week in class, plus homework, and six to eight weeks in work placements in business and industry. In the second year, one-third of the courses are general (French, math, science, etc.) and two-thirds are technical and professional (in the IUT it was about half and half, which gave them more prestige). In 1989 about a third of the students in the STS (including half of those in the tertiary sectors) failed to obtain a diploma in two or three years.[15] The IUT, which were more selective before the reforms of 1991–94, lost only 22 per cent of their students.[16] The percentage of graduates from the STS who continued their studies into the second cycle of higher education rose from 10 per cent in 1982 to 30 per cent in the early 1990s and stands at 40 per cent today, but this does not equal the IUT where over 60 per cent of graduates continue on.[17]

In the early years the STS and IUT had about an equal number of students. In 1975 there were 43,314 in the IUT and 44,428 in the STS.[18] After that, the STS grew much faster, enrolments tripling from 68,000 to 235,000 between 1980 and 1992 and then leveled off, reaching 238,988 in 1997–98.[19] The rapid growth of the STS resulted from the 1983 law partially decentralizing education and placing them under regional education administrators (academy rectors) and regional councils, who increased their number in response to local economic needs.[20] Students are enrolled in ninty-five specialties, with 62 per cent of students in tertiary fields (commerce, accounting, insurance, secretarial, health) and 38 per cent in the industrial sector (electricity, electronics, mechanics). In the IUT the figures are 52 and 48 per cent.[21]

The Instituts Universitaires de Technologie

Along with the STS, the IUT filled a gap between the engineer and the technician. Created in 1966 in the universities, they were given considerable autonomy over budget, programs, and admission standards and so were able to develop programs and methods differing from both the universities and grandes écoles, bringing in faculty from business and industry for the practical side of their programs and introducing work placements in industry.[22] They limited enrolments to increase their prestige and as a result grew slowly during the 1980s. They ended up producing as many engineers as senior technicians, over half the students continuing their studies into the second cycle of higher education, almost always into engineering and technical schools.

Although the STS and IUT were under the jurisdiction of the Ministry of National Education, the IUT answered to the secretary of state for higher education who did not exercise much control, while the STS came under the department of secondary education and were subject to much tighter restrictions over programs and enrolments. Coordination between the two departments was very poor in the labyrinthine education bureaucracy, and the duplication of the ninety-five BTS and

Table 6.2
Diplomas awarded by the Sections de Techniciens Supérieurs and
the Instituts Universitaires de Technologie

Year	Brevet de technicien supérieur	Diplôme universitaire de technologie	Total
1970	10,463	6,482	16,945
1975	11,526	14,746	26,272
1980	17,442	19,769	37,211
1985	29,594	24,045	53,639
1990	52,667	27,825	80,492
1995	77,083	37,362	114,445
1996	76,490	37,433	113,923
1998	84,041	44,189	128,230

Source: L'Enseignement technique, 176 (Oct.–Dec., 1997), 4–13 and 185
(1er trimestre 2000), 35. See Table 4.1.

eighteen DUT programs was also a problem, especially in such fields as electronics, electricity, mechanics, finance, and accounting.[23]

During the 1980s the number of *bacheliers* in France increased by 53 per cent, many of whom were *bacheliers technologiques*, while the number of students in the IUT grew by only 15 per cent.[24] Enrolments in the IUT grew slowly from 43,314 in 1975 to 84,900 in 1992.[25] The IUT admitted progressively fewer bacheliers technologiques, who represented 32 per cent of new students in 1980 and 25 per cent a decade later. In 1994 only 19 per cent of students in the industrial sections of the IUT held that diploma.[26] The bacheliers C-D-E (mathematics and sciences, natural sciences, technology and industry) dominated, especially in more sought-after fields linked to science and engineering (information technology, electronics, chemistry). They were drawn to the IUT because they formed a convenient stepping stone into technical programs in the grandes écoles and universities. Students also found it more convenient to spend two years in an IUT and emerge with a DUT than two or three years in a lycée *cours préparatoire* that granted only the DEUG. The bacheliers technologiques, on the other hand, were more likely to be found in the more traditional sectors, mechanics, industrial maintenance, and business.[27] The restrictive admission policies of the IUT forced many of them, who were frequently of working class origin, into the first cycle of the universities in the DEUG and DEUST programs in industrial technology and management, where many failed because of the difficult university mathematics and language requirements.[28]

The IUT increasingly sought to offer engineering programs in the second cycle of higher education, awarding diplomas at bac + 2, bac + 3 and bac + 4.[29] They developed third and fourth year programs in 165 technical specialties, often in response to local industrial demand, so that by 1990 10 per cent of diplomas awarded by the schools were more advanced than the DUT.[30] It is not surprising that the IUT were accused of trying to become "petites grandes écoles."[31]

In 1989 the Decomps commission, studying ways to increase the output of engineers, recommended against advancing the IUT to engineering schools because of the continuing demand for senior technicians and the growing number of bacheliers technologiques trying to get into the first cycle of higher education. The Forestier commission made the same criticism in 1990 and stressed the importance of keeping the training of senior technicians within the universities as the foundation of a general system of higher technical education, and not leaving this job entirely to the STS situated in the lycées.[32] The commission's argument that the IUT had strayed from their original purpose of providing an outlet for young people moving up from the technical-vocational stream was in fact incorrect. The intention of their founders in the 1960s – De Gaulle, Fouchet, Pierre Laurent and others – had been to divert the excess of mediocre general bacheliers into technical studies.[33]

The biggest blow to the ambitions of the IUT came in 1991 when Jospin suddenly created a new system of IUP (Instituts universitaires professionnalisés) recruiting at bac + 1 and training engineers for graduation at bac + 4 (ingénieur-maître) or a further research diploma at bac + 6. The establishment of the IUP placed the technical stream in the second cycle of higher education. Supporters of the IUT, notably the Fédération nationale des diplômés des Instituts universitaires de technologie, argued that the IUT, not the newly created IUP, had won the right to fill this function, to become a French version of the German Fachhochschulen training technical engineers. They argued that the introduction of the IUP would simply create another layer of schools, adding to an already complex and fragmented system of higher technical schools.[34] The IUP would also block the way of career advancement for IUT graduates, because the bac + 2 level IUT diploma did not corresponded to a clear-cut professional entry level in industry. Graduates had traditionally profited from the void at bac + 4 for on-the-job promotion into management and often, with the aid of continuing education courses, to obtain the title of engineer and executive status (*statut cadre*).[35]

In 1992 the Education ministry authorized the creation of 50,000 more places in the IUT by 1995, to be recruited mainly from among bacheliers technologiques, as part of the Université 2000 Plan to increase the output of engineers and technicians.[36] Since then the number of students has grown very rapidly (more rapidly than the STS) from 84,900 in 1992 to 112,857 in 1998.[37] The percentage of bacheliers technologiques admitted to the IUT has risen from around 25 per cent in 1990 to 36 per cent in 1996, plus 1.5 per cent bacheliers professionnels.[38] New IUT are being established in decidedly unglamorous middle-sized provincial cities deprived of higher education facilities.[39] Rectors have assumed increasing control over them as part of the decentralization policy.[40]

The IUT strongly resisted such government interference in their admission procedures and the inevitable decline in the quality of their students, but they had clearly lost the game. The creation of eighty-three IUP in 1991 destroyed their ambition to become engineering schools. With the rapid growth of the IUT, STS, and technician programs in the universities, and the stagnation in hiring for middle-level positions, IUT graduates found it increasingly difficult to find positions for which they were qualified. The rate of unemployment rose from 5 per cent for holders of the BTS-DUT in 1991 to 14 per cent in 1995, falling to 9.5 per cent in 1997 with better economic times.[41] In 1994, 55.7 per cent of DUT and 67.8 per cent of BTS had to accept first jobs as workers or employees. Graduates managed only slowly to improve their position, frequently by moving to other companies, but the number who continued to work in positions well below their qualifications remained high. By 1996 only 52 per cent of the graduates of the class of 1991 of the STS had reached middle-level positions after five years on the job, and average salaries were the lowest of all higher education graduates. Since then conditions have improved with the economic revival of the late 1990s.[42]

The Instituts Universitaires Professionnalisés (IUP)

The main purpose of the IUP is to train industrial engineers and business graduates capable of moving immediately into professional positions at the conclusion of the three-year program. They were the brainchild of Daniel Bloch, director of higher education in the Ministry of National Education, and Bernard Decomps, Bloch's successor at the Haut Comité Éducation-Économie in 1989. They coordinated several studies on the technical professions and found that half of French engineers were not certified and that Germany produced almost double the number of engineers per year than France (28,000 compared to 14,000 in 1988).[43] Bloch and Decomps concluded that France needed to double the number of engineers graduated each year. They ignored the claim of the IUT that in their advanced (three and four year) programs they were really training technical engineers at about the same level as the German *Fachhochschulen* and that they produced about the same number of graduates each year (the four-year Fachhochschulen, founded in the early 1970s, graduate 17,000 per year – two-thirds of Germany's engineers – while the universities graduated 11,000).[44] The main difference was that the French engineering associations had long refused to create an intermediary category of technical engineers for fear of devaluing the engineering credential.[45]

Claude Allègre, Jospin's advisor on higher education, accepted the advice of Bloch and Decomps to establish a system of IUP. He favoured the bac + 4 (IUP) format because he thought it corresponded to that of other countries in the European Community, differing from the standard format of the French engineering schools which award the engineering diploma at bac + 5 (usually two years in a *cours préparatoire* and three in the school itself).[46] In September 1991, the Ministry of Education opened twenty-one IUP in five fields: engineering, communication, administration, business, and management. By 1992 they had grown to eighty-three schools (about one per department) with around 8,000 students, and by 1996 there were 23,700 students.[47] The three-year program is organized into 187 fields oriented closely to business and industry. The schools recruit at the bac + 1 level at the end of the first year of the DEUG, from the classes préparatoires, and in certain cases from the STS and IUT. This is awkward, because the programs of the STS and IUT run from bac + 1 to bac + 2, so the students have to transfer in mid-stream. Nevertheless by 1996 34 per cent of the IUP students came from an STS or IUT.[48]

The students in the IUP earn a university diploma at the end of each year of study: the DEUP (diplôme d'études universitaires professionnalisées), equivalent of the DEUG or DEUST at bac + 2, the *licence* at the end of the second year (bac + 3), and the *maîtrise*, accompanied by the title *ingénieur-maître* at the end of the third and final year (bac + 4). During this time students spend six months in factory and firm in work placements, and they must study two foreign languages. Half of the faculty are supposed to be "professionals," but in practice well-paid engineers and technicians from business and industry have been reluctant to move to these relatively unknown schools.[49]

The ministry created the schools hastily without consulting the national accreditation commission on engineering diplomas (*commission des titres d'ingénieur*), and consulted only intermittently the Commission of University Presidents and The Commission of Engineering School Directors.[50] It did set up a "habilitation commission," which its chairman admitted was recruited "at random."[51] It also introduced some unusual programs and diplomas which the national accreditation commission was very reluctant to accept, such as "engineering" diplomas in business, banking, sales, tourism and hotel management. Admittedly the term *ingénierie*, borrowed from the English, is vague, but applying the term to the tertiary section stretched credibility and the proposals had to be withdrawn. All this played havoc with the intricate network of French "conventions collectives" and the employment qualification scale established in 1967. Although it was generally accepted that the ingénieurs-maîtres would be defined as "cadres" (executives), their precise designation as cadres intermédiaires (level II) or cadres supérieurs (level I) was far from clear.

Such a slapdash approach was particularly galling to those associated with the IUT, which have developed highly respected programs and diplomas over the years that have proved their worth in practice through close cooperation with business and industry.[52] The applied science departments in the universities were also unhappy with the creation of the IUP about which they were scarcely consulted. The IUP competed with their programs and diplomas while using their faculties, laboratories, and equipment. And of course they set their own entrance requirements while the universities could not – another unfair advantage.[53]

The Student Riots of January and February 1995

The parliamentary elections of 1993 returned the right-centre to power with a large majority. The new prime minister, Edouard Balladur, named François Fillon as Minister of Higher Education and Research. Fillon promised to introduce a comprehensive reform of higher education, naming a study commission under Daniel Laurent to recommend reforms and to sort out the poorly integrated technical programs in higher education hosting 400,000 students in all.[54]

While the study commission was deliberating, the administration issued a series of orders in 1994 that further upset the IUT and their partisans. In January, in an effort to facilitate job placement for young people coming out of school, the government decreed a *contrat d'insertion professionnelle*, the "SMIC-jeunes," in which business and industry would be encouraged to hire young people in return for the right to pay them 80 per cent of the minimum wage (SMIC) for a determined period of time. This measure was extended even to the higher technician level, which the "Iutiens" considered a direct insult to the value of their diploma. This blunder was followed by a ministerial order of April 24 reducing general studies in the IUT by 1000 hours and raising the technical content of the programs of the schools, which weakened the transferability of the program to the second cycle of the universities and to the grandes écoles.[55]

Toward the end of 1994, Fillon and his advisors decided to maintain and indeed even to expand the IUP, integrating them much more closely with the programs and departments in the university.[56] This meant that the IUP would teach the long university program, recruiting mainly from the DEUG programs of the first cycle at bac + 1 (in other words, mainly from among general bacheliers). The IUT and STS were to recruit primarily from among bacheliers technologiques. Their graduates, in possession of the DUT or BTS at bac + 2, were directed toward the job market. They were not normally to be admitted to the IUP because of the awkwardness of the entry year at bac + 1. A government decree of 29 December 1994, drove this point home, tactlessly, by announcing that students possessing a DUT or STS could apply to an IUP "only exceptionally and with the special dispensation of their school director."[57]

Because graduates of the IUT already constituted a third of the students in the IUP, and over half continued their education into the second cycle of higher education, the prospect of being "locked up" in their own schools with no outlet save the job market at the technician level caused consternation in the schools.[58] The administration countered with the offer of a third year, creating a diplôme national de technologie spécialisée (DNTS) at the level of the *licence*. But this was seen as a lame concession to keep the *Iutiens* away from the IUP and to direct them toward the Instituts universitaires de formation des maîtres, the new regional teacher-training institutes (another of Jospin's reforms that had become the object of considerable controversy), because of the scarcity of professors in vocational education with the *licence*. All this simply proved to the IUT students that advancement to the engineering and management level had been blocked and that from now on they would be relegated permanently to the status of technicians and teachers. In early January 1995 student demonstrations began to occur in the IUT.

At the same time the administration announced a freeze on credits for research and a cut in hiring professors and teachers for the following year. On 20 January 1995 the report of the Laurent commission to the minister of higher education on the future of higher education was made public. This document called for "a cultural revolution" and a general "return to the drawing board" in reassessing the entire system of higher education.[59] The commission proposed reinforcing the autonomy of universities, creating regional university institutes to accept the wave of bacheliers technologiques seeking to get into the first cycle of higher education, raising tuition fees, and replacing a certain number of scholarships by loans.[60] These measures, and especially the latter two, provoked an immediate demonstration by university students in Paris and in key provincial cities.

The final blow in a series of remarkably ill-timed moves on the part of the academic administration came with a circular from the director of the department of higher education in the ministry, Jean-Pierre Bardet, on January 26 stating that "the IUT constitute a short stream (*filière courte*) of a technical character, the primary purpose of which is to lead directly to the job market." It reaffirmed that the IUT and STS were to recruit from among bacheliers technologiques rather than bacheliers généraux.[61] Although essentially this was a repeat of the decree of December 29, this was the last straw for the Iutiens. On January 30, thirty IUTs joined the strike begun in the universities.

By early February 1995 the student revolt had spread from the IUT and universities to the lycées and STS and by mid-month had erupted into massive demonstrations by students in Paris and in cities across France.[62] With presidential elections looming in May, Edouard Balladur put pressure on Fillon to resolve the issue, which led him to withdraw the texts citing a "misunderstanding" and "erroneous interpretations" of the administration's intentions, notably the Laurent report, which he said had been published essentially for discussion purposes. He cancelled article 4 of the ministerial order of December 29, eliminating the terms "exceptional" and "by special dispensation" and allowed students from the IUT or STS to transfer at the end of the first or second year to an IUP on the recommendation of their director and on the agreement of a board of admissions. The Bardet circular was to be "rewritten." Fillon added that the admission of bacheliers technologiques to the IUT would no longer be considered as "a priority" but of "special concern" (*attention particulière*). The idea of consolidating university technical studies in the IUP was retained, and the students of the IUT and STS were to have greater access to them and thus to the second cycle of higher education, but the administration continued to warn that the IUT should not be regarded automatically as a "springboard into higher studies."[63]

The riots of early 1995 were the culmination of a series of blunders by the administration that began with the sudden creation of the IUP by Jospin in 1991. While the IUP have an important role to play in extending technical education into the second cycle of higher education, the founding of a new set of specialized schools illustrates all that is wrong with the centralized French education system. While it takes years to pilot a reform bill through the educational bureaucracy, a myriad of commissions, professional associations, and finally parliament, the ministry has the power to impose by decree an entire set of very expensive schools on the country without much consultation. Individual ministers seek to make their mark by introducing attention-getting legislation, often without much planning. The constant overlaying of new institutions on a poorly integrated network of special schools simply makes the system more chaotic. During its audit of 1994 the *Cours des comptes* criticized poor coordination within the department of higher education and the department of secondary education and the professions. It also criticized the overlapping of two-year technical programs in the IUT, STS, the DEUG technologique and DEUST in the universities.[64]

Fillon decided to maintain the IUP and indeed to integrate them into university engineering programs. This sealed the fate of the IUT, which paid the price for their earlier restrictive policies. Instead of being upgraded to institutions training technical engineers, which is essentially what a senior technician is, they were demoted, their programs specialized, their recruitment altered, their students generally oriented into the workplace rather than into higher studies, and they have been forced to expand into geographical areas far from university centres that are not particularly suited to technical studies. Caught between the rapidly growing STS, on one hand and the IUP on the other, and facing a saturated job market for technicians, the future of the IUT did not appear very favourable by the mid-1990s.[65]

The Allègre-Attali Reforms, 1997–98

In 1997 Education Minister Claude Allègre named a work group headed by Jacques Attali and composed of businessmen and academics to study means of consolidating the various branches of higher education and of bringing the grandes écoles and universities closer together in terms of recruitment, research and facilities. The report noted that the old difference between the universities, which traditionally educated students mainly for teaching and the public services, and the grandes écoles, which had trained for professions, had considerably diminished. It argued that they should be encouraged to work closely with business and industry in pursuing research and various common projects.[66] Reporting 5 May 1998, the commission complained of the "disorder" in the organization of French higher education, which over the years had become "confused, bureaucratic and inegalitarian ... a machine to reproduce elites." It stated that the three components of the higher education system, the universities, grandes écoles, and technical schools "do not form complementary parts of a coherent whole ... but rather of poorly coordinated, isolated compartments wasteful of resources and talent."[67] Having started with that dramatic statement the commission made only mild recommendations for reform, proposing to introduce a 3, 5, 8 organization in higher education, with programs more oriented toward the workplace. For example, the DEUG is to become more practical and is to be extended to three years (bac + 3) from two, and would lead to reformed masters' degrees (bac + 5) more closely aligned to the needs of the economy. In November 1999 a new *licence professionnel* was introduced to provide a third year of occupational training for holders of the DUT, BTS, and DEUST (bac + 2). The new professional licence is designed to provide additional competence and skills leading to the job market rather than to prepare for the maîtrise and other advanced credentials. It is unclear as to whether they will train super technicians or lesser engineers, though it is envisaged that graduates will start their careers at the higher technician and middle management level III.[68]

The new system of 3, 5 and 8 is supposed to bring the French system closer to other European systems, but in fact creates a whole new set of exceptions and anomalies. The STS, with their two year program, do not correspond to similar schools in Europe training technical engineers over three years. The IUP, recruiting at bac + 1 and graduating at bac + 4, do not fit into the new numerology. Ironically Allègre recommended the creation of the IUP to Jospin in 1991 on the grounds that bac + 4 came closer to European engineering diplomas than the proposed IUT bac + 3. Had the IUP not been introduced in 1991 and had the IUT simply been allowed to offer a technical engineering diploma at bac + 3, in line with most European countries, much confusion and frustration could have been avoided. The IUT are now preparing for the three-year DNTS and the new licence professionnel anyway, though these are still not considered engineering diplomas. Finally, the "French exception," the grandes écoles and their *cours préparatoires*, remain intact and unreformed. The Attali commission did recommend a quota for technical students at the

Polytechnique and for university graduates in the grands corps, but the reforms ran into opposition from powerful interest groups and failed to pass.

ENGINEERING SCHOOLS

Most of the grandes écoles are engineering and technical schools, notably the École polytechnique, the Écoles des Mines, the École centrale des arts et manufactures and the Écoles d'arts et métiers, plus special schools in aeronautics, electricity, telecommunications, etc. In the 1980s, three-quarters of French senior executives were engineers, a figure that has declined somewhat in the 1990s because of the growth of business schools.

Because of their restrictive admission standards, until recently French engineering schools have graduated too few engineers to meet the demand. This forced companies to promote technicians to engineering posts, mainly in production, a field looked down upon by grande école graduates. A study directed by Bernard Decomps in 1989 found that almost half of French engineers possessed only the baccalauréat or less (about 20 per cent had no more than the CAP-BEP), that is, they had no formal qualifications for their positions and had been promoted as *ingénieurs maison*.[69] This illustrates the gap that existed between the highly educated senior managers and middle-management that came from lesser grandes écoles or in many cases had simply been promoted on the basis of competence, loyalty, and seniority. Decomps estimated that the output of trained French engineers, in 1989 around 16,000 annually, needed to be doubled by the year 2005.[70]

With the upsurge of industrialization during the 1950s and 1960s, governments, unable to force the grandes écoles techniques to increase their output significantly, began to establish new schools and to enlarge existing ones.[71] The result has been a doubling of the number of engineers every decade ever since. In 1940 there were 60,000 engineers in France; by 1995 there were around 650,000 of whom 340,000 were certified.[72] Accredited engineering schools grew from eighty-six in 1940 to 240 in 1998, and student enrolments rose from 43,000 in 1980 to 82,954 in 1998.[73]

The Ministry of Education oversees 48,542 students in 129 schools (58.5 per cent). These are located mainly in the universities (*écoles universitaires*) which today constitute about a third of all schools and students (ninety-four schools, 27,520 students). In addition, there are thirty-five engineering schools with 21,022 students organized under the jurisdiction of the Ministry of National Education but outside the universities (25.6 per cent): the twelve Écoles d'arts et métiers and affiliates (4,447 students), five Écoles nationales d'ingénieurs or ENI (3,439 students), and four Instituts nationaux des sciences appliquées or INSA (7,622), plus fourteen others (5,514).[74] Forty-five schools are under the jurisdiction of seven other ministries (agriculture, defense etc.) with 13,928 students (16.8 per cent), as opposed to 8,100 in 1980, of which the École polytechnique is a well known example (under the jurisdiction of the Ministry of Defense). Finally, there are sixty-six private schools with 20,484 students, which enroll about a quarter of the total number of students in the engineering schools.[75]

Most of the engineering schools recruit at bac + 2 or 3 from the cours préparatoires in the lycées (47 per cent) or at bac + 1 or 2 from the first cycle technical schools and programs (the DEUG, DEUST, DUT and BTS), and have three- or four-year programs, but some (ENI and INSA) recruit at the level of the baccalauréat and have five year courses.[76] A few students (four per cent) come up through work-study programs, the *Nouvelle formation d'ingénieurs* founded by Bernard Decomps in 1990, and through continuing education programs in the Conservatoire national d'arts et métiers and the Centre d'études supérieures industrielles, in which senior technicians with several years of professional experience can continue their studies in engineering while working part time.[77]

Despite the poor job market from 1981 to 1986 and 1991 to 1995, the number of engineers active in France rose from 453,000 to 650,000 and the percentage of executives and higher professionals, many of whom are engineers, rose from 9 to 13 per cent of the labour force.[78] In the computer and electronics industries, the percentage of engineers, technicians, and executives totals 43.5 per cent of employees, up from 29.8 per cent in 1982, the result of increased hiring of educated personnel and the continuing education of employees.[79] With the exception of these industries, France now produces enough engineers to meet the demand. Between 1987 and 1991 the unemployment rate among young engineers who had graduated three years earlier remained below 3 per cent but then rose to 8 per cent in 1994 (graduates of 1992), only to fall again to 5 per cent in 1997 (graduates of 1994).[80] With the economic upswing since 1997, employment prospects for graduates have improved even further in most fields.[81]

THE GRANDES ÉCOLES

The unofficial term grande école can be defined as a diversified ensemble of small (about 400 students each) autonomous establishments existing outside the university stream in response to specialized needs, notably in engineering, applied science, and management studies.[82] The exact criteria for earning the title from among the roughly 300 special schools in France is unclear, but the 160 schools that belong to the *Conférence des grandes écoles* obviously have the best claim.[83] These include a good part of the 240 engineering and some of the business schools, plus schools for the training of professors, the *écoles normales supérieures*, and institutes in the political and social sciences such as the *École nationale d'administration* (ENA).

The grandes écoles absorb 30 per cent of France's higher education budget and educate 5 per cent of the students.[84] They are essentially graduate schools recruiting at bac + 2 or 3 from special *cours préparatoires* at prestigious big city lycées from which they recruit the best students through very difficult entrance examinations (*concours*) for a limited number of places (*numerus clausus*) and then train them in programs lasting three years for school diplomas. They are frequently boarding schools that separate their students from the outside world and enjoy the best facilities, small classes, and distinguished professors. The great majority of their students are the children of professionals, executives, business owners, and senior civil servants. Very few working-class young people ever reach these schools. Over a third of the students are now women, who study mainly in academic, administrative, legal, and medical fields, and are less present in technical and industrial subjects.

In a study done in 1993, Michel Bauer and Bénédicte Bertin-Mourot found that the École Polytechnique and the École nationale d'Administration alone provided the largest number of senior managers in the public and private sector in 1985. The Polytechnique produced 25 per cent of senior managers; in 1993 it was 28 per cent. Even more strikingly, the ENA produced 12 per cent of senior managers in 1985 and 23 per cent in 1993. The École des Hautes Études Commerciales, in third place, fell from 8 to 6 per cent. The place of other grandes écoles has declined slightly, but the big drop has come among university graduates, who made up just 10 per cent of managers in 1984 and only 4 per cent in 1993.[85]

THE GRANDS CORPS, AND THE RECRUITMENT OF SENIOR MANAGERS

Many of the top-ranked graduates of the elite schools move directly into high positions in the great state corporations (*grands corps*): in technical fields into the Corps des Mines and Ponts-et-Chaussées, plus government services in aeronautics, telecommunications, and transport; in finance in the Inspection des finances and the Cour des

Comptes; in administration, the Conseil d'État; and in the military corps. Graduates of the Polytechnique do particularly well in the first corps, those of ENA in the second and third. Top-ranking students can hope to become *directeurs de cabinet* of government ministers, playing an important managerial and political role from which they move easily into senior executive positions in business and industry, usually by the time they are in their mid-thirties. Prominent in the public, private, and financial sectors, the *corpsards* maintain a tight esprit de corps.

The nationalization of companies in 1982–83 followed by privatization into the 1990s augmented the movement of senior managers from the public into the private sector and took place surprisingly smoothly, probably because of the homogeneity of management involved.[86] In 1993, 47 per cent of top executives in major industries were ex-senior civil servants (*grands commis de l'état*), up from 41 per cent in 1985 (the number is higher in the top companies). The percentage of CEOs and senior executives who rose to their posts as founders, heirs, owners, or through family connections rose from 28 to 32 per cent, while those rising through the ranks of business and industry declined from 31 to 21 per cent.[87]

Although the Socialists might have been expected to promote union members or self-made individuals, they are really a party of middle-class professionals and maintained the traditional recruitment of managerial elites. In the Mauroy government, 65 per cent of ministers were former high-level civil servants, often having served in advisory positions to ministers. In the right-centre Chirac government (1986–87) 66 per cent came from those ranks and in the Rocard government (1988–91) the proportion was 70 per cent. In 1990, *énarques* (graduates of the ENA) made up 21 per cent of the cabinet of the President of the Republic, 37 per cent of that of the prime minister, 38 per cent of the Minister of National Education, and 58 per cent of Ministers of Finance, Industry and the Interior. Among recent prime ministers, Laurent Fabius, Jacques Chirac, Michel Rocard, Edouard Balladur, Alain Juppé, and Lionel Jospin are énarques, Edith Cresson graduated from the École des Hautes Études Commerciales and has a doctorate, while only Pierre Mauroy (a teacher) and Pierre Bérégovoy (labour unions, self-taught) came up through the ranks.[88]

Although the grandes écoles recruit theoretically on merit based on rigourous examinations, in practice only middle- and upper middle-class young people, mainly males, can afford the cost, difficulty, and duration of studies, mainly in math and science, in one of the cours préparatoires of the great, big-city lycées that prepare students for the *concours* of the grandes écoles. The *concours* still includes an oral

section which effectively eliminates those unable to discourse eloquently on the place of Guy de Maupassant in French literature. The
percentage of young people of modest backgrounds in four leading
grandes écoles, the Polytechnique, the École normale supérieure, the
École nationale d'administration, and the École des hautes études
commerciales has fallen from 29 per cent in the early 1950s to 9 per
cent in the mid 1990s. Taking into account that the overall representation of workers, peasants, employees, artisans, and shopkeepers in
French society was smaller in the 1990s (58 per cent) than in the early
1950s (91 per cent), one finds that young people of working class
background have today no more chance of graduating from a grande
école than they did almost a half century ago.[89] At ENA in 1992, 69.7
per cent came from the upper middle class (liberal professions, senior
civil servants, corporate executives), 11.1 per cent were the children of
middle managers and none came from the working class. At the Polytechnique, 69.3 per cent were from the upper middle class, 15.1 per
cent were the children of middle managers and workers, and at the
École des Mines the figures were 62.4 and 18.1 per cent. Among pa-
ternal grandfathers, around one third were upper middle class, while
between 30 and 40 per cent were of modest backgrounds, of whom
most were skilled artisans and shopkeepers, with a relatively small
number of workers, farmers and middle managers (8 per cent at ENA,
11.2 per cent at Polytechnique, and 13.5 per cent Mines).[90]

There is some chance for advancement over two generations. Moreover, virtually all European systems of secondary education track
their students into university-preparatory, technical, and vocational-
apprenticeship streams. Like France, since the 1960s they have created
technical-professional schools and programs in higher education,
usually of three years (France is the exception at bac + 2) training
needed specialists, which accommodate the mass of students coming
from expanded secondary systems while protecting the integrity of
university programs. Such measures favour upper-class admission
into the elite schools and universities. This has been the case even in
Scandinavia, despite efforts to democratize the system.[91] In Germany
the difficult six- or seven-year university course discourages young
people of working class origin, though the four-year engineering and
professional schools (*Fachhochschulen*) created in the 1970s are more
accessible. German executives come mainly from universities or engineering schools, but some are promoted from the ranks on the basis of
skills acquired in the national vocational program, continuing education, and achievements on the job.[92] In the United States most come
from universities and business schools, which are of uneven quality.
Studies have found that a high percentage of senior executives in the

US come from prestigious preparatory schools and private Ivy League universities.[93] In Great Britain a greater number come up through the ranks: only 24 per cent of British managers had a higher education in the early 1980s (38 per cent of managers began their careers in manual occupations), as opposed to 65 per cent in France, 62 per cent in Germany, and 85 per cent in the US and Japan.[94] In Japan, which most resembles France, higher executives come mainly from the University of Tokyo, but after graduation they begin their careers in business and industry. Aside from France and Japan, no other country reserves top positions for an elite based on the acquisition of certain types of diplomas, and France alone recruits senior executives from the upper civil service.[95] Only in France are universities regarded as second-level institutions, which makes it difficult to integrate with the higher education systems of countries in the EU.

THE CRITIQUE OF HIGHER EDUCATION

There are three criticisms of French higher education: it is undemocratic, it is poorly organized and badly integrated; and it fails to train effective business leaders conversant with good management techniques.

On the first point, Marxist thinkers during the 1950s and 1960s rejected the optimistic assumptions of the time that educational expansion would serve the purposes of democracy while providing skilled personnel for a growing economy. They argued that educational institutions reflect the social class composition of capitalist society and that the curriculum reproduces the consciousness and the attitudes upon which capitalist society reposes.[96] Children from affluent, well-educated families enjoy a superior linguistic and cultural formation and are in a favourable position to benefit from education by enrolling in academic tracks leading to higher education, thus maximizing their social and professional opportunities. In the words of Pierre Bourdieu, they possess "cultural capital," the ability to master a whole series of codes, social and linguistic, that enable them to achieve success in school and to choose the fields most likely to lead to good jobs and positions of social authority later on. Such groups conceal their domination of society by pointing to the knowledge, competence, hard work, and "merit" necessary to reach their station in life. Children from working class families on the other hand suffer from a "linguistic deficit" and are much less likely to reach higher education, and even when they do they often end up in provincial liberal arts faculties that provide few job opportunities outside of teaching. Much of the rapid expansion of higher education since the

1960s has been directed toward the universities, to the lesser higher schools (*petites grandes écoles*), and to two-year technical-professional schools like the Instituts universitaires de technologie, which are clearly inferior in status to the elite schools and lead only to middle-level jobs.[97] In short, the upper classes are in a superior position to develop successful strategies of self-reproduction, to gain admission into the elite schools and earn the credentials that open the way into the best positions in the public and private sectors.

PIERRE BOURDIEU AND THE NOBLESSE D'ÉTAT

Since the 1960s, Pierre Bourdieu has undertaken major studies of the production of academic knowledge, technical expertise and bureaucratic power in France. In his early work, *La Reproduction*, Bourdieu discussed the multiple processes of elite reproduction in society.[98] In *Homo Academicus* (1988) he analysed the workings of the Paris academic establishment.[99] In *The State Nobility* (1989) he studied the education of academic elites in the grandes écoles and their cours préparatoires by examining the files of prizewinners of national examinations (*concours général*) from 1965 to 1969 and again during the mid-1980s, which appeared to confirm his theories of reproduction, fields of power, and *habitus*.[100]

Bourdieu avoids a narrow, determinist approach by arguing that social classes and groups develop strategies in pursuing their cultural, economic, and social objectives. Upper-class students of course have the advantage because they possess the linguistic capital and *habitus*, a familiarity with abstraction, formalism, intellectualism, and subtlety in expression (including the acquisition of the right body language and comportment) essential to success. Bourdieu argues that the system selects those who already know what they need to know through a "dialectic of consecration and recognition," at the end of which "the elite school chooses those who have chosen it because it has chosen them."[101] Educated and consecrated by the state, increasingly homogeneous and maintaining a strong esprit de corps, they constitute a "new credentialed nobility," uniting all forms of capital, cultural, economic, social and symbolic.[102]

Bourdieu states that the gradual substitution of the academic title for the property title as the instrument for appropriating the profits of economic capital is legitimated by the infusion of the "ideology of public service" and "the illusion of academic neutrality."[103] This signals the consolidation of a new mode of domination and a corresponding transformation in the system of strategies whereby the ruling class maintains and masks itself. The new credentialed elite has all the characteristics of nobility: they monopolize the knowledge and competence necessary in a complex technological society; they possess economic, social, and cultural capital; and they have the "magic" (a quasi-religious consecration of their superior position conferred by the state) that distinguishes them from ordinary people.[104]

Even if the French system of higher education seems an extreme case in the Western world, according to Bourdieu the same process of selection takes place in one form or another through the education systems of all developed countries. As "the central bank of symbolic credit," the state bears upon us all every time we perceive and construct the social world through categories instilled in us by our education. Forms of reason and classification are socially constituted and are really class ideologies that serve particular interests at the very moment they are portrayed as universal. The instruments of knowledge and construction of social reality taught by the school are instruments of symbolic domination. Credential-based nobility is accepted because the state imposes ways of seeing and thinking through the school that cause us to accept forms of domination without our even being aware of them.[105]

Bourdieu attacked the dualisms that reduce people to "mind," mental processes to instrumental rationalism, and learning to the acquisition of knowledge. In criticizing especially the scientific pretentions of structuralist anthropology and Saussurian linguistics, he pointed to the need to demystify scientific attitudes that have become culturally pretentious and imperialistic through association with socially dominant groups. He stressed instead the need to see the whole person acting in the world and to view learning as participation in communities of practice. In *Outline of a Theory of Practice*, he underlined the importance of socially and culturally mediated experience and the interdependence of agent and world. Such views resembled in many ways those developed in the "active pedagogy" of the technical and vocational schools and opened the way to greater understanding of practical activities, human agency, and the workplace as essential components of the learning experience.[106] Bourdieu was active in seeking change and enjoyed considerable influence in Socialist circles. He was named by Chevènement in 1985 to chair a commission on educational reform, especially of secondary and vocational education, and again by Jospin in 1989 to another commission including François Gros, co-chair, Jacques Derrida and Didier Dacunha-Castelle. The second commission in particular influenced the reforms of Jospin and Jack Lang between 1988 and 1993.[107]

Michel Crozier and Business Culture in France

France inherited a system of centralized administration from the *ancien régime* and the Napoleonic Empire and at the same time a tradition of respect for individual rights and suspicion of authority from the Revolution. As Michel Crozier demonstrated in *Le Phénomène Bureaucratique* (1963), centralized decision-making in France has been traditionally limited by unwritten rules defining the boundaries and responsibilities of the various ranks in society. Each rank had a strong sense of identity and an awareness of its rights and duties. In such a system the rights of the individual were protected from unwarranted intervention from above, but communication between groups was difficult. To avoid face-to-face conflicts, decisions were passed up the hierarchy but servile obedience was not required. The bureaucratic system functioned adequately so long as decision-making was routine but it could not deal with situations of uncertainty, hence Crozier's oft-quoted dictum: "A bureaucratic organization is an organization that cannot correct its behaviour by learning from its errors." Crozier described France of the 1960s as a *société bloquée* in which change could only come about through crisis, a comment that was widely taken to have foreseen the uprisings of 1968.[108]

Crozier believed that the same fossilized bureaucratic features that characterized French administration were also present in the education system and in the business world. In his study of eight French companies in the late 1980s, *L'entreprise à l'écoute*, Crozier noted that the old family-owned businesses were giving way to professionally managed companies and that several companies had shown remarkable adaptability and resilience. Businessmen had come a long way from the *dirigisme* and *colbertisme* of the past, increasingly embracing international competition and the principles of a free market economy. He argued however that middle-level management and lesser supervisors were in practice more willing to accept innovation than senior executives. Indeed, the former frequently reproached their bosses for paying lip service to modernization, for failing to progress from bureaucratic to participative management, and for falling back on unilateral, hierarchical, and paternalist approaches.[109]

Crozier blamed this on the grande école and *corpsard* background of many senior managers. Schooled in abstract reasoning rather than problem-solving, they were trained to make decisions from above rather than to consult those of lower rank, hence their isolation even from middle management. Crozier was not opposed to the education of elites in higher schools, but he disliked the *cours préparatoires*, the *concours* and the *grands corps* system for producing a narrow, unimaginative, self-perpetuating bureaucratic elite poorly adapted to the participative requirements of the modern business.[110]

Like Crozier, Philippe d'Iribarne studied work relations in French companies and factories during the 1980s, comparing them with similar firms in the United States and Holland. Less critical of the system than Bourdieu and Crozier, he argued in *La logique de l'honneur* that features of the French company can be traced back to the *ancien régime* in which an employee does not merely do a job but occupies a position that is an indelible part of his identity. The culture of French organizations was based on respect for the individual's dignity and freedom of action within boundaries defined by his or her role and by custom and tradition. These largely unwritten codes of practice provided a strong sense of professional identity for each rank. Thus a spirit of mutual respect between different strata supported both the principle of hierarchy and that of equality between individuals. The hierarchy was based on degrees of nobility. For the senior executive, frequently a graduate of an elite engineering school, the diploma provided legitimacy for his/her superior position; for the works supervisor, craft skills and experience also provided legitimacy, though at a lower level. The relations between these levels were governed by custom, tradition, and professional honour. Higher echelons interfered in the work of the lesser ones only rarely, in cases of breakdown or crisis. The lower ranks were willing to accept the authority of those above them so long as it was exercised by legitimate professionals and so long as they did not threaten their professional autonomy and personal dignity.[111] Thus diplomacy rather than written rules governed the relationships of various strata within the factory, and the individual, working within his/her own sphere, was normally left free to do his job without interference from above.

D'Iribarne argues that in all countries management patterns and work relations incorporate traditional forms of cooperation peculiar to that country. In the US work relations are governed by a contractual approach guaranteeing fairness and in Holland by a consensual approach to dealing with problems. In these countries, as in Germany and Britain, managers hold an instrumental view that considers authority to be an attribute of the job not the person, as is the case in France, Italy and Belgium. D'Iribarne points out however that there is much diversity within countries, between firms, factories and sectors, and that it is difficult to generalize. Not all French companies are authoritarian and bureaucratic, nor are they all run by énarques and polytechniciens. It is impossible to say that French factories are inherently less productive than American or Dutch concerns. French culture has qualities that weigh heavily on productivity, but this is true of all cultures.[112]

Crozier and d'Iribarne agree that in France one finds modern-minded managers, engineers, and workers who are fully aware of the need for change. They note that the French seem better suited to *grands projects* that excite the imagination and sense of adventure, notably in such fields as aviation, aerospace, nuclear power, and telecommunications, and that they have been less effective in market-driven consumer sectors and information technology. D'Iribarne also notes that the grandes écoles have made many changes over the years, notably in introducing extensive facilities for research, and that technical corps such as Mines and Pont-et-Chaussées have proved capable of adapting.[113] The relative independence of top French executives from control by boards of directors and from the influence of middle management and labour unions make possible a level of innovation impossible in more cautious organizations, such as those governed by the Dutch consensual model.[114] D'Iribarne suggests that the logic of honour may be compatible with new approaches, that one can be simultaneously traditional and modern, and that the French elite is capable of adapting to changing circumstances.

Foreign observers of French management performance generally agree with Crozier's conclusion that French businesses are attempting to adapt to change but that this is rendered difficult by the rigidity of French structures and by the weight of past practices. In their recent book, Michael Storper and Robert Salais discuss what they call "the real worlds of production" in which "new worlds," the Interpersonal, Intellectual and Market, are undermining the older Industrial world (mass production, Fordism, Keynesianism) because they provide better possibilities for growth in a global economy and offer economic actors "the possibility of constructing economic identities which position them favourably in the world economy." They argue that France is so deeply rooted in the Industrial World that it integrates the newer Interpersonal and Market factors too slowly.[115] The authors list the most serious obstacles to change: too much state regulation, the bureaucratic mentality, lack of entrepreneurial spirit among French businessmen; weak unions and poor labour organization based on rigid industry-wide collective agreements, the survival of craft consciousness and the notion of "honourable work" among workers; and weak R&D, the importation of too many ideas from abroad, and a system of vocational education too centered in schools and credentials rather than genuine skills training.[116]

While France spends as much money on R&D as the United States, Japan, and Germany, it has not been as successful in integrating new research into productive practices and marketing. For example, the French (and Europeans) have not been able to produce American-style scientist-entrepreneurs such as Steve Jobs (Apple Computers), Bill Gates (Microsoft), and William Hewlett and David Packard.[117] Storper and Salais blame this on the old habit of relying on protected markets, big state contracts, and military-related electronics and aerospace production. As a result, high-technology industries are centred in systems engineering and construction of large-scale, applied technology systems such as military and civilian aircraft and space hardware, large-scale electronics and communications systems. Core high-technology industries such as computers, microelectronics, medical equipment, automated industrial machinery, and semiconductors tend to be dominated by foreign countries. France relies on heavy imports especially in consumer electronics (66 per cent) and computer components (87 per cent).[118]

Other observers take a more optimistic position, pointing to successes in telecommunications and aerospace (the French aviation industry is now number two in the world) and the return to profitability of automobiles and steel. Vivien Schmidt concludes that "a second managerial revolution" began with the nationalization of the major banks and industries in the early 1980s. Nationalization had a salutary effect on business: it served to preserve the industrial base from foreign acquisition and it rationalized, recapitalized, and internationalized French industry.[119] Schmidt credits the top managers, many of whom were ex-*corpsards*, with reversing the economic decline begun in the 1970s by introducing new industrial techniques, quality circles and teamwork, flatter hierarchies, greater employee autonomy, better labour relations, revised employment classification grids, greater emphasis on employee education and training, and improved research and development.[120]

The old *dirigisme* has all but disappeared since the 1980s as a result of governments, businessmen, and EU regulations. Many French executives appear to have acquired a flair for market practices and aggressive entrepreneurship. They have also experimented with new forms of work organization. For example, Renault's unibody "Twingo" was the first model to be produced under the new "project-based" management structure (replacing the old sequential approach to car design and introducing a transversal dimension in the old vertical system) and was completed in record time: four years instead of seven from design to production.[121] After bitter resistance to Japanese imports in the past, the French automobile industry seems prepared now to compete on their own territory with the Japanese. Toyota is building a factory at Valenciennes and under EU regulations will enjoy up to 16 per cent of the French market by the year 2000. One can hardly imagine the French automobile industry prepared to compete with the Japanese, even a decade ago.

From the perspective of the late 1990s, there is considerable evidence that French industry has become more competitive and innovative. After growing at half the rate of the Euro-zone countries from 1990 to 1997, the economy has been averaging between 2.5 and 4 per cent growth per year from 1997 to 2000, higher than the average German rate of 2 per cent, stimulated by rising consumer demand at home and increasing exports in particular to the United States and Europe. Tax revenues are up, jobs created in industry rose by 2 per cent in 1998, and unemployment slipped to 11 per cent. One-quarter of French production is exported, and France has risen from sixth to fourth exporter in volume in the world. Even the machine-tool industry is flourishing after a century in the doldrums, growing by 17.6 per cent in the three years between 1994 and 1996, exporting over half its production and now ranked fifth in the world in output.[122] For the first time in years, industry has made plans to increase production and has even begun to hire more employees after having been a net destroyer of jobs over the previous twenty years.[123] Over its first two years in power (1997–99), the Socialist government of Lionel Jospin oversaw the creation of an estimated 620,000 jobs. The government has continued to sell state-owned assets, worth 30 billion francs, to private shareholders, often from abroad. These shareholders demand good returns on investment and sound long-term strategies. The old cozy relationships between state and business and the bloated economy are disappearing, as companies are forced to slim down in order to compete in an international setting.[124]

Changes in vocational training, in which industry has played an increasingly active role over the last twenty years, accompany steady changes in the workforce. Automation strategies are allied to investments in human resources, improved work organization, and vocational training. This accompanies a much more proactive approach on the part of French management toward the education of youth and manpower training. In 1993, in its *Livre blanc* on the professional education of the young, the French national employers association (Conseil national du patronat français) stated that "French companies are fully aware that their ability to respond successfully to challenges posed by economic competition on a European and world scale is closely linked to the competence and adaptability of their employees and therefore to the capacity of our system of vocational education to respond to changing forms of qualification."[125]

Industry now hires employees possessing credentials at all levels and seldom promotes uncertified people on the job, and today France possesses one of the most skilled workforces in the world. Since 1989 every young person is guaranteed the right to achieve a secondary credential and/or a skill based on a combination of in-school and on-the-job training. An extensive system of apprenticeship provides outlets for those who are unable to obtain school credentials. The argument of Storper and Salais that vocational training is too school-oriented bears less weight today because French technical and vocational schools are based on programs of work-study, from the lycées professionnels to the STS and IUT. The problem today is quite different from the past when people were hired and promoted without benefit of credentials. Today jobs are closely tied to diplomas, which makes promotion on the job difficult, and some who are hired are overqualified for their posts, which engenders a new kind of rigidity.

The most glaring need for reform in the French education system today lies in higher education. The tripartite system is too fragmented and the privileges of the cours préparatoires and grandes écoles excessive. France has become a middle-class society increasingly resentful of the mandarins produced by the grandes écoles and grands corps, who have proved very adept at manipulating the education system to perpetuate their power. Most French people do not believe that the ability to maneuver within the upper echelons of the state bureaucracy adequately prepares a person to manage large industrial corporations. Savary's largely failed reform of higher education in 1984 was on the right track: transfer the grandes écoles to the second cycle of the universities under the jurisdiction of the Ministry of National Education and abolish the cours préparatoires, the numerus clausus and the *concours*. This would open the elite schools to a broader cross-section of the population, put an end to the long-standing inferiority of the universities, and bring France much more in line with the graduate and professional schools of the rest of Europe, which are situated in the universities for the most part. This reform would also have the advantage of leaving university admission open to all those possessing the baccalauréat, but would establish strict standards for continuation into the second cycle (essentially of graduate studies) at bac + 3 or 4. If they passed through the universities, corporation executives would probably be more likely to begin their careers in business and industry and not in the upper civil service. The existing system, whereby the individual must go through three grueling levels of selection for the grandes écoles, the grands corps and then the company itself, restricts access to top posts in business and industry to a privileged and self-perpetuating few.

7 Conclusion

I never negotiate with the state. I explain very clearly what I
want to do, why I want to do it and what the consequences of not
doing it will be. Then I wait for the government to agree.

Jacques Calvet, CEO, Peugeot-Citroën, 1984–97

The French education system has traditionally been concerned with
the transmission of a historically based culture; science, rationality,
and modernity, in other words the rationalist culture of the Enlight-
enment that formed the basis of the ideology of the Third Republic;
centralization, through which the state assures fairness, central planning and direction, and the extension of French culture over local-
isms and particularisms; and the meritocratic selection of elites.
Teaching was based heavily on the old Cartesian assumptions about
the separation of mind from the world, learning as the acquisition of
knowledge, and rationalism as the way of knowing. This, combined
with the Platonic idea that a just society prepares young people for
the occupations for which nature bests suits them, combined with a
modern developmentalism that argued that children pass through
stages of learning according to predetermined stages of biological
development. The result excluded societal, political, and historical
factors from the learning process and led to a mentality among educators that was hardly sympathetic to manual work and to technical
education.

Ironically, in a country where the humanities enjoyed the highest
prestige, part of the French elite including many industrialists were
educated in higher engineering schools such as the École polytechnique and its affiliates Mines and Ponts-et-Chaussées. These schools
were not exactly engineering schools in that they emphasized the
general sciences and the education of leaders of men rather than
technical specialization, and few graduates ever actually became

practising engineers. In this ethos, electrical engineering was considered acceptable because of its more abstract nature while mechanical and industrial engineering were considered too manual and practical and were left to lesser schools such as the Écoles d'arts et métiers. In the secondary lycées, future managers studied little science and received no technical education, only large doses of Greek and Latin, the humanities, and some math, science, and modern languages.

In the 1960s, theoretical mathematics replaced Latin as the *voie royale* into the grandes écoles but this subject bore little more relation to the real world than did the classics. As the technical grandes écoles continued to train for the elite public services rather than for the economy, many industrialists reached their position via the state bureaucracy. Thus the French elite was composed of graduates of engineering schools who were not really engineers, and businessmen who were not trained in business but in the state service. France was and still is unique in the world in the way it educates its senior management *cadres*.

The privileged position of the grandes écoles devalued the universities and this continues to be the case today. Though the latter were partially reformed in 1896 and 1969, higher education in France has never been reformed in its entirety. One result was that France suffered until recently from a chronic shortage of industrial engineers and technicians. This problem has been gradually resolved since the 1960s through the creation of additional schools and diplomas for engineers and technicians.

At the secondary level, the lycée has proved equally difficult to reform. In the early 1880s, the Third Republic introduced compulsory primary education to the age of thirteen, but reserved the lycées for the bourgeoisie. As the economy grew, many ordinary people needed post-elementary education for vocational reasons: to become teachers, skilled workers, technicians, clerks, and employees. Rather than opening the lycées to the common people, governments divided public education into four separate divisions: primary, secondary, higher, and technical. The primary system and the technical education division each had its own secondary and higher schools, and the secondary system had primary schools annexed to its lycées and collèges. In an educational apparatus in which nothing connected, each division had its own administration, hierarchy, clientele, and teacher training schools. The result was wasteful overlapping and continual infighting among the four "feudalities," particularly between the primary and technical divisions, which from the 1880s to 1940 vied for control over the higher primary schools.

Under the Third Republic the education system was designed to serve several clienteles, notably the bourgeoisie, the lower middle class, and the mass of working people. This resulted in a system that was segmented and parcelized both vertically and horizontally. The politicians of the Third Republic responded to rapid economic growth by creating intermediate technical schools, the écoles manuelles d'apprentissage and the écoles nationales professionnelles, during the 1880s without having a very clear idea of what technical education meant or the kind of schools they wanted. The primary education division argued that such schools should have mainly general programs and remain under the Ministry of Education, while the technical education division contended that they should be specialized and vocational in nature and should be placed under the Ministry of Industry and Commerce. While the latter ministry succeeded in winning control over intermediate technical schools in 1892 and 1900, it failed in its campaign to wrest control over several hundred higher primary schools from the Ministry of National Education. The higher primary schools provided a modern instruction to young people aged thirteen to fifteen and were so successful that they competed with the intermediate schools under Commerce as well as with the lycées under the secondary division. The struggle between the primary, secondary, and technical education divisions over the secondary education of the common people paralleled the church-state quarrel and was equally wasteful.

By the eve of the First World War the technical education division controlled a small but complete hierarchy of schools ranging from the higher primary to university level. It had become clear by then that technical education would be provided in schools rather than on the job, that they would train certain types of skilled workers and technicians rather than the mass of ordinary workers, and that they would remain largely separate from the mainstream of public education in France. While the technical education division cooperated closely with the mechanical, metallurgical, and electrical industries, it had little positive contact with the remainder of the education system or with other industries. This made economic and manpower planning for France as a whole extremely difficult.

After the acquisition of the écoles nationales professionnelles and the écoles pratiques in 1892 and 1900, the argument of AFDET and other defenders of the technical education division in favour of further expansion of intermediate technical education failed to carry the day. Many sectors of the French economy were composed of small and technologically backward firms with little need for school-trained engineers, technicians, and workers, notably in textiles, food processing, building, and various artisanal businesses. In the absence of a comprehensive policy of industrial development, the training of large numbers of skilled workers before the First World War would probably have led to unemployment rather than to increased economic activity. In any case the higher primary schools provided the solid intermediate skills in language, maths, science, civics, and some manual training that were potentially useful as a base for technical and vocational programs at the senior secondary level of the sort that began to appear in the 1960s. Their conversion in the early 1940s to collèges modernes, essentially second rank lycées, was a setback for French vocational training.[1]

The decision in 1920 to transfer the technical schools from the Ministry of Commerce to the Ministry of Education did not substantially weaken the autonomy of the technical education division, which obtained its own secretary of state and a strengthened administration. Although the feud between the divisions of technical education and primary education declined during the interwar period, technical education was threatened from many sides, particularly by the école unique movement which appeared after the First World War and which aimed to integrate the schools into a unified, comprehensive junior secondary school. The division managed to survive until the beginning of the Fifth Republic because it allied itself with other divisions in the education system, particularly with the secondary division, against the école unique, and because it had powerful protectors in the mechanical sectors of business and industry who believed that the educational bureaucrats were too ignorant of technico-scientific realities to understand technical education.

The technical education division reached its apogee under the Fourth Republic on the eve of its dissolution in 1960, with several hundred thousand students. In the centres d'apprentissage for workers (established under Vichy), the écoles pratiques, and the écoles nationales professionnelles for skilled workers and technicians, it had the makings of a national system of technical junior secondary and secondary schools closely linked to the mechanical industries. All of these schools selected their own students and were able to provide them with skills that enabled many to advance on the job to supervisory positions as technicians and even engineers.

Right-centre governments under the Fifth Republic from 1958 to 1981, were intent on the modernization of the economy and society, and they moved to consolidate and to integrate a fragmented education system in line with the requirements of rapid industrialization along Fordist lines. This period witnessed three waves of reform that transformed French education: in 1959–60, in 1966–67, and in 1975. In 1960 the school leaving age was raised to sixteen and the technical education division was disbanded, its various branches assimilated into the general education system. A comprehensive junior secondary school (*collège unique*) was established gradually between 1963 and 1975, which made it possible to transfer technical and vocational training to senior high school. Accordingly, the collèges techniques (écoles pratiques), the écoles professionnelles, and other intermediate technical schools were integrated into the new lycées techniques designed to train technicians, and the centres d'apprentissage were transformed into collèges d'enseignement technique for workers, known today as the lycées professionnels.

The reforms of the 1960s and 1970s thus eliminated the varied schools in the first cycle of secondary education and introduced a reasonably unified 6/4/3 system: six years of elementary school, four years of junior secondary education in the collège, and three years of senior secondary school divided into general, technical, and vocational streams in descending order of prestige. The new system opened up secondary education and the first cycle of higher education to the average person, but it was far from democratic and far from efficacious in turning out skilled workers and technicians. The creation of the école unique placed the technical and the vocational schools in the second cycle of secondary education and made them dependent for students on guidance counselors in the new junior secondary schools. The centres d'apprentissage became the collèges d'enseignement technique, which soon had to accept students from the *collèges*, frequently as young as thirteen years of age who did not have the academic ability to complete the course of study. Ironically, the reforms that were supposedly to create a democratic junior secondary school and improve vocational training for the working classes by upgrading vocational training to the second cycle of secondary education instead turned the new collèges d'enseignement technique into dead-end schools for weaker students, many of whom found themselves excluded from further education and from the job market because they did not have diplomas or because their diplomas lacked prestige or were poorly adapted to the job market.

Moreover, the collèges d'enseignement technique were partially cut off from contacts with industry after the dissolution of the technical education division in 1960. Although some attempts were made to upgrade programs, the schools were inadequately financed and continued to teach skills that were too specialized. In many ways this suited the requirements of the Fordist regime that demanded a minority of highly trained skilled workers and a majority of narrowly specialized and docile assembly line operatives. The conservative governments of the 1960s and 1970s were more concerned with the training of technicians and engineers than with workers, but even here they encountered setbacks especially in the education of technicians. The new lycées techniques had so many organizational problems that they actually lost students during the 1960s. Fouchet's introduction of the technical baccalauréat in 1967 was designed to enhance the prestige of the lycées techniques. It led either to the workplace or to the first cycle of higher education – to the new Sections de technicien supérieur and the Instituts universitaires de technologie – which provided the technical stream access for the first time to higher education. The STS and IUT were introduced to train senior technicians. In the early years they had difficulty placing their graduates as business and industry continued to promote skilled workers on the job instead of hiring school-trained technicians.

The remarkable growth of the STS and the IUT since the early 1980s has been one of the most important features of the educational history of the past twenty years. This, and the creation of many engineering schools and programs had by the 1990s overcome the chronic penury of technicians and engineers in France and had even led to some unemployment among them by the middle of the decade. As the lycées techniques increasingly prepared students for the STS and IUT, they graduated fewer and fewer technicians for the marketplace and were integrated during the 1980s into the general lycées as lycées d'enseignement général et technologique (LEGT). This ended the old association of technical and vocational education in France and left the lycées professionnels on their own as the low-status schools training skilled workers and factory technicians. When dramatic changes occurred in techniques of industrial production during the 1970s and 1980s, with rapid advances in information technology and in computer-aided manufacturing, the French labour force was poorly prepared to adapt quickly.

Socialist governments in the 1980s took vigorous action to redress the situation, restructuring industry and reforming technical and vocational education, introducing the lycées professionnels and the baccalauréat professionnel in 1985, and restructuring the programs of the certificat d'aptitude professionnelle and the brevet d'enseignement professionnel in close cooperation with business and industry. The professional baccalauréat was an important departure in two ways: it marked the first time that a baccalauréat was awarded in vocational studies and the first time a diploma was designed from the outset to include work placements in industry in which the company and firm were considered legitimate places of instruction.[2] Even under the old technical education division prior to 1960, characterized by close relations between the mechanical-metallurgical industries, work placements were rare. But during the 1980s they became a standard feature of the programs of the Sections de technicien supérieur, the Instituts universitaires de technologie, and the lycées professionnels. Despite problems in reconciling conflicting methods and goals of school and firm, twenty years of experience has enabled these schools to develop well integrated work placements averaging sixteen to twenty-four weeks a year. The problem remained that the lycées professionnels selected the best students in the vocational stream to become professional *bacheliers* and then factory technicians, for whom there was considerable demand in industry, leaving the rest of the students with only the CAP-BEP or no certification at all in an even more difficult position, thanks to growing deindustrialization and unemployment in the 1970s and 1980s.

Lionel Jospin, the education minister from 1988 to 1992, acknowledged these problems. In a new law in 1989, he declared that every young person has the right to leave secondary school in possession of a skill. This has led to diversification and further decentralization of the education system, notably the expansion of non-academic forms of training such as apprenticeship and continuing education, new work-study programs, new forms of local input and control, and various other reforms frequently borrowed from the German system of vocational training. These programs lead to a revitalized CAP and have brought about a sharp drop in the number of young people leaving school without credentials during the last decade from 12 to 5 per cent (100,000 to 40,000), a significant achievement. Jospin also introduced reforms to establish the lycées professionnels as genuine senior secondary schools to give them some semblance of equality with the LEGT and to stop the premature streaming of young people from the collèges (junior secondary schools) to the lycées professionnels.

Despite their rhetoric, the Socialists are not very different from their opponents on the right in their approach to democratization; both sides accept streaming and the existence of the grandes écoles, major obstacles to the equality of educational opportunity. Governments of the left and right have sought ways to increase the prestige of the lycées professionnels, to associate them with success rather than failure, to make them more equal to the LEGT, to decentralize and lighten programs, to diversify forms of education, and to adapt them more closely to the requirements of business and industry, but they have not altered the essential inferiority of these schools. The students, of working class and often immigrant origin, face the difficulties of residential segregation, social and educational marginalization, and poor employment prospects. Women in these schools are often confined to a narrow set of job outlets and also experience higher than average unemployment. On the other hand, vocational training gives these groups an opportunity to acquire diplomas and offers the possibility of further education that provides improved access to the job market. The introduction of the bac pro and expanded apprenticeship and continuing education programs, better teaching methods and smaller classes, plus the increasing diversification and decentralization of education have provided improved opportunities for young people of working-class backgrounds since the 1980s, though many problems of racism and gender inequality remain.

In the sphere of economic planning, Socialist governments during the 1980s encouraged restructuring and market liberalization as a means of forcing industry to modernize and to compete in a global economy. This involved reversing their old hostility toward business and industry and working to assure the collaboration of business, labour, and government in encouraging the evolution from a crisis-ridden, low-skills Fordist regime toward a high-skills, high value-added economy. The evolution of systems of production from an industrial logic to a services logic meant training people less in specific skills than in more flexible approaches to the job: the ability to cooperate with others, to think strategically, and to take initiative in response to challenges. Such qualities are difficult to define and to build into formal training programs. To do so, the French abandoned their classroom approach to vocational training in favour of the German model combining in-school and on-the-job training, with emphasis on educating adaptable workers possessing in-depth skills.[3]

All this has accompanied a remarkable rapprochement between parties of the left, academics, and business groups. Yet there are still some signs of strain. Industrial groups, notably the Conseil national du patronat français, AFDET, and other associations, now heavily involved in education, warn of the dangers of the "uniformization" of education and the move away from specialization, which they point to as one of the main reasons for the decline of industrial culture. They point to the gradual disappearance of the baccalauréat de technicien and the brevet d'enseignement professionnel as diplomas leading to the workforce, and they fear that the bac pro may go the same way, ceasing to train much-needed factory technicians for industry and leading only to further studies. They also criticize the new Instituts universitaires de formation des maîtres, established by Jospin in 1991 to consolidate teacher-training. The IUFM absorbed the excellent ENNAs, which had trained professors for the vocational schools since the Liberation period. As a result, recruiting good teachers for the lycées professionnels and for apprenticeship programs has been a problem to the present day, undermining the "active pedagogy" of the vocational schools. Such changes reawaken the old fear, dating to the nineteenth century, of academic bureaucrats who fail to understand the needs of industry and who turn everything into a sterile academic exercise. One must note, however, that the position of businessmen and industrialists tends at times to be contradictory; they stress the importance of avoiding early specialization, of teaching flexibility and adaptability for a constantly changing industrial technology, but at the same time they continue to demand specialists and to distrust educators.

Ironically, just as industrialists have begun to play an active role in technical education, the number of people employed by industry has declined steeply, from almost two-thirds to around a third of the workforce. One aspect of deindustrialization in France has been the rapid rise of the tertiary sector. Around two-thirds of students in vocational programs train for work in this sector, which leads to considerable competition for jobs among students holding general, technical, and vocational credentials in virtually the same fields. This problem is particularly severe among young women who are found in a limited number of occupations. This overlapping of programs and credentials raises the question as to whether a unified lycée with diversified programs (as in Scandinavian and other European countries) would be a more democratic and more economical option. The growing importance of the tertiary sector enhances the importance of a core curriculum of general subjects, which could be taught more easily and more cheaply in general secondary schools than in vocational ones.

Most of those who have studied the question of whether France should introduce a unified high school have been critical of the idea. In the early 1980s, Antoine Prost advised Alain Savary against the idea, if only because it meant that the lycées, the least successful pedagogically of French secondary schools, would absorb the technical and professional lycées, the most innovative and creative. In the following years the lycées proceeded to absorb the lycées techniques, reminiscent of their absorption between 1937 and 1941 of the higher primary schools and of the lycées modernes in 1963. The general lycées always seem to prevail over smaller more creative rivals, despite the many defects in their programs and approaches. The response of lycée students to ministerial questionnaires, followed by widespread demonstrations and strikes in the autumn of 1998, has demonstrated once again the long-standing dissatisfaction of lycée students with the lack of activities, the formality of instruction, the overloaded programs, the unwillingness of the "system" to listen, the cramming for exams, and

the frenetic atmosphere of the annual June examinations for the baccalauréat and other diplomas (four million examinations in just over one
month).

Despite the persistence of problems, it is fair to conclude that the
French have made substantial progress in training skilled workers
and technicians and that there is a reasonable consensus as to what
the problems are and considerable willingness on the part of all
parties to explore means to solve them. There is still controversy as to
the suitability of the grandes écoles and the grands corps to form
France's elite in business, industry, and government. Pierre Bourdieu
and others speak of a well-entrenched "state nobility" using its privileged position to acquire the prestigious diplomas necessary to maintain domination over the best jobs in the economy and society. This
elite functioned fairly well in the highly-structured hierarchical organization of Fordism and Taylorism with its close connection between
state and business, but has adapted more slowly to the competitive
challenges of flexible production and participatory management. In
recent years, French businessmen have nevertheless rejected *dirigisme*
and have accepted the free market economy. They have introduced
more informal forms of production and have provided more autonomy and responsibility for workers and employees while playing an
active role in the education system. They are also showing signs of an
augmented entrepreneurial spirit, and recruit and promote executives on the basis of ability as well as education and connections.
Increasingly, French executives competing on an international scale
are judged by their successes in improving the profitability of their
companies. The number of grande école graduates passing through
the grands corps is showing signs of declining as more and more as-
piring young executives seek training abroad. The best positions are
no longer automatically reserved for the academically most successful graduates but sometimes go to those further down in the rankings
who are more likely to produce good corporate results.

There is little doubt that the grandes écoles will survive, but they
should be transferred to the second cycle of the universities where
they can draw on a broader clientele. The cours préparatoires and the
grands corps should be abolished along with the *concours* as the exclusive route toward senior executive posts. Whatever happens, the
international executive is likely to become increasingly homogenous
in style and outlook and the French "difference" less marked. At the
beginning of the twenty-first century most of the big French companies, whether nationalized, privatized, or some combination of the
two, bear little resemblance to the bloated, overstaffed, and state-
dependent corporations of twenty years ago. This is a reflection of the

determination of business, labour, and the state to transform the French economy into a high-skilled, high-value-added accumulation regime.

Bernard Charlot suggests that the vocational stream may well become the *filière de choix* in the future, for this most disdained of all branches has managed the difficult task of combining general and technical studies with practical exercises, of coordinating work-study programs with business and industry, and of preparing young people for the workplace while maintaining reasonably high intellectual standards.[4] Pierre Bourdieu notes that technical and vocational education avoid a purely cognitive approach to education, emphasizing instead the situated character of understanding and communication, the importance of human agency, and the integration in practice of agent, world, and activity. This opens the way to a renewed interest in linking education to the workplace and to a variety of human activities.[5] Ideally, technical education narrows the gap between conception and execution and sees knowledge not as set of abstractions but as responding to challenges in the real world, as achieving projects in cooperation with others.

Despite the rapid rate of change in the economy and in education, studies have shown that young French people know more and are better educated today than they were a generation ago. The French have managed to gear their education system to serve the economy while retaining standards and "a complement of general culture," though there may be a danger in the fact that traditional standards are rapidly giving way to utilitarian goals. Whereas a generation ago economic development was seriously hampered by a poorly adapted education system producing too few skilled workers, technicians, and engineers, the French education system of the 1990s meets the demand for skilled personnel in almost all fields.

In the half century since the Second World War, France has developed from a conservative, semi-rural society in which the great majority of the population had only a primary education, to a highly developed modern one with a remarkably well-educated and well-trained citizenry and labour force. Technical and vocational education, once confined to an enclave within the education system, now permeate the entire system. Business and industry, long isolated from education, today play a major role in educational decision making. Though there are problems associated with such a rapid pace of change, many believe that the adaptation of the education system to the economy under the Fifth Republic provides at least a partial explanation for the revival of French business and industry in recent years.

Notes

INTRODUCTION

1 Dubar, *La Socialisation, Construction des identités sociales et professionnelles*; Boltanski, *Les Cadres*.
2 Kerr, Dunlop, Harbison and Myers, *Industrialism and Industrial Man*, 37.
3 Lane, *Management and Labour in Europe*, 63.
4 Charlot and Figeat, *Histoire de la formation des ouvriers en France*; Tanguy, *L'Enseignement professionnel en France* and *Quelle formation pour les ouvriers et les employés en France?*; Pelpel and Troger, *Histoire de l'Enseignement technique*. See also two short works: Solaux, *Les lycées professionnels*, and Bouyx, *L'enseignement technologique et professionnel*.

CHAPTER ONE

1 Weisz, *The Emergence of Modern Universities in France*; Burney, *Toulouse et son Université*.
2 Belhoste, Delmedico, and Picon, eds., *La formation polytechnicienne 1794–1994*. Shinn, *L'École Polytechnique*. Smith, *The École normale supérieure in the Third Republic*.
3 Ben-David, *The Scientist's Role in Society*. Paul, *From Knowledge to Power*.
4 Day, *Education for the Industrial World*, and Day, *Les Écoles d'Arts et Métiers*.
5 Fontenon and Grelon, eds, *Les professeurs du Conservatoire national des arts et métiers 1794–1955*, vol. 1: 23–57; vol. 2: 311–321. See also Fontenon and Grelon, eds., *Les Cahiers d'Histoire du CNAM*.

6 The Guizot Law inaugurated a period of rapid growth in primary education in France, starting with around three million students in 1834 to 4,336,00 in 1863 and 5,526,000 in 1887. Grew & Harrigan, *School, State and Society,* 55–60.

7 AN F 17 8701–8731, L'Enseignement secondaire spécial. Day, "Technical and Professional Education in France," 177–201.

8 Pelpel and Troger, *Histoire de l'enseignement technique,* 15–16. Another 111 were employed in the liberal professions and 21 as domestics. In 1847 France had 2,494 steam engines; in 1800 England had already 5,000.

9 An investigation by the Paris Chamber of Commerce in 1860 revealed that little progress had been made despite the 1851 law: of 25,540 apprentices under sixteen, only 4,523 had contracts. Gréard, *Des écoles d'apprentis, Mémoire adressé à M. le préfet de la Seine.*

10 Fontenon and Grelon, eds, *Les professeurs du Conservatoire national des arts et métiers,* vol. 1: 23–57, vol. 2: 311–21.

11 Ministère de l'Agriculture, du Commerce, et des Travaux Publics, Commission de l'enseignement professionnel, *Enquête sur l'enseignement professionnel ou recueil de dépositions faites en 1863 et 1864 devant la commission de l'enseignement professionnel.* See also *Rapport et Notes,* and Morin and Tresca, *De l'organisation de l'enseignement industriel et de l'enseignement professionnel.*

12 P. P. Pompée, director of the école professionnelle d'Ivry and M. J. Marguerin, director of the École Turgot of Paris, were spokesmen for this position. See Pompée, *Études sur l'éducation professionnelle en France,* 331, and the following note.

13 Bader, director of the vocational school of Mulhouse, took this position. Ministère de l'Agriculture, *Enquête sur l'enseignement professionnel,* vol. 1, dépositions: 189.

14 Morin & Tresca, *De l'organisation de l'enseignement industriel,* 42–4. Guettier, "Étude sur l'instruction industrielle," 21–48. Guettier preferred the term *université du travail.*

15 Prévot, *L'Enseignement technique chez les Frères des Écoles Chrétiennes.*

16 Ministère de l'Agriculture, *Enquête sur l'enseignement professionnel.*

17 Legoux, *Du compagnon au technicien, L'École Diderot et l'évolution des qualifications 1873–1972, sociologie de l'enseignement technique français.*

18 Gréard, *Des Écoles d'apprentis, Mémoire adressé à M. le préfet de la Seine.*

19 AN F 17 14364, Écoles municipales professionnelles de Paris (seven for boys and for girls), 1890–1900. École Diderot (1873); École d'horlogerie (watch-making) (1880); École d'Alembert (1882), cabinet making and typography; École Bernard Palissy (1883), ceramics and sculpture; École Germain Pilon (1883), ornamental drawing and mechanical drawing; École Dorian (1886), fitting, forging, lathing, carpentry; École Boulle

(1886), furniture-making; Estienne (1887), printing; plus six schools for girls on the rue Fondary (1882), rue de Poitou (1882), rue Bouret (1884), rue Ganneron 1884, rue Bossuet, and rue de la Tombe-Issoire. See Astier and Cuminal, *L'enseignement technique industriel et commercial*, 310.

20 École Turgot (1837), J.-B. Say, Colbert (1868), Lavoisier (1872), Arago (1880), and Chaptal for young men; Sophie Germain and Edgard Quinet for young women. These had about 6,000 students at the turn of the century.

21 Briand and Chapoulie, *Les Collèges du Peuple*.

22 Mallet, *La nouvelle classe ouvrière*, 35–6. Legoux, *Du compagnon au technicien*, 106.

23 Noiriel, *Workers in French Society*, 101.

24 Charlot and Figeat, *Histoire de la Formation des ouvriers*, 238–9. Noiriel, *Workers in French Society*, 58, 73–8, 99.

25 Pasquier, *L'Enseignement professionnel en France*, 63. Nadaud was a former mason from the Creuse and the author of *Mémoires de Léonard* and *L'Histoire des classes ouvrières en Angleterre*.

26 Martel and Ferrand, *Écoles primaires supérieures, Écoles d'apprentissage et écoles nationales professionnelles, Mémoires et documents scolaires*, 51. See also Charmasson, Lelorrain, and Ripa, *L'enseignement technique de la Révolution à nos jours*, 36.

27 Gréard, *Mémoire adressé à M. le préfet de la Seine*.

28 Buisson, *L'Enseignement primaire supérieur et professionnel*, 24.

29 Ollendorf, "Rapport présenté à la commission mixte," 109.

30 AN F 17 14350, Note sur les transformations d'écoles primaires supérieures en Écoles pratiques de commerce et d'industrie. Pasquier, *L'Enseignement professionnel*, 126–33; Guinot, *Formation professionnelle*, 162. Charlot & Figeat, *Histoire de la formation des ouvriers*, 155. Of the sixty-nine EPCI, fifty-six were for boys and thirteen for girls, 10,466 and 2,513 students in 1910.

31 AN F 17 14348–14356, Écoles nationales professionnelles, F 17 14350, "Rattachement des écoles professionnelles au Ministère de Commerce, 1880–1906."

32 AN F 17 14350, Minister of Public Instruction to the Minister of Commerce, 7 October 1893.

33 AN F 17 14356, Ecole nationale professionnelle de Nantes. Bayet, director of primary education, report of 31 August 1898. Letter from E. Corre, director of the school to the Academy Rector, 6 October 1898, 28 August 1898.

34 AN F 17 14356, Nantes. Academy Inspector report, 2 September 1898.

35 *Journal officiel de la République française*, Chambre des Députés, session of 15 Feb. 1895, 315 et suiv. Louis-Modeste Leroy, *Vers l'éducation nouvelle*, 134, 190.

36 *Journal officiel de la République française,* Chambre des Députés, session of
   1 Feb. 1899. F 17 14350, Note du ministère du commerce, s.d. [1899].
   Charmasson et al., *L'enseignement technique,* 50.

37 *Journal officiel,* Chambre des Députés, 27–28 Feb. 1899, 507–22, and
   24 Nov. 1899 and 31 Jan. 1900. The Senate vote was 203 to 44 and the budget was raised from 340,000 francs to 423,000. *Bulletin de l'enseignement
   technique* 2 (Jan. 27 1900), 22–51, 151–68.

38 The school at Cluny was the old École normale de l'enseignement spécial, converted in 1891 to an école pratique de contremaîtres and ten
   years later to an école d'arts et métiers. AN F 17 14319, Note sur les prin-
   cipales améliorations apportées au régime des écoles d'arts et métiers,
   26 February 1901.

39 Ministère du Commerce, *L'enseignement technique en France. Bulletin de
   l'enseignement technique* 2 (Jan. 27, 1900), 202, and 24 (Dec. 8, 1900), 463–5.

40 In 1900, there were thirteen écoles pratiques, four ENP, four écoles d'arts
   et métiers, and fourteen écoles de commerce.

41 *Bulletin de l'enseignement technique* 1 (Jan. 8, 1898), 1–23; and 4 (Mar. 16,
   1912), 76–9. The *Bulletin* was published by the technical education department of the Ministry of Industry and Commerce, 1898–14. Leroy, *Vers
   l'éducation nouvelle,* 189–90.

42 Pasquier, *L'enseignement professionnel,* 132–3. The section at Châlons
   trained sixty teachers from 1891 to 1906. A commercial section was created for men at the École des hautes études commerciales in Paris and for
   women in Le Havre (Lyon).

43 Morin and Henri Tresca, 428–79. See also Ministère du Commerce, Conseil supérieur de l'enseignement technique, *Rapport sur l'organisation de
   l'enseignement technique,* 29.

44 Leroy, *Vers l'éducation nouvelle,* 187.

45 *Technique, Art, Science,* 273–4 (1973), 10–14. AFDET published the *Revue de
   l'enseignement technique* from 1910 to 1913, followed by *La Formation professionnelle* from 1919–20, *Technique, Art, Science* from 1946 to 1977, and the
   Bulletin de l'enseignement technique since 1954. The name of AFDET was
   later changed to Association pour le développement de l'enseignement
   technique.

46 Le Chartier, *La France et son Parlement,* 387–460. Of 114 deputies who gave
   technical education as a priority and/or were active in the technical education movement, seventy-eight belonged to right-centre parliamentary
   parties (fifty-one Républicains, twenty-seven Gauche démocratique),
   twenty-three to the left-centre or left (Radicals thirteen, Socialists ten), and
   thirteen were independents. Placide Astier, Gustave Dron, Fernand
   Dubief, Arthur Groussier, Maruéjols, Jules Méline, G. Mesureur, Henry
   Michel, Alexandre Millerand, Marc Réville, Maurice Sibelle, Jules
   Siegfried, and Constant Verlot were active in the Commerce group.

Mesureur (1895), Siegfried (1897–98), Maruéjols (1898–99), Millerand (1899–02), and Dubief (1905) were ministers of commerce.

47 Louis Modeste Aurèle Leroy, known as Modeste Leroy, the son of a businessman, had a doctorate in law, was deputy from the Eure (Gauche démocratique) from 1893 to 1919, never became a minister, and published *Vers l'éducation nouvelle* and *L'éducation nationale au XXᵉ siècle.*

48 Leroy, *L'Éducation nationale*, 14. *Technique, Arts, Sciences*, 273–4 (1973), 11.

49 Guinot, supports the Commerce thesis that the higher primary schools directed their students toward general rather than vocational studies, orienting them toward bureaucratic rather than productive positions. See Guinot, *Formation professionnelle*, 164.

50 *Bulletin de l'enseignement technique* 2 (Jan. 22, 1898), 19.

51 Pasquier, *L'enseignement professionnel*, 131.

52 Leblanc, *La Réforme des Écoles primaires supérieures*, 11–13, 19, 199–201.

53 Leroy, *L'Éducation nationale au XXᵉ siècle*, 42–3. See also Legoux, *Du compagnon au technicien*, 177–9, 240, who discusses the Commerce group's control over the École Diderot during the 1890s under Emile Kern who turned the school into a mini-factory with very long hours in workshops and much reduced general studies.

54 Leblanc, *La Réforme des écoles primaires supérieures*, 19, 199–201.

55 Ibid., 11–12.

56 Briand and Chapoulie, *Les collèges du peuple*, 166, 273. For 1906 Astier and Cuminal in *L'enseignement technique*, 248–9, list 221 higher primary schools for boys and 111 for girls (322 schools) with 42,393 students (26,930 boys and 15,463 girls). In 1908, Guinot notes 236 EPS for boys with 28,360 pupils, of whom 3,620 were enrolled in industrial sections, 1,351 in commercial sections, and 557 in agricultural sections. Of the 139 girls' schools, 222 out of 19,214 pupils were in industrial sections and 742 in business. See Guinot, *Formation Professionnel*, 164.

57 AN F 17 14350, Note sur les transformations d'écoles primaires supérieures en écoles pratiques de commerce et d'industrie. Note de M. Leblanc relative au projet de rattachement des ENP au Ministère du Commerce, 1900, fearing that the fifty higher primary schools with advanced vocational programs might be annexed to the ENPs.

58 Ibid. Some 351 became machinists, mechanics, metal fitters and turners, and assemblymen (mécaniciens, ajusteurs, tourneurs, monteurs), seventy became woodworkers (modeleurs, menuisiers, ébénistes), sixty-three became draftsmen (dessinateurs), sixty-two became iron workers (chaudronniers, armuriers, fondeurs), forty-eight became electricians, thirty-five became textile workers, 246 were employed in business (these came mainly from the écoles pratiques de commerce), and forty-two worked in miscellaneous industries (bâtiment, travaux publics, horlogers, lunetiers, chimistes, etc.).

59 C. Copland Perry, *L'enseignement technique français*, 84–8.

60 AN F 17 14350, *Statistique graphique des écoles primaires supérieures de garçons*, 1901, and Leblanc's report of 1900. See also Legoux, *Du compagnon au technicien*, 88. In 1890, 29.4 per cent entered industry (31 per cent counting railways), 20.6 per cent commerce or banking, 11 per cent agriculture, around 7 per cent worked in public services and teaching, 22 per cent continued their studies, and 6 per cent entered government service.

61 Nye, *Science in the Provinces, Scientific Communities and Provincial Leadership in France, 1860–1930*. Grelon, "Les universités et la formation des ingénieurs," 65–88.

62 C. Copland Perry, *L'enseignement technique français*, 85.

63 Briand & Chapoulie, *Les Collèges du Peuple*, 220–5. Radicals were split between the Commerce group (Placide Astier) and Public Instruction (Buisson) and were in a good position to bring about a compromise.

64 Leroy, *L'éducation nationale au XXᵉ siècle*, 89–90. *Bulletin de l'enseignement technique* 15 (Mar. 16, 1912), 76–9.

65 Châlons-sur-Marne (1803), Angers (1811), Aix-en-Provence (1843), Cluny (1900), Lille (1901), Paris (1912), and Bordeaux (1964).

66 *Bulletin de l'enseignement technique*, 17 (1914), 212–3. Charmasson et al., *L'Enseignement technique*, 57.

67 Ministère du Commerce, *Rapport sur la situation de l'enseignement technique*. Cohendy provided the following figures, cited by Guinot p. 165: écoles pratiques, 9,901; ENPs, 1,276; Paris vocational schools, 3,027; municipal and private schools and courses, 5,000; for a total of 19,204. Cohendy and Guinot left out the higher primary vocational sections (7,000), the écoles d'arts et métiers and related schools (2,500), the applied science institutes (2,500), and schools under ministries other than Commerce and Public Instruction, such as Agriculture (3000), Public Works, Army, etc. The Cohendy-Guinot estimate of 19,204 is too low – the correct figure is over 30,000. For an estimate on the years 1906–10, see Charlot and Figeat, *Histoire de la formation des ouvriers*, 161. For 1913, Astier and Cuminal, *L'Enseignement technique*, 444; and the *Bulletin de l'enseignement technique*, previous note.

68 Astier and Cuminal, *L'enseignement technique*, 444.

69 Charlot and Figeat, *Histoire de la formation des ouvriers*, 139–62.

70 Ministère du Commerce, de l'Industrie, des Postes et des Télégraphes, *Rapport sur la situation de l'enseignement technique en France en 1904*, procès-verbaux des séances. Also *Bulletin de l'enseignement technique* 8 (1905), 465–556, 569–632. As many as 122 private associations offered 3,593 courses with 80,000 auditors; fifty-six employer associations offered 130 courses with 3,000 auditors, and 408 workingmen's unions welcomed 12,000 auditors.

71 Guinot estimates that no more than 50,000 of the 95,000 got anything out of these courses but provides no evidence to justify his conclusion. Combining 20,000 and 50,000 he estimates 70,000 of 874,941 in the workforce received vocational education, or 8 per cent. See Guinot, *Formation professionnelle*, 165. A more likely figure is around 87,000 of 874,941 or 10 per cent.

72 Grew and Harrigan, *School, State, and Society*, 91–110.

CHAPTER TWO

1 Guinot, *Formation professionnelle*, 184, 197.

2 *Formation professionnelle* 26 (1920), 114. Millerand had said: "Il serait déplorable que, comme parfois des personnes imprudentes ou trop pressées en ont manifesté l'intention, l'Université se proposât d'absorber l'enseignement technique. L'Université n'y gagnerait rien et l'enseignement technique risquerait d'y perdre tout, je veux dire l'originalité qui est sa force et sa raison d'être." ("It would be deplorable for the Ministry of Public Instruction to absorb technical education, as some imprudent people in a hurry have advocated. Public Instruction would gain nothing and technical education would lose everything, including that originality which is its strength and its reason for being.")

3 *Formation professionnelle* 26 (1920), 74, 116.

4 *Formation professionnelle* 25 (1920), 2.

5 *Formation professionnelle* 26 (1920), 66–7.

6 Guinot, *Formation professionnelle* 194. Charlot and Figeat, *Histoire de la Formation des ouvriers*, 244–50.

7 *Formation professionnelle* 26 (1920), 85.

8 *Journal officiel de la République française*, Sénat, sessions of 15 June and 25 July 1920; Chambre des Députés, sessions of 7 and 15 June 1920, cited in *Formation professionnelle* 26 (1920), 86–123, especially 116–19.

9 AN F 17 17843, Ministère de l'Éducation Nationale, Conseil supérieur de l'enseigenement technique, session of July 1941.

10 *Formation professionnelle* 26 (1920), 119.

11 Legoux, *Du compagnon au technicien*, 491–3.

12 AN F 17 17844, Conseil supérieur de l'enseignement technique, session of 22 December 1928.

13 AN F 17 17844, Conseil supérieur de l'enseignement technique, procès-verbaux des réunions, séance du 28 novembre 1922. By 1922 the Education ministry had already transformed twenty-one higher primary schools into écoles jumelées and the primary division had offered thirty-five higher primary schools to the technical education division.

14 AN F 17 17844, Conseil supérieur de l'enseignement technique, procès-verbaux des séances du 20 décembre 1934, 4–6.

15 Les Compagnons, *L'Université nouvelle*. See also Garcia, *L'École unique*, 1994, and Talbott, *The Politics of Educational Reform*.

16 Les Compagnons, *L'Université nouvelle*, vol. I, 64–9, 95–115.

17 Zoretti, *Éducation, un essai d'organisation démocratique*. His ideas were adopted by the Confédération générale du travail: XXe congrès national, Lyon, September 1919. *Compte rendu des travaux*, 325–29.

18 André Duval (pseudonym of Paul Lapie), "Esquisse d'une réforme générale de notre enseignement national," *Revue pédagogique*, 80, 2 (Feb. 1922), 79–101; and Paul Lapie, *Pédagogie française*, 240–73; and *L'École et les écoliers*, Paris: Alcan, 1923. Briand and Chapoulie, *Les Collèges du Peuple*, 402–07.

19 AN F 17 17499. H. Bergson, speech to the Académie des sciences morales et politiques, November 1923.

20 Terral, *Profession: professeur*. See also Vial, *Trois Siècles d'histoire de l'enseignement secondaire*.

21 AN F 17 17499, Paul Crouzet (inspecteur de l'Académie de Paris), Note demandée par Monsieur le Ministre, sur l'état de la réforme après les votes du Conseil supérieur, Feb. 1, 1923. Crouzet was Bréard's main adviser in the formulation of the project.

22 AN F 17 17499, *Politica*, Sept. 23, 1923, 516–27.

23 Chambre de Députés, 22 juin 1923, *Journal Officiel*, June 23, 1923, no. 81, 3124.

24 AN F 17 17499, Association des professeurs des langues vivantes de l'enseignement public, Sept. 29, 1921.

25 AN F 17 17499. The Chambres de Commerce reporting were: Alais, Nov. 9, 1921; Bordeaux, Dec. 13, 1922; Carcassonne, Nov. 8, 1923; Chambéry, Aug. 3, 1923; Dijon, Dec. 5, 1921; Lille, Oct. 8, 1921, and Nov. 11, 1921; Lyons, Nov. 1921; Montpellier, April 11, 1922; Paris, July 6, 1921, Nov. 10 and 25, 1921; Perpignan, Nov. 22, 1921; Saumur, Nov. 10, 1921; Tours, Nov. 14, 1921. Comité central des Houillères de France, Nov. 23, 1921; UIMM, Dec. 15, 1921; Association nationale d'expansion économique, industrielle, commerciale, agricole, July 6, 1923; Chambre syndicale des forces hydrauliques et de l'électro-métallurgie, Oct. 22, 1921; Chambre syndicale des Chaudronniers et fondeurs de France, Nov. 3, 1922; Confédération des Travailleurs Intellectuels, Jan. 25, 1923 (sided with Chambéry and Carcassonne). Syndicat Médical de Paris, Jan. 3, 1923; Union des associations d'anciens élèves des lycées et collèges français, July 12, 1921; Congrès de directeurs et professeurs des écoles primaires supérieures de France, Sept. 16, 1921.

26 Ibid., UIMM, Dec. 15, 1921. Author's translation.

27 F 17 17499, Comité central des Houillères de France, Nov. 23, 1921.

28 F 17 17499. The Confédération des Travailleurs Intellectuels, founded in 1920, representing 120 organizations of artists, writers, journalists,

teachers, etc., defended modern studies and opposed the obsession with educating "les chefs."

29 Bourdieu, *The State Nobility*, 272–315.

30 AN F 17 17499, Conseil supérieur de l'Instruction publique, séances du Jan. 15, 20 and 23, 1923.

31 In 1902: Latin-Greek, Latin-languages, Latin-sciences, and moderne.

32 AN F 17 17500, Notes sur les mesures prises pour réaliser l'École unique, Feb. 18, 1926.

33 Legay, "Histoire de l'enseignement technique, 1895–1960," 19–57. The directors were: Louis Bouquet (1895–1907), Henri Gabelle (1907–15), Henri Tenot (1915–20), Edmond Labbé (1920–33), H. Luc (1933–44), Paul Le Rolland (1944–48), Albert Buisson (1948–60).

34 *Un Grand Commis de l'État, M. Edmond Labbé*, Paris, 1946.

35 Poincaré abolished all secretaryships in 1926 as an economy measure. Four were reestablished in 1929, including technical education. The last secretary of technical education of the interwar period was Alfred Jules-Julien whose term was the longest, 2 1/2 years, 1935–37. The position was then abolished and not reestablished until André Morice was appointed in 1947. *L'Enseignement technique*, 29 (Jan.–Mar. 1961), 21–24; 63 (July–Sept. 1969), 33.

36 *L'Enseignement technique*, 63 (July–Sept. 1969), 24–8.

37 *Recueil des discours prononcé par E. Labbé* (Paris: AFDET, 1937), 8, 76, 90–117, 206, 539, 551.

38 Legoux, *Du compagnon au technicien*, 197–201, 273–4. Prost, *L'Enseignement en France*, 314, 319–20.

39 *Recueil des discours prononcé par E. Labbé* (Paris: AFDET, 1937), 8, 76, 90–117, 206, 539, 551. "We talk about occupations, they reply 'culture.' We explain the needs of French industry: foreign competition, precision mechanics, optics, the cutlery industry that we must defend, create even. But they know only one word: 'Culture! culture! culture! culture! That accounts for everything.'"

40 Planté, *Un grand seigneur de la politique*, 28. "At first view he appeared uncultivated, stubborn, rude in his manners, direct in his relationships. He had the air of a senior foreman ready to grab his workers by the collar to explain their job to them, which he knew better than they. Instead one discovered a refined, cultivated and widely read person interested in everything. His goal was to design a sort of parallel public education system ranging from humble trade schools to the learned chairs of the Conservatoire national d'Arts et Métiers [which offered continuing education courses to workers] which Monzie [Anatole de Monzie, the Education Minister, 1932–1934] persisted in calling the Conservatory of the People."

41 AN F 17 17844, Conseil supérieur de l'enseignement technique, session du 15 décembre 1933, première séance, p. 61, and session du 22 décembre

1938, première séance In the mid 1930s the technical education division had about 7 million francs in state subsidies for its vocational courses, while the city of Bremen alone had 20 million for its courses.

42 AN F 17 17844, Conseil supérieur, session du 20 décembre 1929, deuxième séance, p. 21, and the première séance, 58.

43 AN F 17 17844, Conseil supérieur, session du 15 décembre 1933, deuxième séance, 9. Author's translation.

44 AN F 17 17844, Conseil supérieur, session du 22 décembre 1938, deuxième séance, 8–12.

45 *L'Enseignement technique* 15 (July–Sept. 1957), 10, and 63 (July–Sept. 1969), 33. See also Legoux, *Du compagnon au technicien*, 244.

46 Luc, "Les problèmes actuels de l'Enseignement technique," 8–20. *L'Enseignement technique* 1 (April 1938), 8–20; and 9 (Feb. 1939).

47 Herriot, three times prime minister and education minister from 1926 to 1928, was a sincere supporter of technical education (unlike Ducos): "Toute cette armature me semble nécessaire. Je n'ai jamais voulu y porter atteinte, je ne la laisserai pas démembrer." President of AFDET from 1931 to 1952, he was succeeded by Alfred Jules-Julien from 1955 to 1977. Herriot, *In Those Days*, Berstein, *Edouard Herriot ou la République en personne*.

48 Bayet, chairman of the Radical Party's educational commission, wrote to Zay: "Ne détruisez pas l'Enseignement technique ... ce serait dommageable à une jeunesse modeste et d'autant plus digne d'intérêt; d'ailleurs il faudrait le rétablir un jour ou l'autre." Legay, "L'enseignement technique en France," 54–4. See also Legoux, *Du compagnon au technicien*, 495–6.

49 AN, Archives privées, Papiers Abraham 312/5 (16–17), Albert Châtelet. "This war over occupational training. ... is it admissable that M. Julien, secretary of state [for Technical Education], hiding behind the pen of his chief assistant, Jean Luc, head of the Technical Education division, is fighting a ministerial reform backed by his government. Is the Secretary of State opposing his own government's bill? Is this little war going to continue?"

50 AN F 17 17501, Réforme du ministre Jean Zay, classes d'orientation. Zay, *La Réforme de l'enseignement*.

51 AN F 17 17502, Réforme Langevin-Wallon, 1944–48. Louis Cros, ed., *Gustave Monod, un pionnier en éducation*.

52 Zay, *Souvenirs et solitude*.

53 AN F 17 17502, Commission d'études pour la réforme de l'enseignement, résumé des procès-verbaux, les dix premières séances, p. 1. Capitant (1901–70) was education minister from November 1943 to November 1945.

54 AN F 17 17502, Commission d'études pour la réforme de l'enseignement, procès-verbaux, travaux de la commission, starting with the 15th séance, May 17, 1945.

55 Bayet, director general, Pierre Auger, higher education, Gustave Monod, secondary education, Paul Le Rolland, technical education, and Barré, primary division.

56 Included in the commission were Senèze and Voguet, Paris teachers; Mlle Cabane, primary inspectrice and Mme Seclet, professor at the École normale d'institutrices de Paris; Fernand Canonge and Renaudeau from technical education; and Alfred Weiller and Roger Gal, secondary education division.

57 Rapport général sur les travaux de la Commission pour la réforme de l'enseignement présenté par Marcel Durry, in Luc Decaunes et M. L. Cavalier, eds., *Réformes et projets de réforme de l'enseignement français*, 259. See also AN (*Archives Nationales*) 71 AJ 64 which includes a wide variety of studies and proposals sent to or collected by the Langevin Commission. See the MRP brochure *Pour une réforme de l'enseignement*, Paris, 1945; on the communists, Cogniot, *L'École et les forces populaires*.

58 AN F 17 17502, Commission d'études etc, résumé des procès-verbaux, les dix premières séances, 1–2.

59 AN F 17 17502, Ministère de l'Éducation nationale, La réforme de l'enseignement, projet soumis à M. le Ministre de l'Éducation nationale par la Commission ministérielle d'étude, June 1947, 8–10.

60 AN F 17 17502, 9–15.

61 Wallon, *Principes de psychologie appliquée*, 140–168.

62 Legoux, *Du compagnon au technicien*, 244–46, 263. Langevin, *La pensée et l'action*. Ministre de l'Éducation nationale, Commission ministérielle d'étude, *La Réforme de l'enseignement*, Paris, June 1947.

63 AN F 17 17502, Langevin-Wallon Commission, session du June 12, 1947.

64 AN AP (*Archives privées*) 312/5, "Le Projet de Réforme de l'Enseignement, part 3, 36–45. Naville, *La formation professionnelle*. Quef, *Histoire de l'apprentissage*.

65 *Technique, Art, Science* 9 (June 1947), 1–8.

66 Legay, "Histoire de l'enseignement technique, 1895–1960," 39. Le Rolland, agrégé and docteur-ès-sciences (physics), had been director of the Institut polytechnique de l'Ouest.

67 Legay, "Histoire de l'enseignement technique," 39–40.

68 *Technique, Art, Science* Oct., 1948. Buisson, a former primary teacher and école pratique professor, attended ENSET, was director of the École Diderot and Inspecteur général de l'enseignement technique before being named director in 1948. His main achievement was probably the organization of the centres d'apprentissage in 1949.

69 The industrial section was founded in 1891 in the Écoles d'arts et métiers of Châlons-sur-Marne, then moved to the Paris campus in 1912. The business section was located in the École des Hautes Études Commerciales in Paris since 1894. These sections were consolidated in the École d'arts et

métiers of Paris in 1912, which became the École normale supérieure de l'enseignement technique in 1932 (ENSET). In 1956 it moved to a new campus at Cachan outside of Paris, which included a research centre, a lycée technique, and an ENNA for men and for women. *L'Enseignement technique*, 136 (Oct.–Dec. 1987), 56–60.

70 *Technique, Art, Science* 164 (Dec. 1962), 1–22, 50th anniversary of the founding of ENSET in 1912. See also 145 (Jan. 1961), 38–56.

71 Gal, "Notre Tâche," 5–6, and *Où en est la pédagogie?* See also Canonge and Ducel (ENNA professors), *La Pédagogie devant le progrès technique,* and Terral, *Profession: professeur,* 49–67.

72 *L'Enseignement technique* 10 (Apr.–June 1956), 28–9.

73 *L'Enseignement technique* 4 (Oct.–Dec. 1954), 10–11.

74 Pelpel and Troger, *Histoire de l'enseignement technique,* 93. They grew from 65,000 students to 120,000 students by 1948.

75 *L'Enseignement technique* 14 (Apr.–June 1957), 71–2; 1 (Jan.–Mar. 1954), 14–15; 4 (Oct.–Dec. 1954), 10–11; 5 (Jan.–Mar. 1955), 16. Prost estimates 40,000 students in 1944 and only 150,000 in 1954, *L'École et la famille dans une société en mutation,"* note 1.

76 AN F 17 17857, Conseil de l'enseignement technique, session of 15 June 1956; *L'Enseignement technique* 8 (Oct.–Dec. 1955), 20–2; 9 (Jan.–Mar. 1956), 10–12, 49, 78–80. In 1955 there were 412,000 students in public secondary education, 210,000 in private, as opposed to 321,150 in the schools under the technical education department. Enrolments in the two cycles of secondary education grew from 740,000 in 1948 to 1,350,000 in 1958. Rioux, *The Fourth Republic,* 415. The second cycle grew from 120,000 in 1945 to 270,000 in 1958, mainly as a result of incoming students from the cours complémentaires.

77 Charlot and Figeat, *La formation des ouvriers,* 363.

78 AN F 17 17857, Conseil de l'enseignement technique, section permanente, 15 juin 1956. *L'Enseignement technique* 12 (Oct.–Dec. 1956), 21. In 1952, the ministry granted 2,500 *licences* in law, 2,200 in letters, 1,100 in science, and 33,155 baccalauréats. In 1938 the figures had been 2,300 law, 1,792 letters, 800 sciences, 20,500 baccalauréats. Only 3 per cent of the students in the faculties were the sons of workers, 4 per cent of peasants.

79 *L'Enseignement technique* 20 (Oct.–Dec. 1958), 46. As of June 1957, 2000 professorships of 9,500 in the ENPs, CTs, etc. had not been filled. See also *Technique, Art, Science* 19 (Apr. 1948), 12–17.

80 Wakeman, *Modernizing the Provincial City,* 136.

81 Charlot and Figeat, *La formation des ouvriers,* 411, 549–52.

82 *Technique, Art, Science* 15 (1947), 3–4; 19 (Apr. 1948), 1–4. G. Friedmann, *Humanisme du travail.* See also "Culture et enseignement technique," *Cahiers pédagogiques* (Jan. 1950), 31–8.

83 Naville, *La formation professionnelle à l'école.* Mallet, *La nouvelle classe ouvrière.*

84 AN 17502, séances of the Langevin Commission. The commission held sixty-eight sessions beginning November 19, 1944 and concluding on June 2, 1947.

85 AN F 17 17503, Edouard Depreux project, 1948; Yvon Delbos, 1949; 17504–05, André Marie and Charles Brunold, 1952–54; 17505–06, Jean Berthoin, 1954–55; 17507–08, René Billères. See also Decaunes and Cavalier, *Réformes et projets de réforme*, 259, 275–9.

86 AN F 17 17507–08, Commission pour la démocratisation de l'enseigne-ment de Second Degré, 1956–57, René Billères; 17509, Second projet Berthoin 1958–59.

87 Dreyfus, "Un groupe de pression en action, 213–250.

88 *L'Enseignement technique* 10 (Apr.–June, 1956), 32.

89 Ducos, *Pourquoi l'école unique?*

90 Narbonne, *De Gaulle et l'éducation.*

91 *L'Enseignement technique* 136 (Oct.–Dec. 1987), 45.

92 Legoux, *Du compagnon au technicien*, 496–98. Terral, *Professeurs*, 54. Brucy, *L'État, L'école, les entreprises et la certification.*

CHAPTER THREE

1 Adams and Stoffaës, *French Industral Policy*, 99. Szarka, *Business in France*, 2.

2 Georges Duveau, *La pensée ouvrière.*

3 Ministère du Commerce, de l'Industrie, des Postes et des Télégraphes, *Apprentissage, Rapport de M. Briat au nom de la commission permanente, Enquête et documents.* Paris: Imprimerie nationale, 1902. Ministère du Commerce, de l'Industrie, des Postes et des Télégraphes. Conseil supérieur de l'enseignement technique. *Enquête récente sur l'enseigne-ment professionnel en France. Rapport de M. Briat au nom de la commission permanente: procès-verbaux des séances.* Paris: Imprimerie nationale, 1905.

4 Ministère du Commerce, de l'Industrie, des Postes et des Télégraphes. Direction de l'enseignement technique. *Rapport sur la situation de l'enseignement technique en France en 1904, présenté par Cohendy: procès-verbaux des séances.* Paris: Imprimerie nationale, 1905. See also the *Revue de l'enseignement technique*, 6 (Mar. 1911), 345; and the *Bulletin de l'enseigne-ment technique*, 8 (Oct. 1905), 381–411, 455–488.

5 Charmasson et al., *L'Enseignement technique*, I, 59–60.

6 Dubief, *L'apprentissage et l'enseignement technique. Revue de l'enseignement technique*, 6 (Mar. 1911), 345.

7 Astier, *L'Enseignement technique*, 398–407.

8 Charlot and Figeat, *Histoire de la formation des ouvriers*, 247.

9 Ribes-Christofle, *L'apprentissage et l'enseignement professionnel.*

10 *Revue de l'enseignement technique* 6 (Mar. 1911), 344.

11 Briand and Chapoulie, *Les collèges du peuple*, 396.

12 *L'Enseignement technique* 9 (Jan.–Mar. 1956), 13; and 136 (Oct.–Dec. 1987), 35–6.

13 Charmasson, *L'Enseignement technique*, 470–84. Author's translation. See also Decaunes and Cavalier, *Réformes et projets de réforme*, 80.

14 *Formation professionnelle* 23 (1919), 466–73; *L'Enseignement technique* 136 (Oct.–Dec. 1987), 36.

15 *L'Enseignement technique* 63 (July–Sept. 1969), 26–8.

16 Legoux, *Du compagnon au technicien*, 170.

17 AN F 17 17844, Conseil supérieur de l'enseignement technique, La Direction du travail des jeunes et de l'enseignement technique, July 3, 1935, 13.

18 *Formation professionnelle* 23 (1919), 466–73; and 25 (1920), 70–1. *Technique, Art, Science* 4–5 (Jan.–Feb. 1955), 4–6. Some 700,000 to 800,000 of 2 million young people aged fourteen to eighteen out of a labour force of 20 million lived too far from the courses to attend.

19 Charlot Figeat, *Histoire de la formation des ouvriers*, 240–47.

20 AN F 17 17844, Conseil supérieur de l'enseignement technique, 17 Nov. 1932, second session, 3.

21 *L'Enseignement technique* 136 (Oct.–Dec. 1987), 35–7.

22 Charmasson et al., *L'Enseignement technique*, 536–37.

23 AN F 17 17844, Conseil supérieur de l'enseignement technique, 3 July 1935, and 22 Dec. 1938. *L'Enseignement technique* 27 (July-Sept. 1960), 65.

24 Guinot, *Formation professionnelle*, 205.

25 Guinot, *Formation professionnelle*, 200–2. The deputy Constant Verlot played a key role in the creation of the chambres de métiers and the introduction of the apprenticeship tax.

26 AN F 17 17844, Conseil supérieur de l'enseignement technique, 21 Dec. 1928 and 5 Feb. 1931. Cambon and Butor, *La bataille de l'apprentissage*, 43–7.

27 *L'Enseignement technique* 136 (Oct–Dec. 1987), 39. Guinot, *Formation professionnelle*, 197–8. Forty-five per cent of the courses were offered by 500 cities and towns, 20 per cent by employers groups, 20 per cent by educational associations, 10 per cent labour unions, and 5 per cent by business and industry.

28 Cambon and Butor state that there were 3,000 CAP under the jurisdiction of the UIMM. *La bataille de l'apprentissage*, 45.

29 Brucy, "CAP et certificats de spécialité: les enjeux de la formation au lendemain de la Deuxième Guerre mondiale," *Formation emploi*, 27–28 (July–Dec. 1989), 131–46.

30 Guinot, *Formation professionnelle*, 212–13.

31 Charlot and Figeac, *La formation des ouvriers*, 287–92. Guinot, *Formation professionnelle*, 230–34.

32 Guinot, *Formation professionnelle*, 236. These reeducation centres included the centres de formation professionnelle des chômeurs, les centres de perfectionnement, promotion ouvrière and the centres de formation professionnelle accélérée.

33 Moutet, *Les logiques de l'entreprise*, 419. The UIMM estimated the number of unemployed workers in metallurgy in the Paris area at 38,521 in 1935 and the demand for skilled workers at 14,000.

34 Hatzfeld, "L'école d'apprentissage Peugeot (1930–70): une formation d'excellence, *Formation emploi* 27–28 (July–Dec. 1989), 115–127.

35 Moutet, *Les logiques de l'entreprise*, 140–60, 416–28.

36 Charlot and Figeat, *La formation des ouvriers*, 314–15, 334.

37 *L'Enseignement technique* 8 (Oct.–Dec. 1955), 10–13.

38 *L'Enseignement technique* 14 (Apr.–June 1957), 71–2; 1 (Jan.–Mar. 1954), 14–15; 4 (Oct.–Dec. 1954), 10–11; 5 (Jan.–Mar. 1955), 16.

39 Browaeys and Châtelain, *La France du travail*, 45–6.

40 Raissiguier, *Becoming Women*, 36, 45–6, 155–7.

41 *Technique, Art, Science*, published monthly by the Ministry of National Education and AFDET, 1946–77.

42 *L'Enseignement technique* 25 (Jan.–Mar. 1960), 83.

43 These were originally called commissions consultatives nationales d'apprentissage, then commissions nationales professionnelles consultatives (CNPC) in 1948, and finally commissions professionnelles consultatives that exist today. *L'Enseignement technique* 8 (Oct.–Dec. 1955), 11–13.

44 Brucy, "CAP et certificats de spécialité," 131–46.

45 Noiriel, *Workers in French Society*, 223.

46 Szarka, *Business in France*, 3.

47 Scardigli and Mercier, *Ascension sociale et pauvreté*, 149. Also, Vrain and Gautier, *Les ouvriers vieillissants*, 450.

48 Grelon and Marry, "Entretien avec Bernard Decomps," *Formation emploi* 53 (Jan.–Mar. 1997), 49–63. See also the two preceding notes.

49 AN F 17 17857, Conseil de l'enseignement technique, procès-verbaux des réunions, section permanente, June 15, 1956.

50 Naville, *École et société*.

51 Pelpel and Troger, *Histoire de l'enseignement technique*, 129. There were 340,000 in 1964–65, 677,000 in 1972–73. Solaux, *Les lycées professionnels*.

52 Becker, *Human Capital*.

53 Ross, *Fast Cars, Clean Bodies*, 150–4.

54 Hachem and Fayez, *À quoi sert le Plan?* Charlot and Beillerot, eds., *La Construction des politiques d'éducation*. The third plan covered the years 1958–62, the fourth 1962–66.

55 Pelpel and Troger, *Histoire de l'enseignement technique*, 177. Monaco, *L'Alternance*, 99.

56 Plato, *The Republic*, F.M. Cornford, trans. (London, 1941), 102–11.

57 Piaget, *Introduction à l'épistémologie génétique*.

58 Haby, *Propositions pour une modernisation du système éducatif*, 10–21. See also Legrand, *L'École unique*, 28.

59 Girard, "Enquête nationale sur l'orientation," 597–634. See Baudelot and Establet, *L'École capitaliste en France*, 196, and Grignon, *L'ordre des choses*.

60 Bourdieu and Passeron, *La Reproduction* and *Les Héritiers*. See also Baudelot and Establet, *L'École capitaliste*.

61 Charlot, *La mystification pédagogique*, 65. Garcia, *L'École unique* 178–215. Haby, *Propositions*, 10–21.

62 Charlot and Figeat, *La formation des ouvriers*, 411.

63 Noriel, *Workers*, 198, 211–13.

64 Grignon, *L'ordre des choses*.

65 Crozier, *L'entreprise à l'écoute*, and *Le Phénomène bureaucratique*.

66 Maurice, Sellier, and Silvestre, *The Social Foundations of Industrial Power*, 128–29.

67 Nomenclature nationale des niveaux de formation. In 1985, level six was eliminated, but otherwise the scale exists today.

68 Maurice, Sellier, and Silvestre, *The Social Foundations of Industrial Power*, 107, 132–33.

69 Altmann, Köhler, and Meil, eds., *Technology & Work in German Industry*. Lane, *Management and Labour in Europe*, 42–9, 84.

70 Maurice, Sellier, and Silvestre, *The Social Foundations of Industrial Power*, 87.

71 Cadin and Mendoza, "Tradition and transition," 147–56.

72 Ashton and Green, *Education, Training and the Global Economy*, 141–4.

73 *Le Monde de l'Éducation* 123 (Jan. 1986), 53. *Le Monde*, June 20, 1991, 14.

74 *L'Enseignement technique* 148 (Oct.–Dec. 1990), 63. Maurice et al., *Des entreprises en mutation*. Dalle and Bounine, *L'Éducation en entreprise*, 158–236.

75 Lutz, "Education and Employment," 73–86. *L'Enseignement technique* 110 (Apr.–June 1981), 98–9, 125 (Jan.–Mar. 1985), 92–108. *Éducation-Économie* 17 (Oct.–Dec. 1992), 60–2.

76 Depardieu and Payen, "Disparités des salaires en France et en Allemagne." Lane, *Management and Labour in Europe*, 41–2.

77 Grignon, *L'ordre des choses*; and Charlot and Figeat, *La formation des ouvriers*, 398–411.

78 Ross, *Fast Cars, Clean Bodies*, 136–67, 150–4, 191–6. Wakeman, *Modernizing the Provincial City, Toulouse 1945–75*, 69–145.

79 Storper and Salais, *Worlds of Production*, 228.

80 Delors, "France between reform and counter-reform," 46–71.

81 Laux, *European Automobile Industry*, 248–9.

82 Adams and Stoffaës, *French Industrial Policy*, 44.

83 Compagnie générale d'électricité, CGE (telecommunications), Empain-Schneider (nuclear industry installations), Thomson-CSF (electronics), CII Honeywell Bull (computers), and SNIAS and Dassault (military aviation).

84 Szarka, *Business in France*, 51–3, 60–2.

85 Womack, Jones, and Roos, *The Machine that Changed the World*, 99.

86 Piore and Sabel, *The Second Industrial Divide*. Sabel, *Work and Politics*.

87 Florida and Kenney, "Japanese Automotive Transplants," 51–83. Turner and Auer, "A Diversity of New Work Organization," 233–57.

88 Lane, *Management and Labour in Europe*, 105, 156–53.

89 *L'Enseignement technique* 71 (July–Sept. 1971), 7–14; 72 (Oct.–Dec. 1971), 20–21. Also, 125 (Jan.–Mar. 1985), 97.

CHAPTER FOUR

1 The Popular Front in 1936 nationalized Air France, military aviation, savings banks, and part of the SNCF: the Liberation in 1945 and after: Renault, Elf-Aquitaine, Aérospatiale, Cogema (nuclear energy), CDF-Chimie, EMC, CEA-Industrie, gas, and electricity. In 1982 the Socialists nationalized, among others, Péchiney-Ugine-Kuhlmann (special steels and non-ferrous metals), Saint-Gobain (glass, construction materials), Rhône-Poulenc (chemicals, pharmaceuticals), Thomson-Brandt (electronics, telecommunications), Compagnie générale d'électricité (cables, computers, electronics, telecommunications, now called Alcatel-Alsthom), Compagnie générale des constructions téléphoniques, CII-Honeywell Bull (computers), Dassault-Bréguet (aeronautics), MATRA (weapons), and, in 1984, Usinor & Sacilor (steel). Durupty, "Les privatisations en France," 20.

2 Organization for Economic Cooperation and Development, *Economic Surveys: France* (Paris: OECD, 1984), 9, 22.

3 Huet and Schmitz, "La classe ouvrière en détresse," See also Noiriel, *Workers in French Society,* 223.

4 W. Rand Smith, *The Left's Dirty Job,* 133–47, 213. See also Marklew, *Cash, Crisis, and Corporate Governance.*

5 Joseph Szarka, *Business in France,* 26–34, 60–9. On the decline and recovery of French automobiles and steel, see W. Rand Smith, *The Left's Dirty Job,* 154–209.

6 Schmidt, *From State to Market?,* 53, 106–8, 113–30, 358–9.

7 Szarka, *Business in France,* 31–4. The economy gained 670,000 jobs from 1987 to 1989 and unemployment fell to 8.9 per cent. See also Smith, *The Left's Dirty Job,* 76.

8 Peugeot, for example, had 206,000 employees in 1983 and 157,000 in 1992, down 24 per cent. Employment in the French steel industry fell by 60 per cent between 1974 and 1992, and the production of raw steel fell by 33 per cent during those years, the biggest decline in Europe. Smith, *The Left's Dirty Job,* 157, 192.

9 Zahariadis, *Markets, States and Public Policy,* 134.

10 Schmidt, *From State to Market?,* 369.

11 *Libérer l'École, Plan socialiste pour l'Education nationale,* 1978, stated "l'école est à la fois l'un des terrains et l'un des enjeux de la lutte des classes ... Les patrons hors de l'école". (The school is at once the field where the class struggle occurs and the prize of that struggle ... Bosses stay out of the school.) Savary moved away from the more strident policies of Louis

Mexandeau, education critic for the SP before the victory of 1981. See also Mitterrand's *Cent dix propositions sur l'école*, 1981: "l'unité nationale sera d'autant mieux servie qu'un grand service public unifié et laïque aura été bâti." (National unity will be all the better served once a unified and lay public service has been built.) *Le Monde de l'Éducation*, 124 (Feb. 1986), 11; and 144 (Dec. 1987), 11.

12 Legrand, *Pour un collège démocratique*, and *Pour une politique démocratique de l'éducation*, 1977.

13 Prost, *Les Lycéens et leurs études au seuil du XXIe siècle, rapport du groupe du travail national sur les seconds cycles*, 1983. This report was based in part on a national consultation on the lycées from October 6 to December 13, 1982, in which 2,500 lycées and lycées d'enseignement professionnel participated.

14 de Peretti, *La Formation des personnels de l'Éducation nationale*.

15 *Cahiers de l'Éducation nationale* 1 (Jan. 1982), 19.

16 Prost, *Les lycées et leurs études au seuil du XXe siècle*. See also *Éloge des pédagogues*, 1985, 157–73.

17 Bouyx, *L'enseignement technologique*, 26.

18 Chevènement, *Apprendre pour entreprendre*; and *Le Pari sur l'intelligence*.

19 *Rapport du groupe de travail baccalauréat technologique*, UIMM, June 1984. The UIMM recruits one apprentice per 100 employees, or 200,000 apprentices, half to train in machine repair and maintenance; 55 per cent of the 2 million employees in industries belonging to the UIMM (automobiles, aviation, electricity, steel, mechanical construction, etc.) are the offspring of workers. *Le Monde de l'Éducation* 216 (June 1994), 44–6.

20 Campinos-Dubernet, "Baccalauréat professionnel: une innovation?" 5.

21 Haut Comité Éducation-Économie (HCEE), *Vingt-cinq propositions pour l'avenir de l'école et des entreprises*, 1987. Daniel Bloch was director of the Institut polytechnique de Grenoble. See the commission's *Rapport et recommendations de la mission éducation entreprise*, 1986.

22 Bureau d'information et de prévision économique, *Quels hommes et quelles femmes former pour l'entreprise de demain? Prévision des qualifications à l'an 2000*, Paris, July 1985. Centre d'études et de recherches sur les qualifications (céreq), *Rapport au Ministre de l'Éducation nationale, Direction des Lycées*, "Formation et accès aux emplois industriels," 13, Paris 1993. See also *Éducation-Économie, revue du Haut Comité Éducation-Économie* 11 (Apr.–June 1991), 48–57.

23 *Formation Emploi* 56 (Oct.–Dec. 1996), 47.

24 Campinos-Dubernet, "Baccalauréat professionnel," 3–29.

25 OECD statistics 1989, cited by Campinos-Dubernet: 56.4 per cent in West Germany, 66.4 per cent in the US, 68.5 per cent in the United Kingdom, 75 per cent in Sweden.

26 Eyraud, "Nouvelles technologies et recherche."

27 Campinos-Dubernet, "Baccalauréat professionnel," 17–21.

28 Ibid., 13.

29 *Cahiers de l'Éducation nationale* 38 (Oct. 1985), 8–9.

30 Dauty and Brunet, "Spécialité transversale, Une réponse opérationnelle au rapprochement formation-emploi?" 37–52.

31 *L'Enseignement technique* 168 (Oct.–Dec. 1995), 20.

32 Conseil national du patronat français, *Le livre blanc, Réussir la formation professionnelle des jeunes*, 115–24.

33 Campinos-Dubernet, "Le Baccalauréat professionnel," 3–29.

34 Morin, "La production mécanique française," 25–8.

35 *L'Enseignement technique* 182 (2ème trimestre 1999), 24–6. See also Raissiguier, *Becoming Women, Becoming Workers*.

36 *L'Enseignement technique* 183 (3ème trimestre 1999), 33.

37 *L'Enseignement technique* 182 (2ème trimestre 1999), 8.

38 *L'Enseignement technique* 183 (3ème trimestre 1999), 33. *Le Monde*, June 10, 1997. The figures come from MEN (Ministère de l'éducation nationale), Direction de l'évaluation et de la prospective, December 1996–99.

39 *L'Enseignement technique* 181 (1er trimestre 1999), 22.

40 *Cahiers de l'Éducation nationale,* 55 (May 1987), 15–6; *Le Monde de l'Éducation* 146 (Feb. 1988), 26. Under Savary, thirty-four CAP were created, forty-eight suppressed and fifty-two modified. *Cahiers de l'Éducation nationale* 14 (Apr. 1983), 4; 38 (Oct. 1985), 9.

41 Solaux, *Les lycées professionnels*, 66. *L'Enseignement technique* 156 (Oct.–Dec. 1992), 21, which cites 339,000 in 1985 and 112, 316 in 1992.

42 *L'Enseignement technique* 176 (Oct.–Dec. 1997), 15.

43 Vimont, "Les Besoins des entreprises," 4–9.

44 Rault, *La formation professionnelle*, 24.

45 Bureau international du travail, enquêtes INSI, cited in *L'Enseignement technique* 180 (Oct.–Dec. 1998), 19.

46 Rault, *La formation professionnelle*, 24.

47 The CAP involved fourteen to sixteen hours of general studies (French, math, physical sciences, history, geography, and an optional foreign language), economics, and physical education. In addition there were twelve to seventeen hours of shop work. *Le Monde de l'Éducation* (May 1992), 96.

48 Solaux, *Les lycées professionnels*, 66–8.

49 *L'Enseignement technique,* 179 (July–Sept. 1998), 4–7. The BTS is prepared in the advanced sections of the lycées, while the DUT is prepared for in the IUT located in the universities.

50 Raissiguier, *Becoming Women, Becoming Workers*, 33–40.

51 *L'Enseignement technique* 136 (Oct.–Dec. 1987), 46–7. Author's translation.

52 Combes, "La loi de 1971 sur l'apprentissage," 18–32.

53 *L'Enseignement technique* 177 (Jan.–Mar. 1998), 11–16. Cambon and Butor, *La bataille de l'apprentissage*, 27–53, especially 51–52. In 1987 there were 488 CFA, fifty-six directed by local governments, sixty-one by public schools, thirty-eight by Chambres of commerce, seventy-three by Chambres de métiers and 260 by private corporations.

54 *Cahiers de l'Éducation nationale*, 14, (April 1983), 4–20. See also Léon, *Formation générale et apprentissage du métier.*

55 *L'Enseignement technique* 157 (Jan.–Mar, 1993), 20–3. *Le Monde de l'Éducation* 123 (Jan. 1986), 53. *Le Monde*, June 20, 1991, 14.

56 *L'Enseignement technique* 72 (Oct.–Dec. 1971), 45–47; 73 (Jan.–Mar, 1972), 24; 136 (Oct.–Dec. 1987), 47.

57 Twenty-one per cent of students at the end of the first year of CPPN prepared for the CAP exams, 17 per cent completed the second year of CPPN, 29 per cent transferred into pre-apprenticeship classes (CPA), 4 per cent obtained the one-year certificat d'enseignement professionnel (CEP), and 28 per cent entered the workforce.

58 *Bilan Formation-Emploi*, 1983, 61.

59 Aventur et al., "L'insertion des jeunes," 141–97. Monaco, *L'Alternance*, 98–9.

60 *L'Enseignement technique* 148 (Oct.–Dec. 1990), 22–9; 164 (Oct.–Dec. 1994), 12.

61 *L'Enseignement technique* 165 (Jan.–Mar. 1995), 33. In 1994–95, of a total of 250,011 apprentices, 206,151 were studying at level V of whom 172,829 (69 per cent) the CAP and 27,108 (11 per cent) the BEP, 31,474 (12.5 per cent) the baccalauréat and brevet professionnel (level IV) and 9,285 (4 per cent) the brevet de technicien supérieur (BTS) and diplôme universitaire de technologie (DUT), level 3. The remainder were studying for engineering credentials.

62 Monaco, *L'alternance*, 83, 102: 185,000 in 1976–77.

63 *L'Enseignement technique* 180 (Oct.–Dec. 1998), 5, 177 (Jan.–Mar. 1998), 11–16.

64 *L'Enseignement technique* 146 (Apr.–June, 1990), 42–3; 157 (Jan.–Mar. 1993), 21.

65 Affichard, Combes and Grelet, "Apprentis et élèves de lycées professionnels," 9.

66 *L'Enseignement technique* 164 (Oct.–Dec. 1994), 7–14, especially 7–9. Lhôtel and Monaco, "Deux trajectoires de la formation en alternance."

67 *L'Enseignement technique*, 176 (Oct.–Dec. 1997), 4–13.

68 *L'Enseignement technique* 155 (July–Sept. 1992), 30–1; 164 (Oct.–Dec. 1994), 7–14. *Le Monde*, June 10 1993, 18. Continuing education programs in the secondary schools are grouped together in GRETA (Groupements d'Établissements), of which there were 325 in 1993.

69 *Le Monde de l'Éducation* 216 (June 1994), 36.

70 L'Enseignement technique 165 (Jan.–Mar. 1995), 13–9, 33.

71 L'Enseignement technique 164 (Oct.–Dec. 1994), 7–14. Le Monde de l'Éducation 216 (June 1994), 44–6.

72 Sellier, La confrontation sociale en France. Dubar, Formation permanente. Tanguy, "Les conventions État-patronat." Fouchet introduced work placements in the sections d'éducation professionnelle and the sections d'éducation spécialisée, but these were remedial programs and the experiment stopped there.

73 Charlot and Figeat, La formation des ouvriers, 480. Cambon and Butor, La bataille de l'apprentissage, 73–80. Fifty-four per cent held the CAP or BEP and 24 per cent the bac.

74 Conseil national du patronat français, Journées sur la formation permanente, Deauville, 1978.

75 Ibid.

76 Le Monde de l'Éducation 106 (June 1984), 18.

77 L'Enseignement technique 138 (Apr.–June 1988), 6, 73–9.

78 Schwartz, L'Insertion professionnelle. See also Schwartz, Une autre école, and L'Éducation demain. Le Monde de l'Éducation 75 (Sept. 1981), 15–6; 105 (June 1984), 23; 146 (Feb. 1988), 27.

79 L'Enseignement technique 155 (July–Sept. 1992), 72.

80 Monaco, L'Alternance, 130–44.

81 Rault, La formation professionnelle, 23.

82 Conseil national du patronat français, Le livre blanc, Réussir, La formation professionnelle des jeunes, 85.

83 Le Monde de l'Éducation, 106 (June 1984), 18–22; 124 (Feb. 1986), 11. Cahiers de l'Éducation nationale 5 (May 1982), 16–18; Éducation-Économie 13 (Dec. 1991), 15. L'Enseignement technique 125 (Jan.–Mar. 1985), 111; 144 (Oct.–Dec. 1989), 32–6; 147 (July–Sept. 1990), 28–9, 36–8.

84 Monaco, L'Alternance, 170–4.

85 Le Monde, Dec. 27, 1996.

86 Monaco, L'Alternance, 175–6.

87 Cambon and Butor, La bataille de l'apprentissage, 102.

88 Cambon and Butor, La bataille de l'apprentissage, 86–7, 102. Le Monde de l'Éducation, 216 (June 1994), 39. Recent programs include: Expo-jeunes (1991), designed to encourage small companies to hire the unskilled; DIJEN (dispositif d'insertion des jeunes de l'Éducation nationale); CIPPA (cycles d'insertion professionnelle par alternance); and MOREA (modes de préparation d'examen en alternance).

89 Le Monde, June 25, 1997; Sept. 17, 1997, March 24 and 25, 2000.

90 Le Monde de l'Éducation 216 (June 1994), 33–36. In 1993–94 the Germans spent 70 billion francs on work study and apprenticeship programs, the French 5 billion.

91 Le Monde de l'Éducation 224 (Mar. 1995), 37, 42–50.

92 Tanguy, *Quelle formation pour les ouvriers en France?*, 19–20. *Le Monde de l'Éducation* 110 (Nov. 1984), 10–13.

93 *Formation Emploi* 58 (Apr.–June 1997), 79–89.

94 *L'Enseignement technique* 145 (Jan.–Mar. 1990), 64–7.

95 *L'Enseignement technique* 145 (Jan.–Mar. 1990), 64–7.

96 "Travail: la France est-elle archaïque?" *Le Monde Économie*, Nov. 18, 1997. Bergeron and Bourdelais, *La France, n'est-elle pas douée pour la production?*.

97 "Le dossier 'noir' des chefs d'entreprise," *Le Monde*, Nov. 18, 1998.

98 OECD, *France, National Policies for Education* (1996), 95–8, 166. On a base of 100 in 1972, French GDP rose to 150 in 1992, Germany 153 and US 153, but in terms of employment growth, France was 105 in 1992, Germany 111 and the US 137.

99 *Le Monde*, Apr. 8, 1998. Vimont, "Les besoins des entreprises," 4–9.

100 *Le Monde*, Nov. 18, 1997. See also the OECD figures for 1989: in France for men over fifty-five the rate of activity was 47.5 per cent; in the Federal Republic of Germany, 56.4 per cent; in the US 66.4 per cent; in the UK 68.5 per cent; and in Sweden 75 per cent.

101 Couppie, Epiphane, and Fournier, "Insertion professionnelle et début de carrière." See also *L'Enseignement technique*, 181 (1er trimestre 1999), 20–2; 182 (2ème trimestre 1999), 24–6.

102 Storper and Salais, *Worlds of Production*, 225–26.

103 OECD, *France, National Policies*, 102–5, 248.

104 Ibid., 232.

105 Monaco, *L'Alternance*, 25–8. See also Dubar, *La Socialisation* and Rose, *En quête d'emploi-formation*.

106 Monaco, *L'Alternance*, 34–6.

107 Pelpel, *Les Stages de formation* and Pelpel and Troger, *Histoire*, 288.

108 Ashton and Green, *Education, Training and the Global Economy*, 101–2.

109 Pelpel and Troger, *Histoire de l'enseignement technique*, 152.

110 OECD, *Reviews of National Policies for Education, France* (Paris: OECD, 1996), 24.

111 Tanguy, *Quelle formation pour les ouvriers?*, 25–89. In the mid-1980s the figure was 61 per cent in companies employing less than 200 and 35 per cent less than fifty. See also *Éducation-Économie*, 13 (Dec. 1991), 17–20.

112 Tanguy, *Quelle formation pour les ouvriers?*, 115–25.

113 *Le Monde*, June 20, 1991, 13.

114 *Éducation-Économie*, 13 (Dec. 1991), 15–6.

115 Tanguy, *Quelle formation pour les ouvriers?* 105–8, 123–36. See also *L'Enseignement professionnel en France, des ouvriers aux techniciens* (Paris: Presses universitaires de France, 1991), which deals mainly with vocational education of teachers.

116 Ministère de l'Éducation nationale, Loi d'orientation sur l'enseignement du 10 juillet 1989. Plan de développement de l'apprentissage et de l'alternance, Sept. 1991.

117 *L'Enseignement technique* 173 (Jan.–Mar. 1997), 4.

118 OCDE, "La formation initiale en France: efficacité interne et maîtrise des coûts," *Études économiques*, no 2.352–3, Dec. 1993, 20–34.

119 Laurent, "Projet de la loi d'orientation et de programme sur la formation professionnelle," *Technique, Art, Science* 204 (Dec. 1966), 1–10. *L'Enseignement technique* 173 (Jan.–Mar. 1997), 4; 160 (Oct.–Dec. 1993), 19; also 157 (Jan.–Mar. 1993), 11; and 156 (Oct.–Dec. 1992), 21. In 1966 girls formed 50 per cent of the students in the CET, one quarter in higher education, mostly in the STS.

120 *L'Enseignement technique* 180 (Oct.–Dec. 1998), 4–5; 173 (Jan.–Mar. 1997), 4; 160 (Oct.–Dec. 1993), 19, also 157 (Jan.–Mar. 1993), 11, and 156 (Oct.–Dec., 1992), 21. In 1992–93, a total of 1,455,800 were enrolled in technical-vocational programs, public and private, out of 2.4 million students in all lycées, of which 716,000 were in lycées professionnels, 527,800 in bac technologique programs in the LEGT, and 212,000 in apprenticeship programs.

121 *L'Enseignement technique* 168 (Oct.–Dec. 1995), 23. The percentage of technical studies in the general lycées fell from 35.6 to 34.4 per cent in the early 1990s.

122 *L'Enseignement technique* 183, (3ème trimestre 1999), 33; 176 (Oct.–Dec. 1998), 8, 15–6; 173 (Jan.–Mar. 1997), 4–7.

123 Campinos-Dubernet, "Le Baccalauréat professionnel," 3–29.

124 *L'Enseignement technique* 182 (2ème trimestre 1999), 9. *Le Monde*, Oct. 24, 1995.

125 Hoffmann, "Look Back in Anger," 45–49.

126 Bel, "Le rôle des établissements," 47.

127 Gonnin-Bolo, *Écoles-entreprises*.

128 HCEE, *Vingt-cinq propositions pour l'avenir de l'école. Éducation-Économie* 28 (Oct. 1996), 1–2.

129 Conseil national du patronat français (CNPF), *Livre blanc*.

130 *Le Monde de l'Éducation*, 123 (Jan. 1986), 53–7.

131 Feenberg, *Critical Theory of Technology*, 117.

132 *Le Monde*, Oct. 30, 1995. See also *Le Monde*, May 6, 1997, and Compagnon and Thévenin, *L'École et la Société française*.

133 Madelin, *Quand les Autruches relèveront la tête*, 166.

134 Ashton and Green, *Education, Training and the Global Economy*, 111.

CHAPTER FIVE

1 Guillon, *Techniciens en formation*, 9.

2 Legoux, "Regards sur une nouvelle génération de techniciens," 33–48. *L'Enseignement technique*, 38 (Apr.–June 1963), 21–6.

3 AN F 17 17844, Conseil supérieur de l'enseignement technique, séance du 12 décembre 1923.

4 Legoux, *Du compagnon au technicien*, 389–98. 520. Pierre Bézier, "Évolution des techniques d'usinage," 13–15.
5 *L'Enseignement technique* 17 (Jan.–Mar. 1958), 35–6.
6 Naville, "L'évolution des techniques," 17–24.
7 Bourdieu, *The State Nobility*, 131–161.
8 Guillon, *Enseignement et organisation du travail*, 50.
9 The percentage of clerks and employees in the workforce grew from 11.5 per cent in 1926 to 15.1 per cent in 1946. Boltanski, *Making of a Class*, 63.
10 M. Virmaud, *Mémoire de l'Association des anciens élèves des Écoles d'Arts et Métiers sur l'orientation et la formation professionnelle de la jeunesse*. Paris: CNAM, 1942. The report estimated that 67 per cent of 13,556,000 males of employment age did not need specialized vocational education, 26 per cent did so either in industry or agriculture, 4 per cent needed training in business, 1 per cent in the pure sciences and 1.1 per cent in the liberal arts. See also *L'Enseignement technique*, 136 (Oct.–Dec. 1987), 37–8.
11 Boltanski, *Cadres in French Society*, 68–70, French edition, 111–3.
12 Boltanski, *Cadres in French Society*, 66–7, French edition, 108–9.
13 *Bulletin administratif*, 3 (Mar. 1926), 156. Day, *Education for the Industrial World*, 90–118. The schools were at Châlons-sur-Marne (1803), Angers (1811), Aix-en-Provence (1843), Cluny (1891), Lille (1900), Paris (1912), Bordeaux (1964).
14 AN 17844, Conseil supérieur de l'enseignement technique, séance du 12 décembre 1923.
15 Troger, "Les centres d'apprentissage," 150.
16 AN F 17 14348–14356. Écoles nationales professionnelles, Troisième République: personnel, élèves. F 17 14350, Note sur l'organisation de l'enseignement technique français, cr. 1899–1900. *Les Écoles Nationales Professionnelles*. Paris: Société amicale des anciens élèves des écoles nationales professionnelles, 1926, 17–9. 53–112.
17 *L'Enseignement technique* 1 (Jan.–Mar. 1954), 30–41.
18 Enquête sur la situation des anciens élèves des écoles nationales professionnelles, in *Bulletin mensuel de la société amicale des anciens élèves des écoles nationales professionnelles* (henceforth *Bulletin des écoles nationales professionnelles*, no. 1 bis (1947), 1 (February 1948), 68, and 3 (May–June 1948), 6. See also *Les Écoles Nationales Professionnelles*, 1926, 23–24.
19 AN F 17 17844, Conseil supérieur de l'enseignement technique, séance du 17 novembre 1932, 13. *Les Écoles Nationales Professionnelles*, 1926, 15.
20 AN F 17 17844, Conseil supérieur de l'enseignement technique, séance du 26 février 1936, pp. 65–66. *Bulletin des écoles nationales professionnelles*, 167 (Aug. 1936), 189–90.
21 *Bulletin des écoles nationales professionnelles* 167 (Aug. 1936), 189–97.
22 *Bulletin des écoles nationales professionnelles* 70 (July 1928), 114; and 94 (July 1930), 109. *L'Enseignement technique* 136 (Oct.–Dec. 1987), 39.

23 Day, *Education for the Industrial World,* chap. 6–7.

24 There were approximately 32,000 graduates by 1936. Not counting the 30 per cent who continued their studies in the Arts et Métiers or elsewhere, one comes to about 20,000, although some of these did not finish their studies or did not work in industry. Graduates of the newer schools were not allowed into the alumni association until 1937. Thus 3,000 graduates belonged to the society in 1923, 6,500 in 1936, 12,500 in 1947, and 18,000 in 1955. *Bulletin des écoles nationales professionnelles* (Aug. 1936), 199.

25 AN F 17 17844, Conseil supérieur de l'enseignement technique, séance du 12 décembre 1923.

26 *Les Écoles Nationales Professionnelles,* 1926, 98.

27 *L'Enseignement technique* 12 (Oct.–Dec. 1956), 90–100, *Technique, Art, Science* 4–5 (Jan.–Feb. 1955), 19–110.

28 The 39,258 bacs were divided as follows: baccalauréat mathématiques et techniques, 1,571; technique et économique, 86; mathématiques élémentaires 8,783; sciences expérimentales, 11,154; philosophie 17,664.
   AN F 17 17507, Henri Belliot, Les perspectives d'emploi des élites intellectuelles françaises, March 27, 1956.

29 AN F 17 17845, Conseil de l'enseignement technique, procès-verbaux des réunions, section permanente (1946–47), séance du 5 décembre 1946, and 17852, Conseil de l'enseignement technique, séance du 22 avril 1953. 17857, Conseil de l'enseignement technique, section permanente, 15 juin 1956, 13.

30 M. Fourgeaud, "Une véritable révolution dans l'apprentissage du maniement de la lime," 70. *Technique, Art, Science* 8 (1949), 66. AN F 17 17856, Conseil de l'enseignement technique (1955), procès-verbaux des réunions, section permanente, séances du 28 septembre & 21 novembre 1955, rapport Jean Fieux.

31 *L'Enseignement technique* 10 (Apr.–June 1956), 50–1. Pelpel and Troger, *Histoire de l'enseignement technique,* 97.

32 *L'Enseignement technique* 1 (Jan.–Mar. 1954), 33. Twenty-one per cent came from other technical schools, and 4.7 per cent from miscellaneous schools and programs.

33 *L'Enseignement technique* 25 (Jan.–Mar. 1960), 12. The number of students rose from 10,000 in 1946 to 18,500 in 1956. *Le Technicien,* 39 (May–June 1958), 33.

34 *Bulletin des écoles nationales professionnelles* 3 (May 1959), 25–8. Société amicale nationale des techniciens supérieurs, brevetés des lycées techniques et des anciens élèves des écoles nationales professionnelles.

35 *L'Enseignement technique* 8 (Oct.–Dec. 1955), 20–2.

36 *Bulletin des écoles nationales professionnelles* 70 (July 1928), 114; 167 (August 1936), 186–203.

37 *L'Enseignement technique* 1 (Apr. 1938), 23–4. "It is necessary to defend women against the material and moral despotism of the occupation …

Vocational education must double as a very broadly conceived domestic education that permits the woman to play her role as educator and facilitator in the home."

38 *Technique, Art, Science* 1 (Oct. 1946), 10–11. See the accounts of Simone Weil of her year working in the Renault factory in the mid 1930s: *L'Enracinement*, 1949, *La condition ouvrière*, 1951, and *Oppression et Liberté*, 1955.

39 *L'Enseignement technique* 5 (Jan.–Feb. 1955), 63–5.

40 *L'Enseignement technique* 71 (July–Sept. 1996), 50; and 72 (Oct.–Dec. 1996), II.

41 AN F 17 17843, Conseil supérieur de l'enseignement technique, La Direction du Travail des Jeunes et de l'Enseignement technique, July, 1941. Les cours et les écoles. F 17 17846, Conseil supérieur de l'enseignement technique, procès-verbaux des réunions, section permanente, 22 avril 1948.

42 AN 14350, Note sur l'organisation de l'enseignement technique, cr. 1899–1900. Charlot and Figeat, *La Formation des ouvriers*, 253.

43 Guinot, *Formation professionnelle*, 283, cites 65,000. Legay, *L'Enseignement technique* 136 (Oct.–Dec. 1987), 39, cites 70,000 attending écoles pratiques and affiliated schools in 1938. Pelpel and Troger cite "around 200 schools" in 1939 with around 46,000 students (between 34,500 and 35,000 boys and between 11,200 and 11,800 girls), but they do not cite their sources, *Histoire de l'enseignement technique*, 69.

44 *L'Enseignement technique* 19 (July–Sept. 1958), 39–40.; 25 (Jan.–Mar. 1960), 12; 27 (July–Sept. 1960), 12.

45 *L'Enseignement technique* 10 (Apr.–June, 1956), 50–1.

46 Workers and employees were mainly artisans (10.8 per cent) and petty officials (19.4 per cent) plus managers, 10.4 per cent; liberal professions 2.4 per cent; agriculture 7.1 per cent; miscellaneous 1.4 per cent. *L'Enseignement technique* 1 (Jan.–Mar. 1954), 33–5. The CTs recruited 26.6 per cent from their own preparatory sections, 51.2 per cent from primaire, 6.2 per cent from the cours complémentaires, 10.5 per cent from lycées and collèges, 2.5 per cent other technical schools, and 3 per cent misc. The centres d'apprentissage recruited 84 per cent directly from primaire (fin d'études primaires); cours complémentaires 5.6 per cent; lycées and collèges 3.6 per cent; other technical 4.5 per cent; and 2.3 per cent misc. Pierre Naville, *École et Société*. Paris, 1959.

47 Buisson, "L'avenir des Écoles nationales professionnelles," 1–7. *Technique, Art, Science* 101 (new series), (Nov. 1956), 1–2. *L'Enseignement technique* 5 (Jan.–Mar. 1955), 77; and 9 (Jan.–Mar. 1956), 51.

48 Union des industries métallurgiques et minières UIMM, *Enquête sur la situation des ingénieurs* 1956: 51.2 per cent agents de maîtrise, 40.2 per cent chefs d'ateliers, and 46.5 per cent draftsmen had no diploma for their position. Only 9.3 per cent of foremen had the CAP. See also *L'Enseignement technique* 12 (July–Sept. 1958), 21–7; 34 (Apr.–June 1962), 71–88; 45 (Jan.–Mar. 1965), 39–41.

49 UIMM *Le Personnel dans l'industrie des métaux*, Paris, 1963.

50 Guillon, *Techniciens en formation continue d'ingénieur*, 11–2.

51 Friedmann, *Où va le travail human?* 284–345; and *Le Travail en miettes*, Paris, 1956.

52 Friedmann, *Problèmes humains du machinisme industriel*, 215–244 (his thesis, defended in 1946). Naville, *Essai sur la qualification du travail*, 8.

53 See Legoux, "Regardes sur la nouvelle génération de techniciens," 71–88; and Naville, "L'Évolution des techniques et la formation humaine et scolaire," 17–24.

54 AN F 17 17509, Charles Brunold, Le projet de réforme de l'Enseignement du second Degré, 1953. See also Brunold, *Demain ils seront des hommes*, 20. Legoux, *Du compagnon au technicien*, 498.

55 AFDET estimated 66,000 students, see *L'Enseignement technique* 4 (Oct.–Dec. 1954), 21. H. Legay, an inspector in the technical education division, estimated 70,000 students, see his "Histoire de l'enseignement technique," in *L'Enseignement technique* 136 (Oct.–Dec. 1987), 39. Charlot and Figeat, *La formation des ouvriers*, 297, estimated 64,000 in 1939: 46,695 students in the écoles pratiques and the balance in écoles de métiers and other schools. They estimated 32,000 in the écoles techniques secondaires (ENPs, EPS with vocational sections) plus the schools in higher education, eighteen Écoles supérieures de Commerce, and various engineering schools. *L'Enseignement technique* 143 (July–Sept. 1989), 9, estimated 200,000 in the Centres d'apprentisssage, 180,000 in the collèges techniques et sections techniques, 25,000 in the Écoles nationales professionnelles, and 4,000 in engineering schools for a total of 410,000 in 1960.

56 *L'Enseignement technique* 27 (July–Sept. 1960), 12; 9 (Jan.–Mar. 1956), 49; and 8 (Oct.–Dec. 1955), 20–2. Charlot and Figeat's figures for 1951, in *La formation des ouvriers*, 357, are comparable to Buisson's. Pierre Laurent, secretary general to the minister of education, estimated 800,000 in 1966. See *Technique, Art, Science* 204 (Dec. 1966), 1–10.

57 *L'Enseignement technique* 57 (Jan.–Mar. 1968), 16–30.

58 *L'Enseignement technique*, 73 (Jan.–Mar. 1972), 21.

59 Bouyx, *L'Enseignement technologique et professionnel*, 50.

60 Ministère de l'Éducation nationale, de l'enseignement supérieur et de la recherche, Direction de l'évaluation et de la prospective, "Les sections de techniciens supérieurs 1996–1997," Note d'Information 97.20, April 1997. *L'Enseignement technique* 177 (Jan.–Mar. 1998), 8–13; 160 (Oct.–Dec. 1993), 19. The IUTs had 43,336 students in 1976, and 84,900 in 1993.

61 *L'Enseignement technique* 173 (Jan.–Mar. 1997), 4.

62 *L'Enseignement technique* 173 (Jan.–Mar. 1997), 4; 160 (Oct.–Dec. 1993), 19; also 157 (Jan.–March 1993), 11; and 156 (Oct.–Dec. 1992), 21. In 1992–93, a total of 1,455,800 were enrolled in technical-vocational programs, public and private, out of 2.4 million students in all lycées, 716,000 in lycées

professionnels, 527,800 bac technologique programs in general lycées, and 212,000 in apprenticeship programs.

63 *Le Monde*, June 10, 1997. Also Bouyx, *L'Enseignement technologique*, 29, 104.

64 Ministère de l'Éducation nationale, *Repères et références statistiques*. *L'Enseignement technique* 172 (Oct.–Dec. 1996), II.

65 Lelièvre and Lelièvre, *Histoire de la scolarisation des filles*. Baudelot and Establet, *Allez les filles*. See also Mayeur, *L'Enseignement secondaire des jeunes filles*.

66 These commissions were chaired by Antoine Prost in 1983, Pierre Bourdieu in 1985, J. Lesourne in 1987, Pierre Bourdieu and François Gros (including philosopher Jacques Derrida and mathematician Didier Dacunha-Castelle) in 1989. *L'Enseignement technique* 144 (Oct.–Dec. 1989), 63–8. *Éducation-Économie* 9 (Nov.–Dec. 1990), 15–8. *Le Monde de l'Éducation* 182 (May 1991). *Le Monde*, Apr. 29–30, 1998.

67 J. Lesourne, *Éducation et société demain*.

68 OECD, *France, Reviews of National Policies*, 1996, 109–118.

69 *L'Enseignement technique* 155 (July–Aug. 1992), 35–44; and 172 (Oct.–Dec. 1996), II–XI.

70 The STI is divided into five specialties corresponding to the old industrial categories: génie mécanique, génie électronique, génie civil, génie électrotechnique, génie énergétique. Génie mécanique, for example, is divided into six options: productique mécanique, systèmes motorisés, structures métalliques, bois et matériaux associés, matériaux souples, microtechniques. *Le Monde de l'Éducation* 201 (Feb. 1993), 22–4; and 203 (Apr. 1993), 12–5.

71 *Le Monde*, 24 and 25 March, 1 April 2000.

72 Legoux, *Du compagnon au technicien*, 389.

CHAPTER SIX

1 Dubois, "Universités, croissance et diversité," 7–12. In 1984, the doctorats d'état et du troisième cycle were replaced by a new doctorate. In 1996 there were 280 diplômes nationaux: 35 DEUG, 103 *licences*, 121 maîtrises, 21 diplômes d'IUP, plus 126 DEUST, 270 maîtrises professionnalisées, 1,136 DESS, 1,215 DEA, 42 diplômes de recherche technologique.

2 *Cahiers de l'Éducation nationale* 12 (Feb. 1983), 16–17; 15 (May 1983), 4–12.

3 *Arts et Métiers* 2 (March, 1983), 5; 4 (May 1983), 25–31; and 6 (July-August 1983), 5. Two powerful organizations led the opposition to the Savary reform: the Comité national pour le développement des grandes écoles and the Comité national des ingénieurs français representing 200 higher technical schools, 250,000 engineers, and 50,000 techniciens supérieurs. See also *Le Monde de l'Éducation* 126 (April 1986), 10–3.

4 *Le Monde de l'Éducation* 124 (Feb. 1986), 15.

5 Ministère de l'Éducation nationale, de l'Enseignement supérieur et de la Recherche, *Les États généraux de l'université*, Paris: ONISEP, 128 p. *L'Enseignement technique* 171 (July–Sept. 1996), 51. Pierre Dubois, "Universités, Croissance et diversité," 58 (Apr.–June 1997), 7–12.

6 *Le Monde*, Sept. 29, 1997, 8. *Le Monde de l'Éducation*, 219 (Oct. 1994), 35.

7 *L'Enseignement technique* 176 (Oct.–Dec. 1997), 9.

8 "In 1997–98, 1,444,038 enrolled in universities. Les étudiants inscrits à l'université en 1996–97, Ministère de l'Éducation nationale, de l'enseignement supérieur et de la recherche, Direction de l'évaluation et de la prospective, Note d'information, March 1997. See also *L'Enseignement technique* 176 (Oct.–Nov. 1997), 8–13; and 179 (July–Sept. 1998), 24–7.

9 *Le Monde de l'Éducation* 195 (July–August 1992), 30.

10 *Le Monde de l'Éducation* 219 (Oct. 1994), 34–6.

11 *Le Monde*, Dec. 7–8, 1997. Boltanksi, *Making of a Class*, 202; *Les Cadres*, 335.

12 *L'Enseignement technique* 18, (1er trimestre 2000), 16–17; 182 (2ème trimestre 1999), 24–5; 171 (July–Sept. 1996), 48; 162 (April–June 1994), 35–7.

13 L'Enseignement technique, 185 (1re trimestre 2000) 35. *Le Monde de L'Éducation* 90 (Jan. 1983), 14–6.

14 *L'Enseignement technique* 179 (July–Sept. 1998), 23.

15 *L'Enseignement technique* 179 (July–Sept. 1998), 23.

16 *Dossiers de l'ONISEP*, (July 1990), 9. *Éducation-Économie* 11 (Apr.–June 1991), 28–34. In the tertiary section more students failed to obtain a diploma (23,700) than were successful in 1990 (21,850), and the drop-out and failure rate was higher in private STS than in the public ones.

17 *L'Enseignement technique* 181 (1er trimestre, 1999), 21.

18 *L'Enseignement technique* 181 (1er trimestre, 1999), 21; 158 (Apr.–June 1993), 30; 152 (Oct.–Dec. 1991), 82.

19 Guillon, *Enseignement*, 112. *Éducation-Économie* 11 (Apr.–June 1991), 29.

20 *L'Enseignement technique* 183 (3ème trimestre, 1999), 12, 185 (1re trimestre 2000), 35.

21 *Éducation-Économie* 12 (July–Sept. 1991), 58–61. *Cahiers de l'Éducation nationale*, 61 (Jan. 1988), 16.

22 AFDET, "Liste des sections et specialités," 1998. The number of specialities stood at 120 early in the decade. *Le Monde de l'Éducation*, 187 (Nov. 1991), 30. *Le Monde*, June 10, 1993, 18.

23 Pierre Laurent, series of articles in *Technique, Art, Science* 201–202 (Sept.–Oct. 1966), 15–26; 204 (December 1966), 1–10; and 213 (November 1967), 1–9.

24 *Le Monde de l'Éducation* 90 (Jan. 1983), 14–8. Cours des Comptes, *Les Instituts universitaires de technologie*.

25 *Éducation-Économie* 12 (July–Sept. 1991), 59. The percentage of students admitted to the IUT as a percentage of total university enrolments fell from 12 to 9 per cent between 1980 and 1990.

26 Ministère de l'Éducation nationale, de l'enseignement supérieur et de la recherche, Direction de l'évaluation et de la prospective, "Les sections de techniciens supérieurs 1996–1997," Note d'information 97.20. April 1997. *L'Enseignement technique* 177 (Jan.–Mar. 1998), 8–13; 160 (Oct.–Dec. 1993), 19. *Éducation-Économie* 12 (July–Sept. 1991), 59; *Cahiers de l'Éducation nationale*, 51 (Jan. 1987), 24–5.

27 *Le Monde*, February 11, 1995.

28 *L'Enseignement technique* 155 (July–Sept. 1992), 66–7 and 158 (Apr.–June 1993) 30–1. For the class of 1992–93, the figures were 71 per cent general bac, 26.4 per cent technological bac, 0.6 per cent bac pro, 0.4 per cent brevet de technicien, and 1.7 per cent miscellaneous. The number of bacheliers technologiques who repeated at least one year at the secondary level was double that of bacheliers généraux, 80 per cent versus 41 per cent.

29 *Le Monde*, Feb. 11, 1997, 10.

30 *L'Enseignement technique* 158 (Apr.–June, 1993), 29–31; 162 (Apr.–June, 1994), 35.

31 *Éducation-Économie* 12 (July–Sept. 1991), 61. *Le Monde de l'Éducation* 225 (Apr. 1995), 82–83; and 194 (June 1992), 99. Two-thirds came from the IUT, over a quarter from the STS and a tenth from the DEUG.

32 *Dossiers de l'ONISEP*, July 1990, 7. *Éducation Économie* 11 (Apr.–June 1991), 29.

33 Narbonne, *De Gaulle et l'éducation*, 115–17, 130–3, 170–5, and 194. Laurent, "Les aspects de la réforme de l'enseignement," 15–26. *Technique, Art, Science* 204 (Dec. 1966), 1–10.

34 Forestier, "Les IUT 25 ans après leur création," 59–63.

35 *Le Monde de l'Éducation* 90 (Jan. 1983), 16.

36 ID, 1 (Sept.–Oct. 1992), 14–6. Report of the Conseil national des Ingénieurs et des Scientifiques de France.

37 *L'Enseignement technique* 155 (July–Sept. 1992), 66–7; 179 (July–Sept. 1998), 24.

38 *L'Enseignement technique* 183 (3ème trimestre 1999); 176 (Oct.–Dec. 1997), 10–12. *Le Monde*, February 12–13, 1995; Feb. 11, 1997 (96,200 students 1996, 50,800 tertiary, 45,400 industrial).

39 *Le Monde de l'Éducation* 187 (Nov. 1991), 28. *Le Monde*, Feb. 11, 1997, 10.

40 *L'Enseignement technique* 152 (Oct.–Dec. 1991), 80–3; *Le Monde de l'Éducation* 187 (Nov. 1991), 28–33.

41 *L'Enseignement technique* 176 (Oct.–Dec. 1997), 8–13.

42 In 1995, 14.8 per cent for the DUT and 13.7 per cent BTS; in 1997, 14 per cent for the DUT and 7.8 per cent for the BTS. *L'Enseignement technique* 179 (July–Sept. 1998), 26; 182 (2ème trimestre 1999), 24–26; and 155 (July–Sept. 1992), 45–54.

43 *L'Enseignement technique* 181 (1er trimestre 1999), 22; *Le Monde*, Feb. 11, 1998, XII–XIV. Among the DUT, 4.3 per cent started as cadres, 6.3 were cadres 3 years later; BTS, 4.2 and 5.6 per cent.

44 Daniel Bloch, *Université 2000 – La formation des ingénieurs. Éducation-Économie* 4 (Dec. 1988), 4. *L'Enseignement technique* 157 (Jan.–Mar. 1993), 43–4.

45 Grelon and Marry, "Entretien avec Bernard Decomps," 49–63, especially 55.

46 FASFID, Fédération des Associations, Sociétés et Syndicats français d'ingénieurs diplômés, commission des titres. Conférence des Directeurs des Établissements de Formation d'Ingénieurs. See its review ID *(Ingénieurs diplômés)*, 1 nouvelle série, Sept.–Oct. 1992.

47 Allègre, *L'âge des savoirs. Le Monde de l'Éducation* 223 (Feb. 1995), 34.

48 *Le Monde*, Feb. 11, 1997. Of the 187 fields, twenty-three are in systems engineering, twenty-two in management, seventeen MIAGE (maîtrise de méthodes informatiques appliquées à la gestion), sixteen electrical and computer engineering, fifteen in computer studies, fourteen in commerce and sales.

49 *Le Monde*, Feb. 11, 1997.

50 *ID*, 1 (Sept.–Oct. 1992), 5–6. Daniel Bloch, *Université 2000 – La formation des ingénieurs*.

51 *ID*, 1 nouvelle série (Sept.–Oct. 1992), 17–9. Conférence des Présidents d'Universités and Conférence des Directeurs des Établissements de Formation d'Ingénieurs. Interview with M. Michel Lavalou, president of the Université de Technologie de Compiègne.

52 *ID*, 1 (Sept.–Oct. 1992), 7–11, especially 8.

53 *Le Monde de l'Éducation* 187 (Nov. 1991), 22–7.

54 *L'Enseignement technique* 157 (Jan.–Mar. 1993), 43–4.

55 *Le Monde*, Feb. 12–13, 1995. See Table 6.2.

56 *Le Monde*, Feb. 2 and 12–13, 1995; *Libération*, February 8, 1995.

57 *Libération*, Feb. 4–5, 7–8, 1995; *Le Monde*, Feb. 9, 1995.

58 *Libération*, Feb. 8, 1995.

59 *Le Monde*, Jan. 25, 1995.

60 Ministère de l'Éducation nationale. Groupe de réflexion sur l'avenir de l'enseignement supérieur, Daniel Laurent, chairman. Universités: relever les défis du nombre, rapport sur l'adaptation de l'université actuelle aux missions de l'enseignement supérieur, aux exigences de son environnement économique et social et à la demande de formation. Paris, Jan. 20, 1995. Daniel Laurent was president of the University Marne-la-Vallée and former cabinet director of Alice Saunier-Seïté, Secretary of State and minister for Universities under the Barre government, 1976–81.

61 *Le Monde*, Feb. 16, 1995; *Le Monde de l'Éducation*, 219 (Oct. 1994), 34; 225 (Apr. 1995), 42–5.

62 *Le Monde*, Feb. 12–13, 1995.

63 *Le Monde*, Feb. 9, 1995.

64 Cours des Comptes, *Les Instituts universitaires de technologie.*

65 *Le Monde, Guide*, Feb. 11, 1998.

66 *Le Monde*, May 6, 1998.

67 Ministère de l'éducation nationale, *Pour un modèle européen d'enseignement supérieur.* See also C. Allègre, *L'Âge des Savoirs.*

68 *L'Enseignement technique* 187 (3ᵉ trimestre 2000), 11.

69 Christel Lane, *Management and Labour in Europe*, 93. In 1996 there were forty-two business schools in France of which ten were classified as *grandes écoles de commerce.* The École des hautes études commerciales (HEC) was founded in 1881, the École supérieure de commerce de Paris in 1819, and the École supérieure des sciences économiques et commerciales (ESSEC), in 1913. There are also about twenty Écoles supérieures de commerce et d'administration des entreprises (ESCAE). See Crawshaw, *The European Business Environment*, 11.

70 Bernard Decomps, "L'adaptation du système de formation aux emplois de l'an 2000." *L'Enseignement technique* 176 (Oct.–Dec. 1997), 13. The number of certified engineers in France grew from 55,089 in 1920 to 256,290 in 1975 (+238%), compared to a growth of 136 per cent for non-technical managers (*cadres administratifs supérieurs*), 82 per cent for middle level administrative personnel (*cadres administratifs moyens*), 91 per cent for office workers, and 14 per cent for the labour force in general. Technicians formed the fastest growing profession in France, rising from 193,206 in 1954 to 758,690 in 1975 (+293 per cent). Together engineers and technicians grew from less than 1.5 per cent of the labour force in 1954 to almost 5 per cent in 1975. Comité d'études sur les formations d'ingénieurs. *Les formations d'ingénieurs en France.* Paris: CEFI, 1979; *Les Dossiers de l'ONISEP* (July, 1990), 5–9. Stephen Crawford, *Technical Workers in an Advanced Society*, 2.

71 Grelon, ed., *Les Ingénieurs de la crise.*

72 Grelon and Marry, "Entretien avec Bernard Decomps," 49–63.

73 Duprez, "Jeunes ingénieurs diplômés en France," 31–46.

74 *Le Monde*, Feb. 11, 1997, 10. *L'Enseignement technique* 176 (Oct.–Dec. 1997), 11. The various écoles de commerce have risen from 10,000 students to 30,000 since 1980. The years from 1747 to 1899 saw the creation of forty-one engineering schools; twenty-three from 1900–18; twenty-two during 1918–40 and fifty-seven from 1946–78. "Les écoles d'ingénieurs," *Notes et études documentaires* (4045–4047), Paris: CEFI, 1973 and Comité d'études sur les formations d'ingénieurs, *Les formations d'ingénieurs en France*, Paris: La documentation française 1973.

75 *Formation Emploi* 58 (Apr.–June 1997), 7–12. The ENI were established in 1947 based on the old applied science institutes and various independent

engineering schools. The INSA were established in Lyon in 1957 and then at Rennes and Toulouse. Compiègne was established in 1973. *Le Monde de l'Éducation* 2 (Feb. 1975), 38; 5 (May 1975), 45; 96 (July–Aug. 1983), 31–2; and 187 (Nov. 1991), 9. The ENI, established in 1969, recruit 56.6 per cent bacheliers, and the INSA, established in the 1950s, 68.7 per cent. *Le Monde de L'Éducation* 2 (Feb. 1975), 38; 105 (May 1984), 30–76. *Le Monde*, Feb. 11, 1997. See also Bousquet and Grandgérard, "Du modèle des grandes écoles aux formations en partenariat," 77.

76 *L'Enseignement technique*, 1re trimestre 2000, 16–17.

77 Decomps, "L'adaptation du système de formation aux emplois de l'an 2000," 48–57.

78 Guillon, *Techniciens en formation continue d'ingénieur.*

79 Martinelli, "Essor des emplois d'ingénieurs," 21–28. Fifty-five per cent of French engineers work in industry, 38 per cent in the tertiary sector, and 6 per cent in building and public works. Sixty per cent work in companies employing over 1,000 people. Half of French engineering schools are located in just five academies: Paris (17 per cent), Versailles (12.7 per cent), Lyon (9.5 per cent), Toulouse (7.6 per cent), and Lille (7.2 per cent). Over half are employed in the Paris region. *ID*, n° spécial Jan. 1994.

80 *L'Enseignement technique* 165 (Jan.–Mar. 1995), 13–9.

81 *L'Enseignement technique* 179 (July–Sept. 1998), 26 and 180 (Oct.–Dec. 1998), 19. Unemployment rates at level 1 (engineering and business school graduates, 2nd and 3rd cycle university) were as follows: 2.9 per cent in 1983; 4.1 per cent in 1987; 3.3 per cent; 1990; 7.4 per cent, 1996–97; 6.8 per cent in 1998. Centre d'études et de recherches sur les qualifications, "Taux de chômage en mars 1993 et décembre 1994 des diplômés de 1992," Céreq bref 107, March 1995. As many as 29.5 per cent of graduates of engineering schools were unemployed nine months after leaving school, though after thirty months that figure had fallen to 8 per cent. Among graduates of the third cycle of higher education, the figures were 26.5 per cent unemployed, falling to 10 per cent thirty months later.

82 *Le Monde*, May 6, 1998.

83 Barsoux and Lawrence, *Management in France*, 31.

84 *L'Enseignement technique* 176 (Oct.–Dec. 1997), 11; 186 (2^{e} trimestre 2000), 13. The number of students in these higher schools has increased from 95,000 in 1980 to 203,000 in 1998.

85 Bauer and Bertin-Mourot, *Les 200 en France et en Allemagne*, 40–1. *Le Monde*, Sept. 9, 1997, II–VII.

86 Schmidt, *From State to Market?*, 334.

87 Bauer and Bertin-Mourot, *Les 200, Comment devient-on un grand patron. Libération*, Feb. 16, 1995. *Le Monde*, June 16, 1997. Renaut, *Les Révolutions de l'Université.*

88 Fabius and Juppé reached ENA via the École normale supérieure; Balladur, Chirac and Rocard came up from the Institut d'Études Politiques. Balladur criticized the grandes écoles and grands corps as against the free market and as contributing to "the existence of a synarchy created by the collusion of political and economic power for the profit of a small group of technocrats." Balladur, *Je Crois en l'Homme plus qu'en l'État*, 48.

89 Euriat and Thélot, "Le recrutement social de l'élite scolaire en France." *Le Monde*, Nov. 21, 1997; May 6, 1998; and Aug. 30, 1995. "Pour un modèle européen d'enseignement supérieur," *Le Monde*, May 5, 1998 (Report of the Attali Commission).

90 Bourdieu, *La noblesse de l'état: Grandes écoles et esprit de corps*, 352–3.

91 OECD, *Review of National Policies for Education, France*, 16–8, 72–3, 115–8.

92 Philips, ed., *Education in Germany*. Muller, ed., *Universities in the Twenty-First Century*. In West Germany, higher education enrolment grew from 265,000 in 1960 to 440,000 in 1969; in France during the 1960s, it grew from 247,000 to 612,000.

93 Bourdieu notes that even in the United States, with its democratic mythology, that graduates of "prep schools" (Andover, Choate, Exeter, etc.), are more likely to be admitted to Ivy League universities, and are disproportionately represented in higher positions in business and industry. However a study by Peter W. Cookson Jr. and Caroline H. Persell, *Preparing for Power: America's Elite Boarding Schools*, found that an increasing number of students in these schools experienced "burn out" or for other reasons refused to accept the sacrifices necessary to academic success.

94 Lane, *Management and Labour in Europe*, 84.

95 France has the highest percentage of outside recruitment of managers in Europe at 76 per cent as opposed to 24 per cent internal promotion. Germany and Italy have the lowest outside recruitment at 57 per cent against 43 per cent internal. France also has the highest percentage of managers compared to employees overall, 14 per cent, versus only 9.3 per cent in Germany and a European average of 12.5 per cent. Bauer and Bertin-Mourot, *Les 200*, 190.

96 For background, see Bowles and Gintis, *Schooling in Capitalist America*; Baudelot and Establet, *L'École capitaliste*, on social inequality; and Bernstein, ed., *Class, Codes and Control*, on cultural inequality.

97 There is an elaborate hierarchy of higher technical schools in France: at the upper middle level are the Écoles nationales supérieures d'Arts et Métiers (ENSAM), the Institut polytechnique de Grenoble, various Écoles de Chimie industrielle de Lyon, de Lille, etc.; somewhat further down are the École spéciale de Mécanique et d'Électricité, Sudria, the Institut industriel du Nord, the École des Arts et Industries textiles de Roubaix, and the École nationale supérieure des PTT (postes, télégraphes, télé-

phones), and the various Écoles supérieures de Commerce et d'Administration des Entreprises. Bourdieu, *La Noblesse d'état*, 131–52.

98 Bourdieu and Passeron, *La Reproduction, 1970* and *Les Héritiers* Paris: Les Éditions de Minuit, 1964. Bourdieu, *La Distinction*, Paris: Les Éditions de Minuit, 1964 and 1979.

99 Bourdieu, *Homo Academicus*.

100 Bourdieu, *State Nobility,* 9–11, 188–97.

101 Ibid., 104.

102 Ibid., 116–19, 331–5.

103 Ibid., 34.

104 Ibid., 116–17.

105 Wacquant, foreword, *State Nobility,* xvii-xviii.

106 Bourdieu, *Outline of a Theory of Practice*. See also Robbins, *The Work of Pierre Bourdieu*, 140–160; and Lave and Wenger, *Situated Learning*, 49–51.

107 *L'Enseignement technique*, 144 (Oct.–Dec. 1989), 63–8. *Éducation-Économie* 9 (Nov.–Dec. 1990), 15–18. *Le Monde de l'Éducation* 182 (May 1991). *Le Monde*, April 29–30, 1998.

108 Crozier, *Le phénomène bureaucratique*; and Crozier, *La Société bloquée*.

109 Crozier, *L'Entreprise à l'écoute*, 89–97.

110 Crozier, *La crise de l'intelligence*, 90–101.

111 d'Iribarne, *La logique de l'honneur*, 40–2, 70–7, 258–65.

112 Ibid., 50–1, 112, 227.

113 Ezra Suleiman emphasizes the capacity of French elites to adapt to change in *Elites in French Society, the Politics of Survival*. See also his *Politics, Power, and Bureaucracy in France, the Administrative Elite*.

114 d'Iribarne, *La logique de l'honneur*, 131–202, 205–51.

115 Storper and Salais, *Worlds of Production*, 22.

116 Storper and Salais, *Worlds of Production*, 84–98, 180.

117 Ibid., 178–80.

118 Ibid., 130–48.

119 Schmidt, *From State to Market*, 334, 347–8, Crawshaw, *European Business*, 78.

120 Schmidt, *From State to Market*, 174, 392–5, 417–8, 434–7, 445–57.

121 Midler, *L'auto qui n'existait pas*. See also Cadin and Mendoza, "Tradition and transition," 147–65.

122 Morin, "La production mécanique française," 25–28. *Le Monde*, May 29, 1998 and 25 March 2000.

123 *Le Monde*, May 29, 1998; June 12, 1991.

124 *Guardian Weekly*, April 11, 1999; *Globe and Mail*, May 10, 1999, national edition. *National Post*, June 2 and September 2, 1999.

125 Conseil National du Patronat Français, *Livre blanc*, 115.

CHAPTER SEVEN

1 Ashton and Green, *Education, Training and the Global Economy*, 39.
2 Monaco, *L'école-production*, 13.
3 Galambaud, "The development of the human resource function," 166–75.
4 Charlot, "Technique et formation des enseignants," 26–9.
5 Bourdieu, *Outline of a Theory of Practice*. See also Lave and Wenger, *Situated Learning*, 50, and Vygotsky, *Mind in Society*.

Bibliography

ARCHIVAL SOURCES

Archives Nationales (AN)

F 12 (Ministère de l'Industrie et du Commerce) 6359–6363. Office du travail: Enquête sur l'apprentissage industriel, 1901

F 17 (Ministère de l'Éducation nationale) 17499. Réforme Léon Béard, 1923

F 17 17500. Organisation de la scolarité. Commissions, rapports, projets, 1924–36

F 17 17501. Réforme du ministre Jean Zay, réglementation classes d'orientation, 1936–39

F 17 17502. Vichy – réglementation, 1940–44. La réforme Langevin-Wallon 1944–48

F 17 17503. Projets des ministres Edouard Depreux et Yvon Delbos (enseignement public) 1948–1949, correspondance relative aux projets, 1948–1950

F 17 17504. Réforme de l'enseignement du second degré, Projet Brunold, 1952–54

F 17 17505. Projets des Ministres André Marie, 1954, et Jean Berthoin, 1954–55

F 17 17506. Comité d'étude pour la réforme de l'enseignement, 1954–55. Compte rendu des séances, December 1954 to April 1955

F 17 17507. Commission pour la démocratisation de l'enseignement du second degré, 1956–57, René Billères

F 17 17508. Projet du Ministre René Billères et "petite réforme de 1956" sur l'enseignement du second degré, 1955–59

F 17 17509. Second projet Berthoin 1958–59, Enseignement du deuxième degré, 1949–58, les classes nouvelles

F 17 17777. Correspondance Gustave Monod, 1947–51

F 17 17843. Ministère de l'Éducation Nationale, Conseil supérieur de l'Enseignement technique, la Direction du Travail des Jeunes et de l'Enseignement technique, 1920–1946

F 17 17844. Conseil supérieur de l'Enseignement technique. Procès-verbaux des réunions, 1922–38

F 17 17845–17847. Conseil supérieur de l'Enseignement technique, procès-verbaux des réunions, 1946–49

F 17 17849–17857. Section permanente du Conseil de l'Enseignement technique, réunions 1950–57

F 17 8701–8731. L'Enseignement secondaire spécial, 1847–1890

F 17 14317–14326. Écoles nationales d'arts et métiers, 1814–1923: origins, inspection, programs, alumni association

F 17 14348–64. Écoles nationales professionnelles, creation, personnel, programs, recruitment, placement, scholarships

Archives privées (AP)

312–316, Marcel Abraham, chef du cabinet d'Anatole de Monzie, 1932–34, et de Jean Zay, 1936–39

PERIODICALS

L'Agrégation, published by the Société des Agrégés since 1914

Arts et Métiers, Revue mensuelle. Published by the Société des Ingénieurs Arts et Métiers, since 1951

Bulletin administratif (mensuel) de la Société des anciens élèves des Écoles d'arts et métiers, 1861–1937

Bulletin de l'enseignement technique. Published monthly by the Ministry of Industry and Commerce, 1898–1914

Bulletin mensuel de la Société amicale des anciens élèves des Écoles nationales professionnelles, 1920–50

Cahiers de l'Éducation nationale, published by the Ministry of National Education, 1982–90

Les dossiers de l'ONISEP (Office national d'information sur les enseignements et les professions), 1990s

Éducation-Économie, revue du Haut Comité Éducation-Économie, since 1987

L'Enseignement technique, published quarterly by the Association française pour le développement de l'enseignement technique (AFDET), since 1954

Formation-Emploi, published by the Centre d'études et de recherches sur les qualifications (Céreq), under the auspices of the Ministry of National Education and Ministry of Work, Paris: La Documentation française, since 1983

La Formation professionnelle. Published quarterly by AFDET, 1904–14, 1919–20

ID (Ingénieurs diplômés), published by the Conseil national des ingénieurs et scientifiques de France, since 1992

Ingénieurs Arts et Métiers. Published monthly by the Société des Ingénieurs Arts et Métiers, 1938–50

Le Monde de l'Éducation, 1974–1996, since 1997 called *Le Monde de l'Éducation, de la Culture et de la Formation*

Revue de l'enseignement technique. Published monthly by AFDET, 1910–14

Le Technicien. Published monthly by the alumni association of the Écoles nationales professionnelles, 1950–61

Technique, Art, Science. Published monthly by AFDET and the Ministry of National Education, 1946–77

PUBLISHED WORKS AND STUDIES

Adams, William James and Christian Stoffaës. *French Industrial Policy*. Washington D.C.: the Brookings Institution, 1986

Affichard, J., M.-C. Combes and Y. Grelet. "Apprentis et élèves de lycées professionnels: où sont les emplois stables?" *Formation-Emploi* 38 (Apr.–June 1992): 5–15

Agulhon, Catherine. *L'Enseignement professionnel, Quel avenir pour les jeunes?* Paris: Les Éditions ouvrières, 1994

Albert, Michel. *Capitalism against Capitalism*. Translated by Paul Haviland. London: Whurr Publishers, 1993. Originally published as *Capitalisme contre Capitalisme*. Paris: Éditions du Seuil, 1991

Allègre, Claude. *L'Âge de Savoirs, Pour une Renaissance de l'Université*. Paris: Gallimard, 1993

Altmann, Norbert; Christoph Kölhler; and Pamela Meil, eds. *Technology and Work in German Industry*. London: Routledge, 1992 and Munich: The Institute for Social Science Research, 1992

Ashton, David and Francis Green. *Education, Training and the Global Economy*. Cheltenham, UK: Edward Elgar, 1996

Association pour le développement de l'enseignement technique en France (AFDET), Liste des sections et spécialités, brevet de technicien supérieur, 1998

Astier, Placide and Isidore Cuminal. *L'Enseignement technique industriel et commercial en France et à l'étranger*. 2d ed. Paris: G. Roustan, 1912

Aventur, F., O. Bouquillard, G. Guasco, and X. Jansolin. "L'insertion des jeunes: les contrats et stages de formation en alternance." *Dossiers statistiques du travail et de l'emploi* 23–24 (Dec. 1986): 141–97

Balladur, Edouard. *Je Crois en l'Homme plus qu'en l'État*. Paris: Flammarion, 1987

Barsoux, Jean-Louis and Pamela Lawrence. *Management in France*. London: Cassell Educational Limited, 1990

Baudelot, Christian and Roger Establet. *Allez les filles*. Paris: Le Seuil, 1992

– *L'école capitaliste en France*. Paris: Maspero, 1971

Bauer, Michel and B. Bertin-Mourot. *Les 200, Comment devient-on un grand patron?* Paris: Éditions du Seuil, 1987

- *Les 200 en France et en Allemagne.* Paris: CNRS and Heidrick and Struggles International, 1994

Becker, G.S. *Human Capital: A Theoretical and Empirical Analysis,* 2d ed. New York: Columbia University Press, 1975

Bel, Maïten. "Le rôle des établissements dans la construction de l'offre de formation professionnelle et technique initiale." *Formation Emploi* 56 (Oct.–Dec. 1996): 47

Belhoste, B., A. Dahan Delmedico, and A. Picon, eds. *La formation polytechnicienne 1794–1994.* Paris: Dunod, 1994

Ben-David, Joseph. *The Scientist's Role in Society: A Comparative Study.* Englewood Cliffs, N.J.: Prentice-Hall, 1971

Bergeron, Louis and Patrice Bourdelais. *La France, n'est-elle pas douée pour la production?* Paris: Belin, 1998

Bernstein, Basil, ed. *Class, Codes and Control.* 3 vols. London: Routledge and Kegan Paul, 1973, 1974, 1976

Berstein, S. *Edouard Herriot ou la République en personne.* Paris, 1985

Bézier, Pierre. "Évolution des techniques d'usinage." *Technique, Art, Science* 229–230 (Mar.–Apr. 1969): 13–15

Bloch, Daniel. *Université 2000 – La formation des ingénieurs-maîtres.* Paris: Ministère de l'Éducation nationale, 1991

Boltanski, Luc. *The Making of a Class, Cadres in French Society.* Translated by Arthur Goldhammer. Paris and London: Cambridge University Press and Éditions de la Maison des Sciences de l'Homme, 1987. Originally published as *Les cadres: La formation d'un groupe social.* Paris: Les Éditions de Minuit, 1982

Bouffartigue, Paul and Charles Godéa. "Un héritage à l'épreuve, bref panorama des évolutions dans la formation et l'emploi des ingénieurs en France." *Formation Emploi* 53 (Jan.–Mar. 1996): 5–13

Bourdieu, Pierre, and Jean-Claude Passeron. *Les Héritiers.* Paris: Les Éditions de Minuit, 1964

Bourdieu, Pierre, and Jean-Claude Passeron. *La Reproduction, éléments pour une théorie du système d'enseignement.* Paris: Éditions de Minuit, 1970

Bourdieu, Pierre. *Homo Academicus.* Translated by Peter Collier. Cambridge, UK: Polity Press, 1988, and Stanford, Calif.: Stanford University Press. Originally published as *Homo Academicus.* Paris: Les Éditions de Minuit, 1984

- *La noblesse de l'état: Grandes écoles et esprit de corps.* Paris: Éditions de Minuit, 1989. Translated by Lauretta Clough as *The State Nobility, Elite Schools in the Field of Power.* Cambridge, UK: Polity Press, 1996

- *Outline of a Theory of Practice.* Cambridge, UK: Cambridge University Press, 1977

- *La Distinction.* Paris: Les Éditions de Minuit, 1979

Bousquet, Nelly and Colette Grandgérard. "Du modèle des grandes écoles aux formations en partenariat, quelles logiques de modernisation?" *Formation Emploi* 53 (Jan.–Mar. 1996): 75–84

Bouyx, Benoît. *L'Enseignement technologique et professionnel.* Paris: Centre national de documentation pédagogique, 1997

Bowles, Samuel and Herbert Gintis. *Schooling in Capitalist America.* New York: Basic Books, 1976

Briand, Jean-Pierre and Jean-Michel Chapoulie. *Les Collèges du Peuple, l'enseignement primaire supérieur et le développement de la scolarisation prolongée sous la Troisième République.* Paris: Éditions du CNRS, 1992

Browaeys, X. and P. Châtelain, *La France du travail.* Paris: PUF, 1984

Brucy, Guy. *L'État, L'école, les entreprises et la certification des compétences, 1880 à 1965.* Paris: Belin, 1998

Brucy, Guy. "CAP et certificats de spécialité: les enjeux de la formation au lendemain de la Deuxième Guerre mondiale." *Formation Emploi* 27–28 (July–Dec. 1989): 131–46

Brunold, Charles. *Demain ils seront des hommes, Aspects divers du problème scolaire.* Paris: Hattier, 1963

Buisson, Albert. "L'avenir des Écoles nationales professionnelles" *Technique, Art, Science* 33 (July 1956): 1–7

Buisson, Ferdinand. *L'Enseignement primaire supérieur et professionnel.* Paris, 1887

Bureau d'information et de prévision économique, *Quels hommes et quelles femmes former pour l'entreprise de demain? Prévision des qualifications à l'an 2000.* Paris, 1985

Burney, John M. *Toulouse et son Université, Facultés et Étudiants dans la France provinciale du 19e siècle.* Translated by Philippe Wolff. Paris: Éditions du Centre National de la Recherche Scientifique, 1988

Cadin, Loïc and Carla Mendoza. "Tradition and transition: the implementation of organisational principles." In *The European Business Environment,* edited by R. Crawshaw and Jean-Yves Eglem. London: International Thomson Business Press, 1997

Cambon, Christian and Patrick Butor. *La Bataille de l'Apprentissage, une réponse au chômage des jeunes.* Paris: Descartes and Cie, 1993

Campinos-Dubernet, Myriam. "Baccalauréat professionnel: une innovation?" *Formation Emploi* 49 (Jan.–Mar. 1995): 3–29

Canonge, Fernand and René Ducel. *La Pédagogie devant le progrès technique.* Paris: PUF, 1969

Capelle, Jean. *L'Éducation nationale dans la France de demain.* Paris: Éditions du Rocher, 1967

Centre d'études et de recherches sur les qualifications (Céreq), *Rapport au Ministre de l'Éducation nationale, Direction des Lycées, Formation et accès aux emplois industriels.* March 1993

– "Taux de chômage en mars 1993 et décembre 1994 des diplômés de 1992." *Céreq bref* 107, March 1995

Charlot, B. "Technique et formation des enseignants." *L'Enseignement technique* 149 (Jan.–Mar. 1991): 26–9

Charlot, Bernard and Jacky Beillerot, eds. *La Construction des politiques d'éducation et de formation*. Paris: PUF, 1995

Charlot, Bernard, and Madeleine Figeat. *La formation des ouvriers en France, 1789–1984*. Paris: Minerve, 1985

Charlot, Bernard. *La mystification pédagogique*. Paris: Payot, 1977

Charmasson, Thérèse; Anne-Marie Lelorrain; and Yannick Ripa. *L'Enseignement technique de la Révolution à nos jours*. Vol. 1. Paris: INRP/Economica, 1987

Chevènement, J.-P. *Apprendre pour entreprendre*. Paris: Librairie générale française, 1985

– *Le Pari sur l'intelligence: entretiens avec Hervé Hamon et Patrick Rotman*. Paris: Flammarion, 1985

Cogniot, G. *L'École et les forces populaires*. Paris, 1946

Combes, M.-C. "La loi de 1971 sur l'apprentissage, une institutionalisation de la formation professionnelle." *Formation Emploi* 15 (July–Sept. 1986): 18–32

Commission ministérielle d'étude, Ministre de l'Éducation nationale (Langevin commission). *La Réforme de l'enseignement*, Paris, June 1947

Comité d'études sur les formations d'ingénieurs. *Les formations d'ingénieurs en France*. Paris: CEFI, 1979

Compagnon, Béatrice and Anne Thévenin, *L'École et la société française*. Paris: Complexe, 1995

Conseil national du patronat français. *Le livre blanc, Réussir la formation professionnelle des jeunes*. Paris: Les Éditions d'organisation, 1993

Conseil national du patronat français. *Journées sur la formation permanente*. Deauville, 1978

Cookson, Peter W. Jr. and Caroline H. Persell. *Preparing for Power: America's Elite Boarding Schools*. New York: Basic Books, 1985

Copland-Perry, Charles. *L'enseignement technique français jugé par un Anglais*. Grenoble, 1899

Couppie, T., D. Epiphane, and C. Fournier. "Insertion professionnelle et début de carrière, les inégalités entre hommes et femmes résistent elles au diplôme?" *Bref Céreq* 135 (Oct. 1997)

Cours des Comptes. *Les Instituts universitaires de technologie et leur place dans le plan de développement des enseignements supérieurs*. Paris, June 1994

Crawford, Stephen. *Technical Workers in an Advanced Society: The Work, Careers and Politics of French Engineers*. Cambridge: Cambridge University Press, 1989

Crawshaw, Robert and Eglem, Jean-Yves, eds. *The European Business Environment, France*. London: International Thomson Business Press, 1997

Crozier, Michel. *L'Entreprise à l'écoute, apprendre le management post-industriel*. Paris: Interéditions, 1989

– *Le Phénomène bureaucratique*. Paris: Le Seuil, 1963

- *La Société bloquée*. Paris: Interéditions, 1970
- *La Crise de l'intelligence, essai sur l'impuissance des élites à se réformer*. Paris: Interéditions, 1995
Dalle, François and Jean Bounine. *L'Éducation en entreprise, contre le chômage des jeunes*. Paris: Éditions Odile Jacob, 1993
Dauty, Françoise and Hugues Brunet. "Spécialité transversale, Une réponse opérationnelle au rapprochement formation-emploi?" *Formation Emploi* 59 (July–Sept. 1997): 37–52
Day, C. *Les Écoles d'Arts et Métiers, l'enseignement technique en France XIXe–XXe siècle*. Translated by Jean-Pierre Bardos. Paris: Belin, 1991
- *Education for the Industrial World: The Écoles d'Arts et Métiers and the Rise of French Industrial Engineering*. Cambridge, Mass.: MIT Press, 1987
- "Technical and Professional Education in France: The Rise and Fall of L'Enseignement Secondaire Spécial, 1865–1902." *Journal of Social History* 6, no. 2 (Winter 1972–73): 177–201
Decaunes, Luc and M.L. Cavalier. *Réformes et projets de réforme de l'enseignement français de la Révolution à nos jours (1789–1960)*. Paris: IPN, 1962
Decomps, Bernard. "L'adaptation du système de Formation aux emplois de l'an 2000." *Éducation-Économie* 11 (Apr.–June 1991): 48–57
Delors, Jacques. "France between reform and counter-reform." In *Europe's Economy in Crisis*, edited by R. Dahrendorf. London: Weidenfeld and Nicholson, 1982
Depardieu, D. and J.-F. Payen. *Disparités des salaires en France*. Paris: Colin, 1950
Deyo, Frederic C., ed. *Social Reconstructions of the World Automobile Industry, Competition, Power and Industrial Flexibility*. New York: St. Martin's Press, 1996
D'Iribarne, Philippe. *La logique de l'honneur*. Paris: Le Seuil, 1989
Donndieu, G. and Denimal, P. *Classification-Qualification, De l'Évaluation des Emplois à la Gestion des Compétences*. Paris: Éditions Liaisons, 1993
Dreyfus, F.G. "Un groupe de pression en action: les syndicats universitaires devant le projet Billères de réforme de l'enseignement (1955–59)." *Revue française de sciences politiques* 15, 2 (Apr. 1965), 213–50
Dubar, C. *Formation permanente et contradictions sociales*. Paris: Éditions sociales, 1980
Dubar, Claude. *La Socialisation, Construction des identités sociales et profession-nelles*. Paris: Armand Colin, 1991
Dubief, F. *L'apprentissage et l'enseignement technique*. Paris, 1910
Dubois, Pierre. "Universités, croissance et diversité de l'offre de formation." *Formation Emploi* 58 (Apr.–June 1997): 7–12
Ducos, H. *Pourquoi l'école unique?* Paris: F. Nathan, 1932
Duprez, Jean-Marie. "Jeunes ingénieurs diplômés en France, Insertion, déqualification, professionalisation: retour sur trois problèmes classiques de la sociologie du travail." *Formation Emploi* 56 (Oct.–Dec. 1996): 31–46

Durupty, M. "Les privatisations en France." *Notes et études documentaires.* Paris: La Documentation française, 1988

Duveau, Georges. *La pensée ouvrière sur l'éducation pendant la Seconde République et le Second Empire.* Paris: Domat, 1948

Euriat, Michel and Claude Thélot. "Le recrutement social de l'élite scolaire en France." *Revue française de la sociologie* 3 (July–Sept. 1995)

Eyraud, François, Annette Jobert, Patrick Rozenblatt, and Michelle Talard. *Les classifications dans l'entreprise, production des hiérarchies professionnelles et salariales.* Paris: La Documentation française, 1989

Fédération des associations et sociétés françaises d'ingénieurs diplomés. *Enquêtes socio-économiques sur la situation des ingénieurs diplômés,* Paris: 1958, 1963, 1967, 1971, 1974, 1977, 1983

Feenberg, Andrew. *Critical Theory of Technology.* New York: Oxford University Press, 1991

Florida, Richard and Martin Kenney. "Japanese Automotive Transplants and the Transfer of the Japanese Production System." In *Social Reconstructions of the World Automobile Industry, Competition, Power and Industrial Flexibility* edited by Frederic C. Deyo. New York: St. Martin's Press, 1996

Fontenon, Claudine and André Grelon, eds. *Les professeurs du Conservatoire national des arts et métiers, dictionnaire biographique 1794–1955.* 2 vols. Paris: Institut national de recherche pédagogique, 1994

Fourgeaud, M. "Une véritable révolution dans l'apprentissage du maniement de la lime." *Technique, Art, Science* 4 (1949): 70

Friedmann, Georges. *Industrial Society, the Emergence of the Human Problems of Automation,* edited by H.L. Sheppard. Glencoe, Ill.: Free Press, 1955 (published originally as *Problèmes humains du machinisme industriel,* Paris: Gallimard, 1946)

– *Le travail en miettes.* Paris: Gallimard, 1956

– *Où va le travail humain?* Paris: Gallimard, 1950

Frommer, Judith and Janice McCormick. *Transformations in French Business, Political, Economic and Cultural Changes from 1981 to 1987.* New York: Quorum Books, 1989

Gal, Roger "Notre Tâche," *Technique, Art, Science,* 1 (October 1946), 5–6, and *Où en est la pédagogie?* Paris: Buchet-Chastel, 1961

Galambaud, Bernard. "The development of the human resource function and the inadequacies of discourse." In *The European Business Environment,* edited by R. Crawshaw and J.-Y. Eglem. London: International Thomson Business Press, 1997

Galland, Olivier. *Les Jeunes.* Paris: La Découverte, 1990

Garcia, J.-F. *L'École unique.* Paris: PUF, 1994

Girard, Alain. "Enquête nationale sur l'orientation et la sélection des enfants d'âge scolaire." *Population* 65, no. 4 (Oct.–Dec. 1954): 597–634

Gonnin-Bolo, Annette. *Écoles-entreprises, des partenariats en marche, analyse des pratiques et des représentations en collèges et lycées.* Paris: Institut National de Recherche Pédagogique, 1994

Gréard, Octave. *Éducation et instruction,* 2 vols. Paris: Hachette, 1887 et 1889

Gréard, Octave. *Des écoles d'apprentis, Mémoire adressé à M. le préfet de la Seine par l'Inspecteur général de l'Instruction publique, direction de l'enseignement primaire de la Seine.* Paris: Mourgues, 1872

Grelon, André and Catherine Marry. "Entretien avec Bernard Decomps." *Formation Emploi* 53 (Jan.–Mar. 1997): 49–63

Grelon, André, ed. *Les ingénieurs de la crise. Titre et profession entre les deux guerres.* Paris: EHESS, 1986

Grelon, André. "Les universités et la formation des ingénieurs en France (1870–1914)." *Formation Emploi* 27–28 (July–Dec. 1989): 65–88

Grew, Raymond and Patrick J. Harrigan. *School, State, and Society, the Growth of Elementary Schooling in Nineteenth-Century France, A Quantitative Analysis.* Ann Arbor: University of Michigan Press, 1991

Grignon, Claude. *L'ordre des choses, les fonctions sociales de l'enseignement technique.* Paris: Éditions de Minuit, 1971

Groupe de réflexion sur l'avenir de l'enseignement supérieur, Daniel Laurent, chairman. *Universités: relever les défis du nombre, rapport sur l'adaptation de l'université actuelle aux missions de l'enseignement supérieur, aux exigences de son environnement économique et social et à la demande de formation.* 20 Jan. 1995

Guettier, André. "Étude sur l'instruction industrielle." *Bulletin administratif de la Société des anciens élèves des Écoles nationales d'arts et métiers,* 17 (Jan.–Mar. 1864): 21–48

Guillon, Roland. *Techniciens en formation continue d'ingénieur.* Paris: Centre d'Études et de Recherches sur les Qualifications, 1985

Guillon, R. *Enseignement et organisation du travail du XIXe siècle à nos jours.* Paris: La Documentation française, 1979

Guinot, Jean-Pierre. *Formation professionnelle et travailleurs qualifiés depuis 1789.* Paris: Domat, 1946

Haby, René. *Propositions pour une modernisation du système éducatif.* Paris: La Documentation française, 1975

Hachem, El and Thèrese Fayez. *À quoi sert le Plan? Un regard sur le système éducatif.* Paris: Economica, 1992

Hatzfeld, Nicolas. "L'école d'apprentissage Peugeot (1930–1970): une formation d'excellence." *Formation Emploi* 27–28 (July–Dec. 1989): 115–27

Haut Comité Éducation-Économie (HCEE). *Vingt-cinq propositions pour l'avenir de l'école et des entreprises.* Paris: La Documentation française, 1987

Herriot, E. *In Those Days.* New York: 1952

Hoffmann, Stanley. "Look Back in Anger." *New York Review of Books,* 17 July 1997: 45–49

Huet, M. and N. Schmitz. "La classe ouvrière en détresse." *Le Monde*, December 1984

Institut national de la statistique et des études économiques (INSEE). *Tableaux de l'Économie française*. Paris: INSEE, 1995–96

Institut national de la statistique et des études économiques (INSEE). *Enquête formation-qualification professionnelle*. Paris: INSEE, 1970

Journal officiel de la République française, Chambre des Députés, 1895–1900, 1920–23, Sénat, 1920–23

Kerr, C., J.T. Dunlop, F.H. Harbison, and C.A. Myers. *Industrialism and Industrial Man: the Problems in Labor and Management in Economic Growth*. London: Heinemann, 1962

Labbé, Edmond, *Recueil des discours prononcés par E. Labbé*. Paris: AFDET, 1937

Landes, David. "French Business and the Businessman: A Social and Cultural Survey." In *Modern France*, edited by E.M. Earle. Princeton: Princeton University Press, 1951

Lane, Christel. *Management and Labour in Europe, the Industrial Enterprise in Germany, Britain and France*. Aldershot, UK: Edward Elgar, 1989

Langevin, Paul. *La pensée et l'action, textes recueillis*. Paris, 1950

Lapie, Paul. *Pédagogie française*. 2d ed. Paris: Alcan, 1926

Lapie, Paul (written under the pseudonym André Duval). "Esquisse d'une réforme générale de notre enseignement national." *Revue pédagogique*, 80, 2 (Feb. 1922): 79–101

– *L'École et les écoliers*. Paris: Alcan, 1923

Laurent, Pierre. "Projet de la loi d'orientation et de programme sur la formation professionnelle." *Technique, Art, Science* 204 (Dec. 1966): 1–10

Laux, James M. *The European Automobile Industry*. New York: Twayne Publishers, 1992

Lave, Jean and Etienne Wenger. *Situated Learning, Legitimate Peripheral Participation*. Cambridge: Cambridge University Press, 1991

Le Chartier, Eugène. *La France et son Parlement*. Paris, 1912

Leblanc, René. *La Réforme des Écoles primaires supérieures*. Paris: Larousse, 1907

Legay, F. "Histoire de l'enseignement technique, 1895–1960." *L'Enseignement technique* 63 (July–Sept. 1969): 19–57

Legoux, Yves. *Du compagnon au technicien, L'École Diderot et l'évolution des qualifications 1873–1972, sociologie de l'enseignement technique française*. Paris: Techniques et Vulgarisation, 1972

– "Regards sur les nouvelles générations de techniciens." *L'Enseignement technique* 34 (Apr.–June 1962): 71–88

– "Regards sur les nouvelles générations de techniciens." *L'Enseignement technique* 37 (Jan.–Mar. 1963): 33–48

Legrand, L. *L'École unique, à quelles conditions?* Paris: CEMEA, 1981

Legrand, Louis. *Pour un collège démocratique, mission d'étude pour l'amélioration du fonctionnement des collèges. Rapport au ministère de l'Éducation nationale.* Paris: la Documentation française, 1982

Legrand, Louis. *Pour une politique démocratique de l'éducation.* Paris: PUF, 1977

Lelièvre, F. and C. Lelièvre. *Histoire de la scolarisation des filles.* Paris: Nathan, 1991

Léon, Antoine. *Formation générale et apprentissage du métier.* Paris: PUF, 1965

Léon, Antoine. *Histoire de l'éducation technique.* Paris: PUF, 1968

Leroy, Louis Modeste. *Vers l'éducation nouvelle.* Paris, 1906

– *L'Éducation nationale au 20e siècle.* Paris, 1914

Les Compagnons de l'Université nouvelle. *L'Université nouvelle,* 2 vols. Paris: Librairie Fischbacher, 1918–19

"Les écoles d'ingénieurs," *Notes et études documentaires* (4045–4047). Paris: La Documentation française, 1973

Les Écoles nationales professionnelles. Paris: Société amicale des anciens élèves des écoles nationales professionnelles, 1926

Lesourne, Jacques. *Éducation et société demain. À la recherche des vraies questions.* Paris: Éditions de la Découverte, 1988

Lévy-Leboyer, M. "Le patronat français." In *Le patronat de la seconde industrialisation,* edited by M. Lévy-Leboyer. Paris: Les Éditions ouvrières, 1979

Lhôtel, Hervé and Antonio Monaco. "Deux trajectoires de la formation en alternance: l'apprentissage et les contrats de qualification." *Formation-Emploi* (Apr.–June 1993)

Luc, Hippolyte. "Les problèmes actuels de l'enseignement technique." *L'Enseignement technique* 1 (Apr. 1938): 8–20

Lutz, B. "Education and Employment: Contrasting Evidence from France and the Federal Republic of Germany." *European Journal of Education* 16 (1981): 73–86

Madelin, A. *Quand les Autruches relèveront la tête.* Paris: Robert Laffont, 1995

Mallet, Serge. *La nouvelle classe ouvrière.* Paris: Éditions du Seuil, 1963

Marklew, Victoria. *Cash, Crisis, and Corporate Governance, the Role of National Financial Systems in Industrial Restructuring.* Ann Arbor: University of Michigan Press, 1995

Martel, Félix and Georges Ferrand. *Écoles primaires supérieures, Écoles d'apprentissage et écoles nationales professionnelles, Mémoires et documents scolaires.* Paris: Musée pédagogique, 1889

Martinelli, Daniel. "Essor des emplois d'ingénieurs mais déclin des fonctions de fabrication." *Emploi Formation* 53 (Jan.–March 1996): 21–8

Martinelli, J., J.C. Sigot, and J.F. Vergnies. "Diplômés de l'enseignement supérieur, l'insertion professionnelle se stabilise mais les écarts s'accentuent." *Bref Céreq* 134 (Sept. 1997)

Maurice, M., F. Eyraud, A. d'Iribarne, and F. Rychener. *Des entreprises en mutation dans la crise.* Aix-en-Provence: LEST, 1986

Maurice, Marc, François Sellier, and Jean-Jacques Silvestre. *The Social Founda-tions of Industial Power, A Comparison of France and Germany.* Translated by Arthur Goldhammer. Cambridge, Mass.: The MIT Press, 1986. Originally published as *Politique d'éducation et organisation industrielle en France et en Allemagne.* Paris: PUF, 1982

Mayeur, Françoise. *L'Enseignement secondaire des jeunes filles sous la IIIᵉ Répu-blique.* Paris: Presses de la fondation nationale des sciences politiques, 1977

Midler, C. *L'auto qui n'existait pas.* Paris: Interéditions, 1993

Minc, Alain. *La France de l'an 2000.* Paris: Odile Jacob/La Documentation française, 1994

Ministère de l'Agriculture, du Commerce, et des Travaux Publics, Commis-sion de l'enseignement professionnel, *Enquête sur l'enseignement profession-nel ou recueil de dépositions faites en 1863 et 1864 devant la commission de l'enseignement professionnel.* 2 vols., Paris, 1864–65

Ministère de l'Éducation nationale, Commission ministérielle d'étude, *La Ré-forme de l'enseignement,* Paris, June 1947

Ministère de l'Éducation nationale, de l'enseignement supérieur et de la re-cherche (MENESR), Direction de l'évaluation et de la prospective, "Les étu-diants inscrits à l'université en 1996–97." *Note d'information,* March 1997

Ministère de l'Éducation nationale. Groupe de réflexion sur l'avenir de l'enseignement supérieur, Daniel Laurent, chairman. *Universités: relever les défis du nombre, rapport sur l'adaptation de l'université actuelle aux missions de l'enseignement supérieur, aux exigences de son environnement économique et social et à la demande de formation.* Jan. 20, 1995

Ministère de l'Éducation nationale. *Loi d'orientation sur l'enseignement du 10 juillet 1989. Plan de développement de l'apprentissage et de l'alternance.* Sept. 1991

Ministère de l'Éducation nationale. Note d'information, données de 1980–81. Paris, 1982

Ministère de l'Éducation nationale, de l'enseignement supérieur et de la re-cherche, Direction de l'évaluation et de la prospective, "Les sections de techniciens supérieurs 1996–1997," *Note d'information 97.20.* April 1997

Ministère de l'Éducation nationale, de l'enseignement supérieur et de la recherche. *Les enseignement supérieurs,* 106, Jan.–Feb. 1994

Ministère de l'Éducation nationale, de l'enseignement supérieur et de la recherche. *Les États généraux de l'université.* Paris: ONISEP, 1996

Ministère de l'Éducation nationale, de la recherche et de la technologie. *Pour un modèle européen d'enseignement supérieur.* Paris, 1998

Ministère de l'Éducation nationale, Département de l'évaluation et de la per-spective (DEP). *Repères et références statistiques sur l'enseignement et la forma-tion.* Paris, 1992 and 1995

Ministère de l'Éducation nationale. *Encyclopédie générale de l'Éducation française, L'Enseignement technique.* Paris: Rombaldi, 1954

Ministère de l'Éducation nationale. *Note d'information,* 82–16, SEIS, données de 1980–81

Ministère du Commerce et de l'Industrie. Conseil supérieur de l'enseignement technique. *Rapport sur l'organisation technique,* by H. Tresca. Paris: Imprimerie nationale, 1885

Ministère du Commerce, de l'Industrie, des Postes et des Télégraphes. Direction de l'enseignement technique. *Rapport sur la situation de l'enseignement technique en France en 1904, présenté par Cohendy: procès-verbaux des séances.* Paris: Imprimerie nationale, 1905

Ministère du Commerce, de l'Industrie, des Postes et des Télégraphes, Direction de l'enseignement technique. *L'Enseignement technique en France, Étude publiée à l'occasion de l'exposition de 1900.* 5 vols. Paris, 1900

Ministère du Commerce, de l'Industrie, des Postes et des Télégraphes. *Apprentissage, Rapport de M. Briat au nom de la commission permanente, Enquête et documents.* Paris: Imprimerie nationale, 1902

Ministère du Commerce, de l'Industrie, des Postes et des Télégraphes. Conseil supérieur du Travail. *Enquête récente sur l'enseignement professionnel en France, Rapport de M. Briat au nom de la commission permanente: procès-verbaux des séances.* Paris: Imprimerie nationale, 1905

Ministère du Commerce, de l'Industrie, etc. Conseil supérieur de l'enseignement technique. *Rapport sur la situation de l'enseignement technique en France en 1904, présenté par Cohendy: procès-verbaux des séances.* Paris: Imprimerie nationale, 1905

Monaco, Antonio. *L'Alternance école production, Entreprises et formation des jeunes depuis 1959.* Paris: PUF, 1994

Morin, Arthur and Henri Tresca. *De l'organisation de l'enseignement industriel et de l'enseignement professionnel.* Paris, 1862

Morin, Henri. "La production mécanique française." *L'Enseignement technique* 177 (Jan.–Mar. 1998): 25–8

Moutet, Aimée. *Les logiques de l'entreprise, la rationalisation dans l'industrie française de l'entre-deux guerres.* Paris: EHESS, 1997

Mouvement républicain populaire. *Pour une réforme de l'enseignement.* Paris, 1945

Muller, Steven, ed. *Universities in the Twenty-First Century.* Oxford: Berghahn Books, 1996

Narbonne, Jacques. *De Gaulle et l'éducation, une rencontre manquée.* Paris: Denoël, 1994

Naville, Pierre. *La formation professionnelle à l'école.* Paris: PUF, 1948

– "L'Évolution des techniques et la formation humaine et scolaire." *L'Enseignement technique* 35 (July–Sept 1962): 17–24

– *École et Société.* Paris, 1959

– *Essai sur la qualification du travail*. Paris: Rivière, 1956

Noiriel, Gérard. *Workers in French Society in the 19th and 20th Centuries*. Translated by Helen McPhail. New York: St. Martin's Press, 1990. Originally published as *Les ouvriers dans la société française, XIX–XXe siècle*. Paris: Éditions du Seuil, 1986

Nye, Mary Jo. *Science in the Provinces, Scientific Communities and Provincial Leadership in France, 1860–1930*. Berkeley: University of California Press, 1986

Organization for Economic Co-operation and Development (OECD). *Reviews of National Policies for Education: France*. Paris: OECD, 1996

Ollendorf, Gustave. "Rapport présenté à la commission mixte." *Mémoires et documents scolaires*. Paris, 1887

Organisation de coopération et de développement économiques (OCDE), "La formation initiale en France: efficacité interne et maîtrise des coûts." *Études économiques*, no 2.352–3 (Dec. 1993)

Pasquier, J.-B. *L'Enseignement professionnel en France*. Paris: Colin, 1908

Paul, Harry. *From Knowledge to Power, The Rise of the Science Empire in France, 1860–1939*. Cambridge, UK: Cambridge University Press, 1985

Pelpel, P. *Les stages de formation*. Paris: Bordas, 1989

Pelpel, Patrice and Vincent Troger. *Histoire de l'enseignement technique*. Paris: Hachette Éducation, 1993

De Peretti, André. *La Formation des personnels de l'Éducation nationale*. Paris: la Documentation française, 1982

Philips, David, ed. *Education in Germany, Tradition and Reform in Historical Context*. London: Routledge, 1995

Piaget, Jean. *Introduction à l'épistémologie génétique*. 3 vols. Paris: Presses universitaires de France, 1950

Piore, Michael J. and Charles Sabel. *The Second Industrial Divide*. New York: Basic Books, 1984

Planté, Louis. *Un grand seigneur de la politique, Anatole de Monzie (1876–1947)*. Paris: Clavreuil, 1955

Pompée, Philippe. *Études sur l'éducation professionnelle en France*. Paris, 1863

Poulot, Denis. *Le Sublime, ou le travailleur comme il est en 1870 et ce qu'il peut être*. Paris: Éditions Maspero, 1982

Prévot, André. *L'Enseignement technique chez les Frères des écoles chrétiennes au XVIIIe et XIXe siècles*. Paris: Ligel, 1932

Prost, Antoine. *Éloge des pédagogues*. Paris: Seuil, 1985

– *Histoire générale de l'enseignement et de l'éducation en France*. Vol. 4 of *L'École et la Famille dans une société en mutation*. Paris: Nouvelle Librairaie de France, 1981

– *L'enseignement en France, 1800–1967*. Paris: Colin, 1968

– *Les Lycéens et leurs études au seuil du XXIe siècle, rapport du groupe du travail national sur les seconds cycles*. Paris: CNDP, 1983

– *Éducation, Société et Politiques, Une histoire de l'enseignement en France de 1945 à nos jours*. Paris: Éditions du Seuil, 1992

Quef, P. *Histoire de l'apprentissage, aspects de la formation technique et commerciale*. Paris: Librairie générale de droit et de jurisprudence, 1964

Raissiguier, Catherine. *Becoming Women, Becoming Workers, Identity Formation in a French Vocational School*. Albany, N.Y.: Suny Press, 1994

Rand Smith, W. *The Left's Dirty Job. The Politics of Industrial Restructuring in France and Spain*. Pittsburgh and Toronto: University of Pittsburgh Press, University of Toronto Press, 1998

Rault, Christiane. *La formation professionnelle initiale, Contrastes et similitudes en France et en Europe*. Paris: La Documentation française, 1994

Renaut, Alain. *Les Révolutions de l'Université. Essai sur la démocratisation de la culture*. Paris: Calmann-Lévy, 1996

Reynaud, J. *Les Syndicats, les Patrons et l'État*. Paris: Éditions ouvrières, 1978

Ribes-Christofle, F. de. *L'apprentissage et l'enseignement professionnel en France, Rapport présenté à la Fédération des industriels et commerçants français*. Paris, 1905

Rioux, J.-P. *The Fourth Republic 1944–58*. Cambridge, UK: Cambridge University Press, 1987

Robbins, Derek. *The Work of Pierre Bourdieu, Recognizing Society*. Buckingham, UK: Open University Press, 1991

Rose, J. *En quête d'emploi-formation*. Paris: Economica, 1984

Ross, Kristen. *Fast Cars, Clean Bodies, Decolonization and the Reordering of French Culture*. Cambridge, Mass.: MIT Press, 1995

Sabel, Charles. *Work and Politics: the Division of Labour in Industry*. Cambridge, UK: Cambridge University Press, 1982

Savary, Alain. *En toute liberté*. Paris: Hachette, 1985

Scardigli, V. and P.-A. Mercier. *Ascension sociale et pauvreté: la différentiation d'une génération de fils d'ouvriers*. Paris: CNRS, 1978

Schmidt, Vivien A. *From State to Market? The Transformation of French Business and Government*. Cambridge, UK: Cambridge University Press, 1996

Schwartz, Bertrand. *L'Insertion professionnelle et sociale des jeunes, Rapport au Premier Ministre*. Paris: La Documentation française, 1981

– *Une autre école*. Paris: Flammarion, 1977

– *L'Éducation demain: Une étude de la Fondation européenne de la culture*. Paris: Aubier-Montaigne, 1973

Sellier, F. *La confrontation sociale en France, 1936–81*. Paris: PUF, 1984

Shinn, Terry *L'École Polytechnique, Savoir scientifique et pouvoir social*. Paris: Presses de la fondation nationale des sciences politiques, 1980

Smith, Robert J. *The École normale supérieure in the Third Republic*. Albany: SUNY Press, 1982

Solaux, Georges. *Les lycées professionnels*. Paris: Hachette Éducation, 1994

Storper, Michael and Robert Salais. *Worlds of Production, the Action Framework of the Economy*. Cambridge, Mass.: Harvard University Press, 1997

Suleiman Ezra. *Politics, Power, and Bureaucracy in France, the Administrative Elite*. Princeton, N.J.: Princeton University Press, 1974

– *Elites in French Society, the Politics of Survival*. Princeton, N.J.: Princeton University Press, 1978

Szarka, Joseph. *Business in France. An Introduction to the Economic and Social Context*. London: Pitman, 1992

Talbott, John E. *The Politics of Educational Reform*. Princeton N.J.: Princeton University Press, 1969

Tanguy, Lucie. *Quelle formation pour les ouvriers et les employés en France?* Paris: La Documentation française, 1991

– "Les conventions État-patronat 1949–61; un régime de transition." *Formation-Emploi* 27–28 (July–Dec. 1989): 163–87

– *Quelle formation pour les ouvriers en France?* Paris: La Documentation française, 1991

– *L'Enseignement professionnel en France, des ouvriers aux techniciens*. Paris: PUF, 1991

Terral, Hervé. *Profession: professeur, Des écoles normales maintenues aux Instituts universitaires de formation des maîtres 1945–90*. Paris: PUF, 1997

Troger, Vincent. "Les centres d'apprentissage de 1940 à 1960: le temps des initiatives," *Formation Emploi* 27–28 (July–Dec. 1989): 147–62

Turner, Lowell and Peter Auer. "A Diversity of New Work Organization: Human-centered, Lean and In-between." In *Social Reconstructions of the World Automobile Industry, Competition, Power and Industrial Flexibility*, edited by Frederic C. Deyo. New York: St. Martin's Press, 1996

Un grand commis de l'État, M. Edmond Labbé. Paris, 1946

Union des industries métallurgiques et minières, de la construction mécanique, électrique et métallique et des industries qui s'y rattachent (UIMM). *Enquête sur la situation des ingénieurs et cadres supérieurs et sur la prévision et les besoins dans les industries des métaux*. Paris: UIMM, 1956, 1962, 1970, 1977

Vial, F. *Trois Siècles d'histoire de l'enseignement secondaire*. Paris: Delagrave, 1936

Vimont, Claude. "Les Besoins des entreprises en emploi et en formation pour les dix prochaines années." *Éducation-Économie* 19 (June 1993): 4–9

Virmaud, M. *Mémoire de l'Association des anciens élèves des Arts et Métiers sur l'orientation et la formation professionnelle de la jeunesse*. Paris: CNAM, 1942

Vrain, P. and G. Gautier. *Les ouvriers vieillissants de la région parisienne: activité professionnelle et conditions de travail*. Paris: PUF, 1979

Vygotsky, Lev S. *Mind in Society*. Cambridge, Mass.: Harvard University Press, 1978

Wakeman, Rosemary. *Modernizing the Provincial City: Toulouse 1945–75*. Cambridge, Mass.: Harvard University Press, 1997

Wallon, Henri. *Principes de psychologie appliquée*. Paris: Colin, 1930

Weisz, George. *The Emergence of Modern Universities in France, 1863–1914*. Princeton, N.J.: Princeton University Press, 1983

Weil, Simone. *La condition ouvrière*. Paris: Gallimard, 1951

Womack, James P., Daniel T. Jones, and Daniel Roos. *The Machine that Changed the World*. New York: MacMillan, 1990

Zahariadis, Nikolaos. *Markets, States, and Public Policy, Privatization in Britain and France*. Ann Arbor: University of Michigan Press, 1995

Zay, Jean. *Souvenirs et solitude*. Paris: Julliard, 1945

Zoretti, L. *Éducation, un essai d'organisation démocratique*. Paris: Plon, 1918

Index